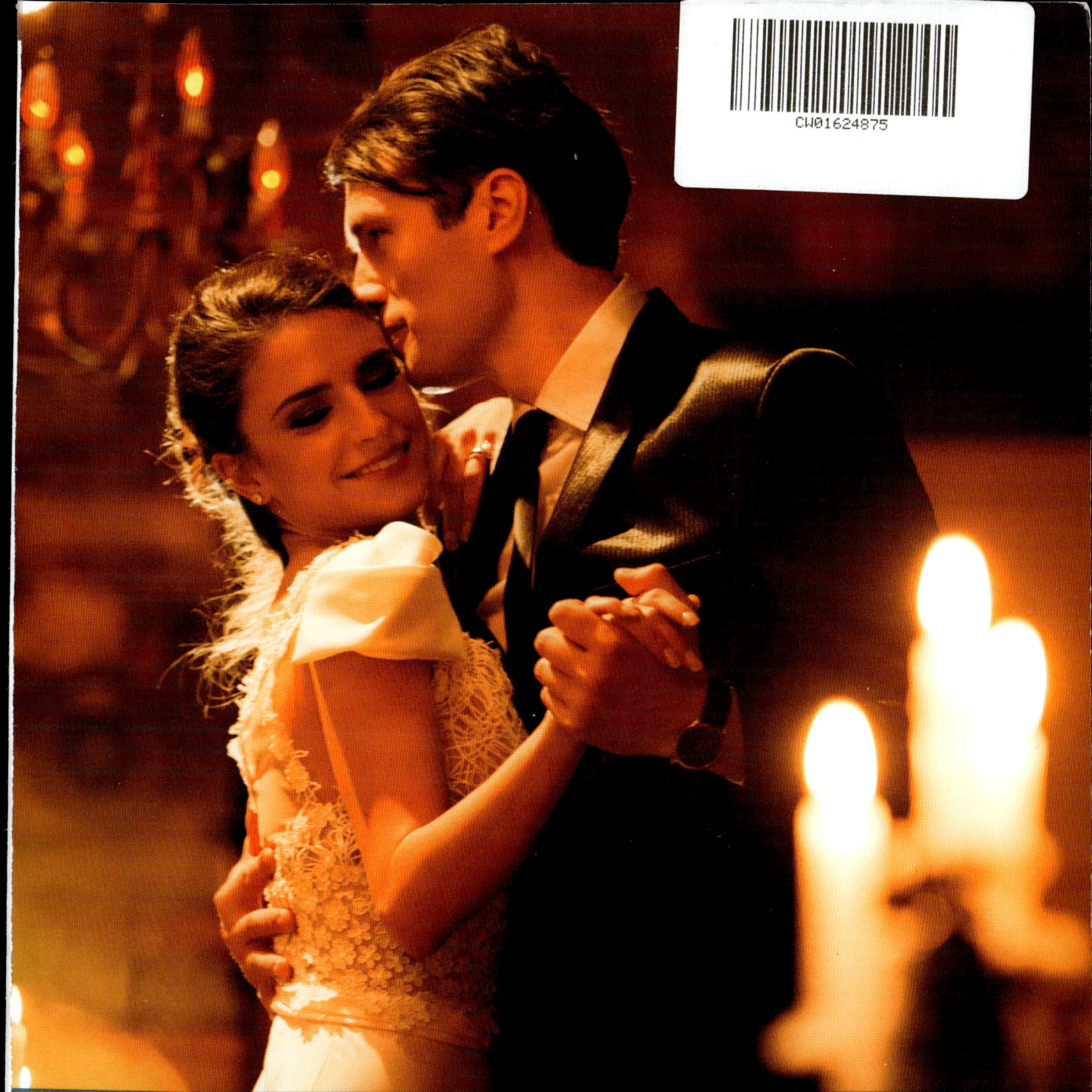

SHOT IN THE DARK

Low-Light Techniques for Wedding & Portrait Photography

Brett Florens

AMHERST MEDIA, INC. ■ BUFFALO, NY

This book is dedicated to the memory of Bill Hurter, whose guidance, friendship, and influence on my career were immeasurable.

Author photograph by Samantha Lauren.

Published by:
Amherst Media, Inc., P.O. Box 586, Buffalo, N.Y. 14226, Fax: 716-874-4508
www.AmherstMedia.com

Publisher: Craig Alesse
Senior Editor/Production Manager: Michelle Perkins
Editors: Barbara A. Lynch-Johnt, Harvey Goldstein, Beth Alesse
Associate Publisher: Kate Neaverth
Editorial Assistance from: Carey A. Miller, Sally Jarzab, John S. Loder
Business Manager: Adam Richards
Warehouse and Fulfillment Manager: Roger Singo

ISBN-13: 978-1-68203-008-0
Library of Congress Control Number: 2015953687
Printed in The United States of America.
10 9 8 7 6 5 4 3 2 1

www.facebook.com/AmherstMediaInc
www.youtube.com/c/AmherstMedia
www.twitter.com/AmherstMedia

Contents

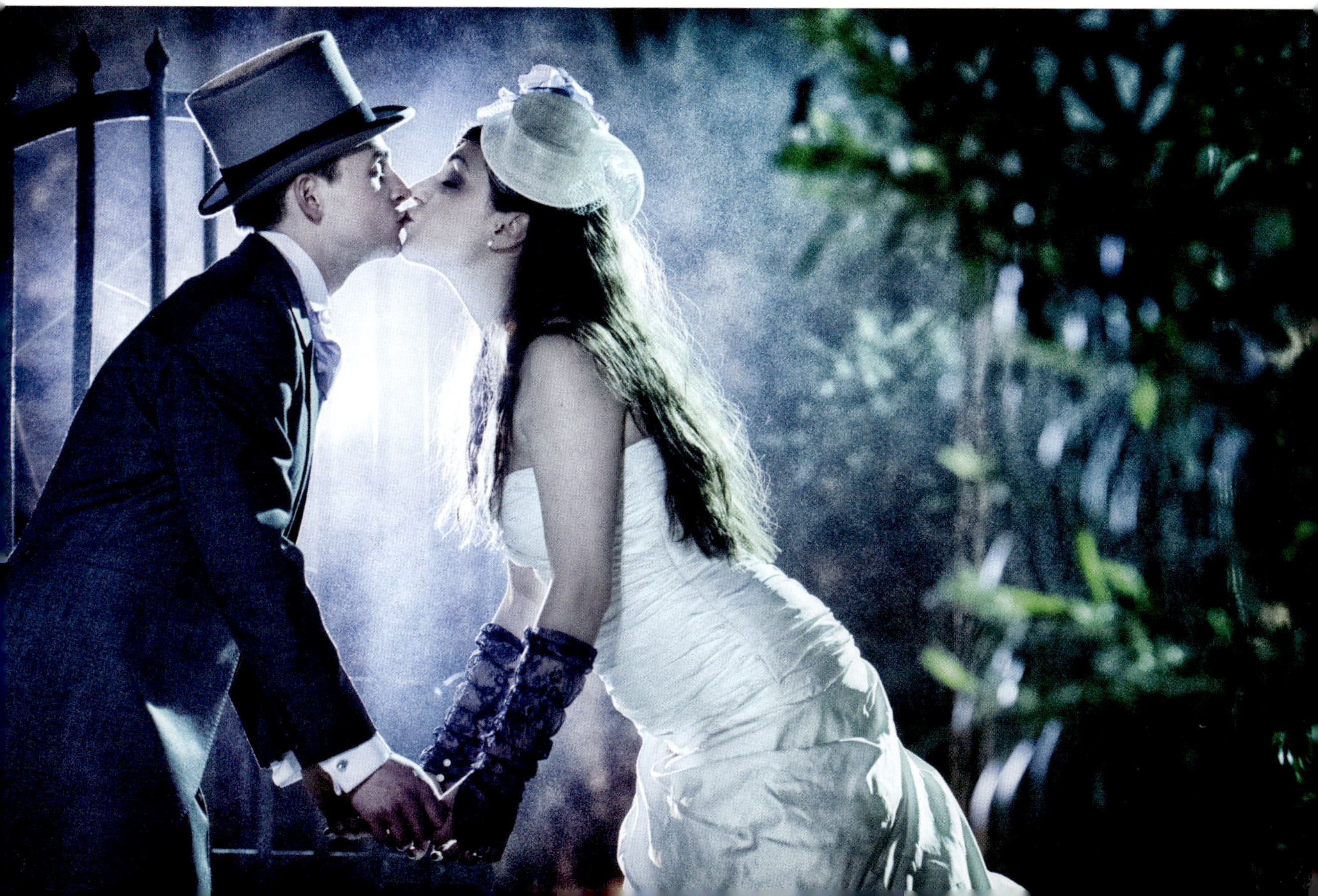

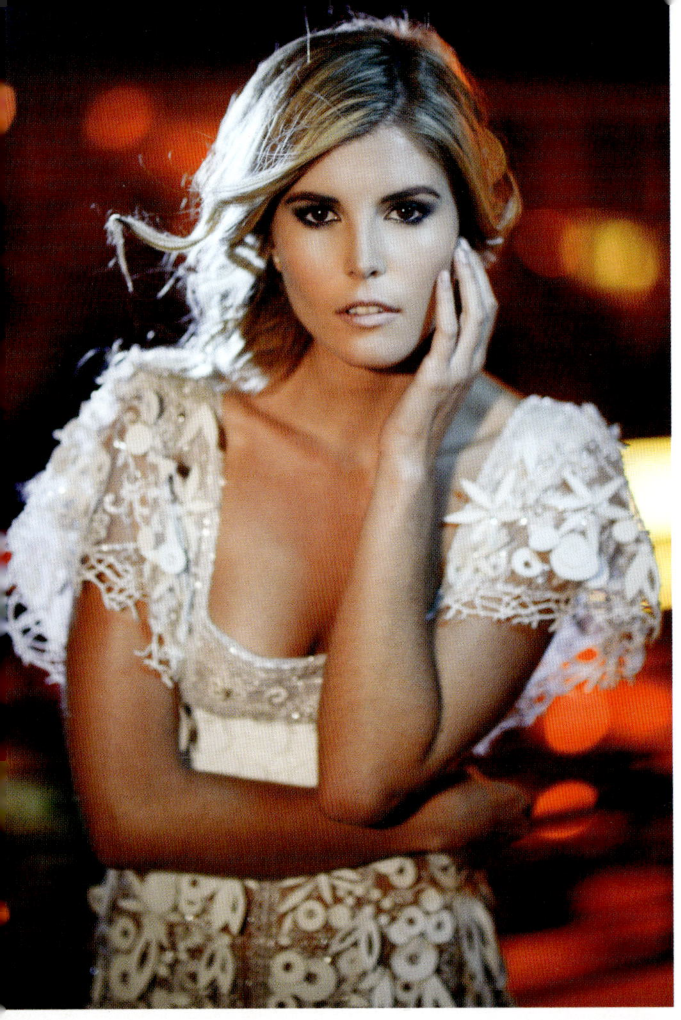

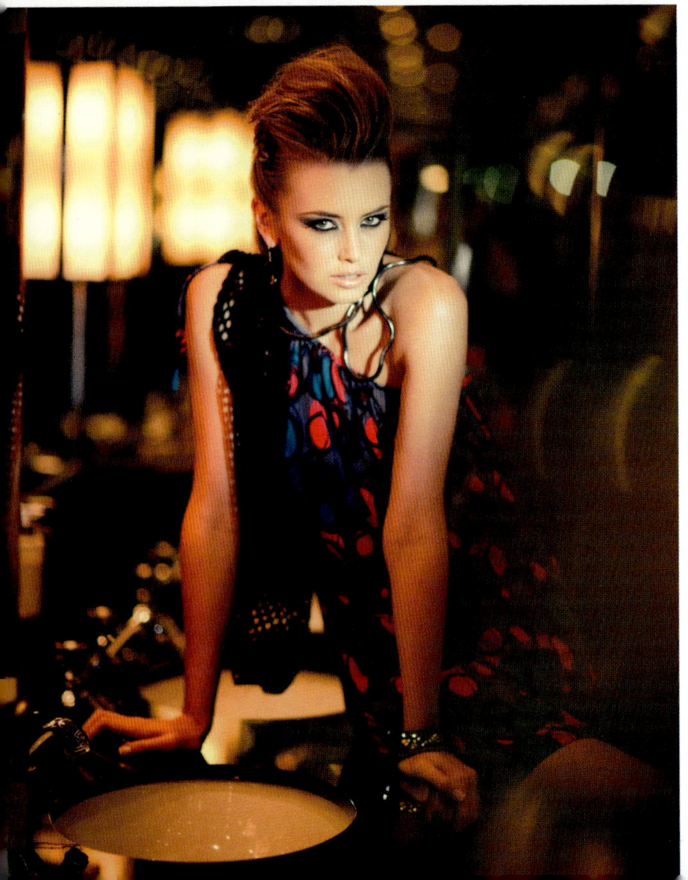

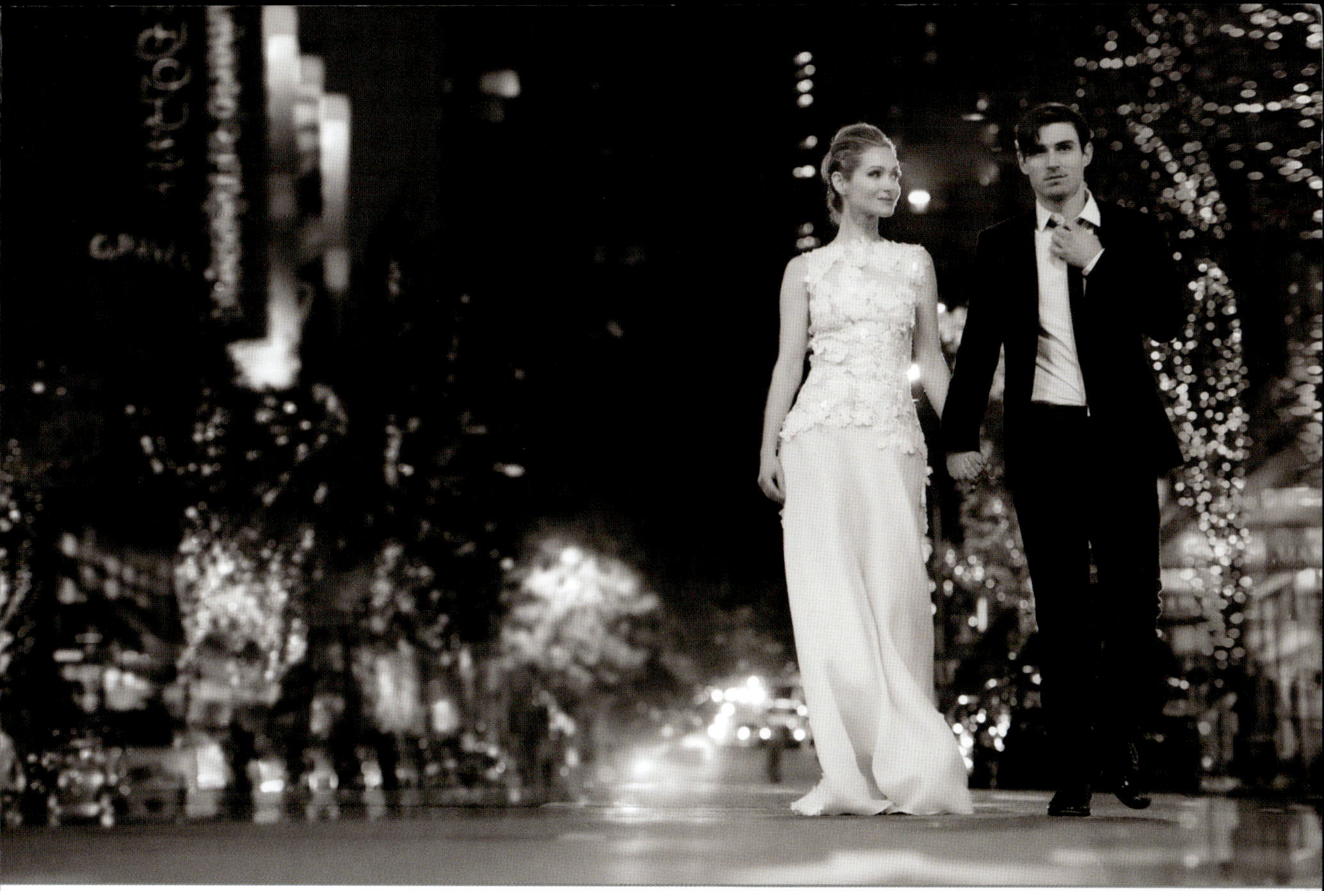

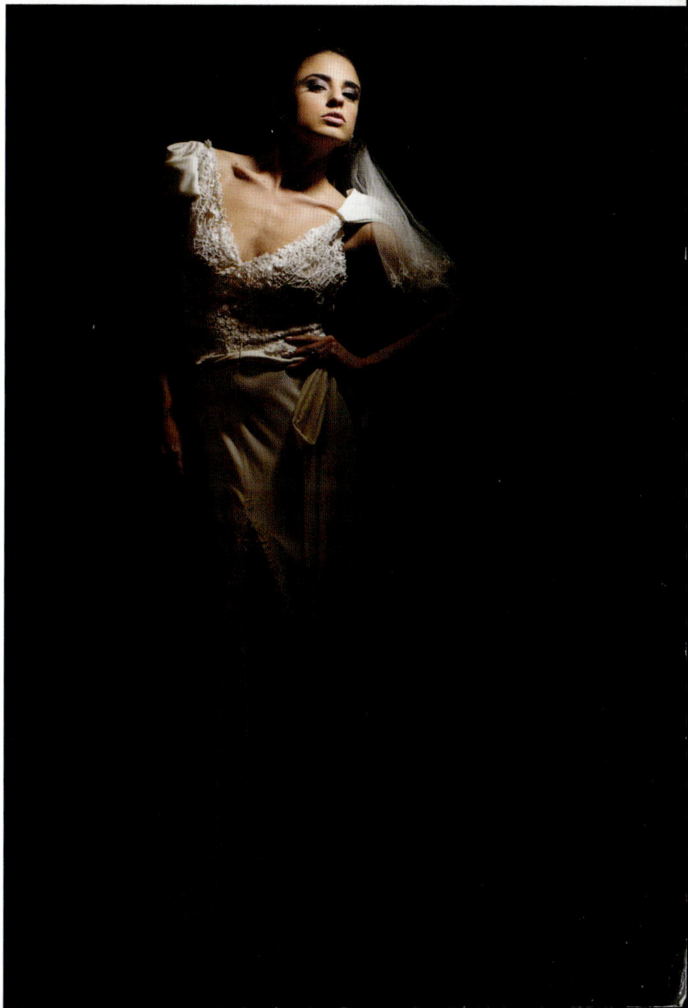

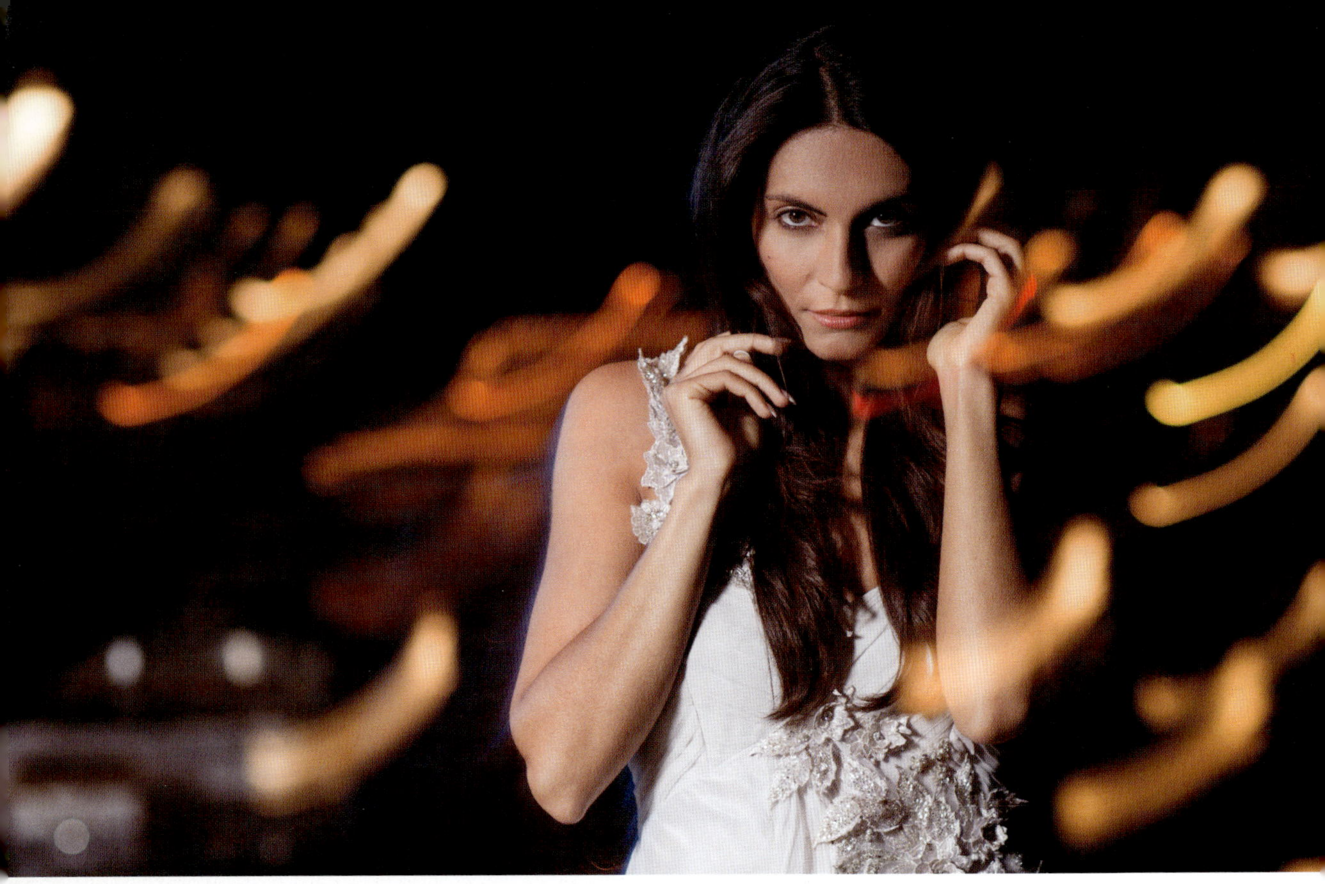

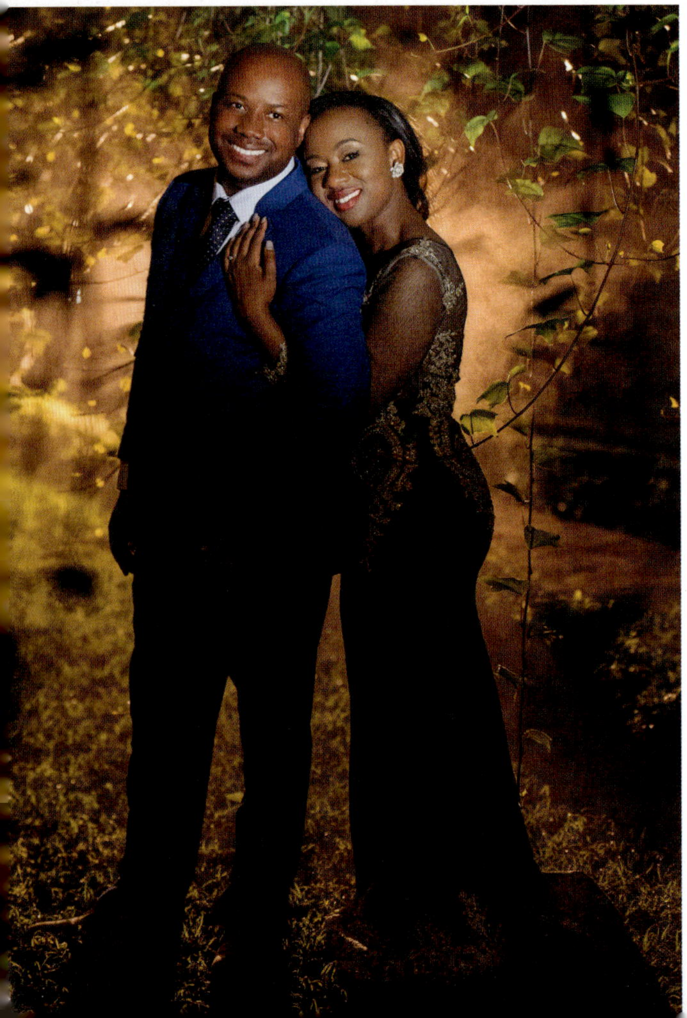

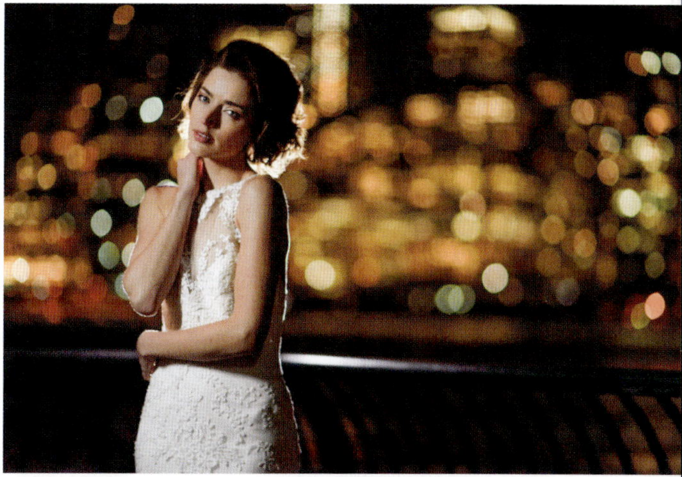

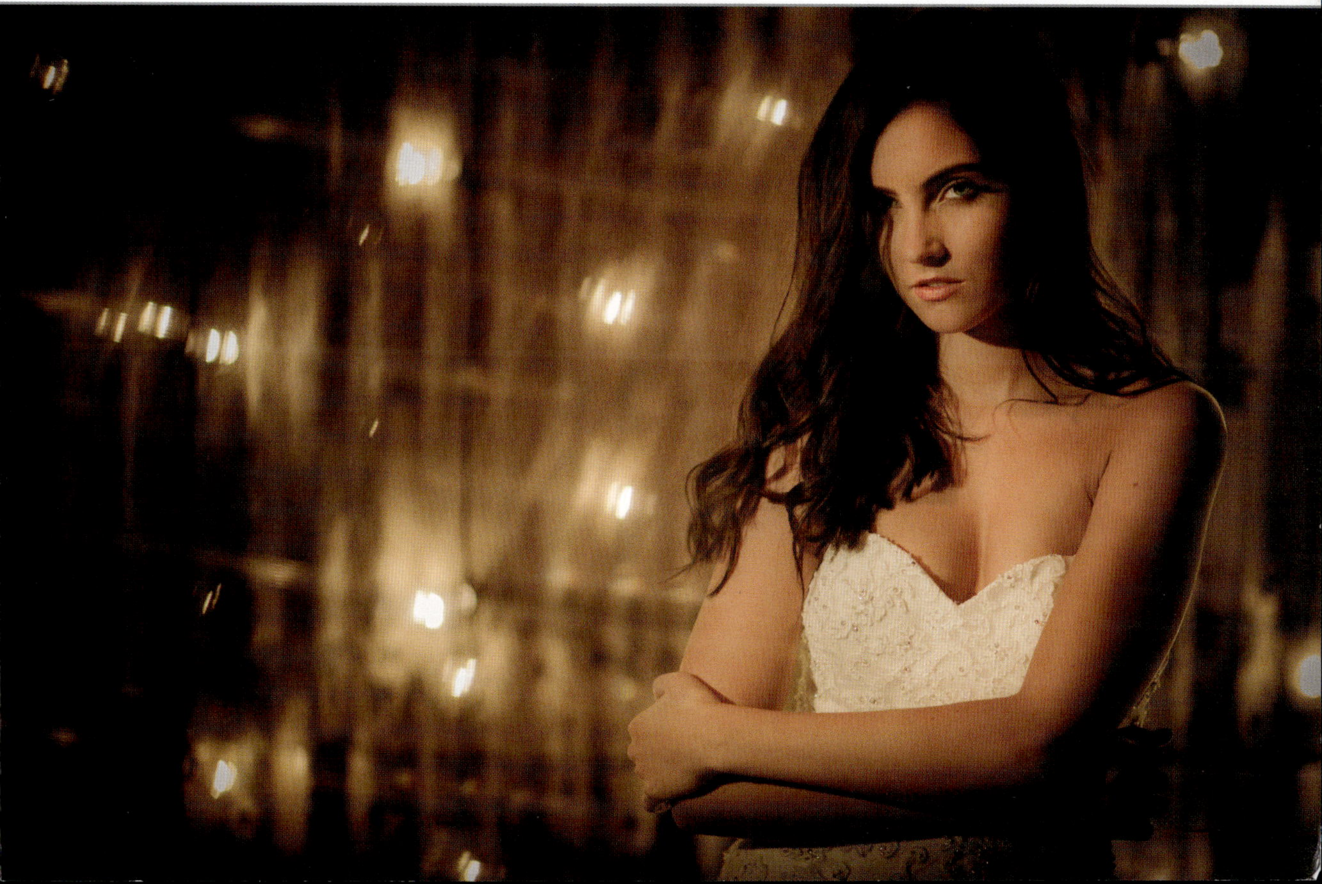

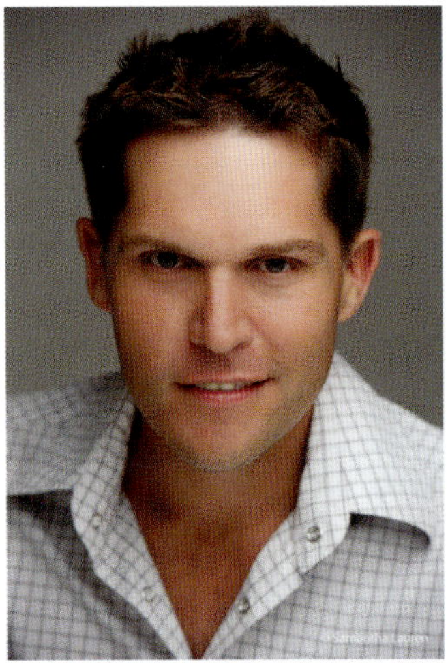

About the Author

Brett Florens launched his career as a photojournalist in 1992, while fulfilling national service obligations in his native South Africa. Since then, his devotion to photography has taken Brett from covering police riot squads to a highly successful career as a wedding, commercial, and fashion photographer—with long-standing clients such as Wonderbra, Playtex, Quiksilver, and Roxy. Recently, he received the distinction of being chosen as the representative Nikon Wedding Photographer, making him one of twelve photographers chosen worldwide as the best in their particular field. Brett is also the author of *Brett Florens' Guide to Photographing Weddings*, *Modern Bridal Photography Techniques*, and *One Wedding* (all from Amherst Media®). He currently travels extensively, shooting and hosting professional seminars. Visit www.brettflorens.com for more information on Brett or to check out the video companion to this book.

The Dark Age

The Date: Saturday, 15 January, 2002
My Assignment: Wedding
Checklist: Fuji Superia 100 (8 rolls); Fuji Reala 400 (4 rolls); Fuji Superia 400 (5 rolls); Ilford XP2 Black & White (3 rolls); Nikon F4 camera for color; Nikon F90 camera for black & white

We arrive at the bridal preparation room and start shooting details. My Nikon is F4 loaded with the 400 Superia. As I'm shooting indoors with window light, I'll be able to get a shutter speed of around 1/125 second. Using my Nikon F90, loaded with the 400 ISO black & white film, I shoot the bridesmaids' activities, as well as the ladies' makeup being applied. The bride is now ready for her portraits. So far, I have shot twenty-two images of the details on the color roll, and now I need to change to the Fuji Reala because the skin tones look better than they do on the Fuji Superia. (The Reala, however, is prohibitively expensive—hence the two types of film I am carrying). I don't want to waste the remaining fourteen frames on the Superia roll, though, so I manually rewind the film to just before the tongue is swallowed by the cassette and, before putting the partially used film into my pocket, make a mental note that I have shot twenty-two frames. I shoot around eighteen carefully lit and posed images on the Reala before repeating the process of manually rewinding the film and putting that one into my other pocket.

> "Oh my word – I get exhausted just remembering the rigmarole I had to go through!"

Now it's time to head off to the church, where I shoot some more photojournalist-styled images with the Nikon F90 camera and the Ilford black & white film. I have replaced the Reala with the partially used Superia roll. To advance the film to the correct place, I set my camera to manual, put it on the highest shutter speed and smallest aperture, then hold my hand in front of the lens to ensure no stray light enters the frame as I shoot off twenty-three frames (to ensure that I don't have any double exposures). I fire off the remaining thirteen images of the bride getting out of the car and take a portrait with her father. As I rush into the church, I insert a new roll of Superia 400 as I need a high ISO for the low light inside the dark church. The ceremony goes well, with me shooting around thirty color images on the Superia 400 and fifteen black & white on the Ilford film. Done and dusted.

I now prepare for the family formals and load my camera with the Superia 100, since we are shooting outside with good light. I use a roll and a half for that and—as before—I manually rewind the film to replace it with the partially shot Reala roll I had used for the bride's portraits. Now I need the best film available for the bridal couple together. It's the same procedure. The daylight fades fast, so we concede defeat and head to the reception.

The first dance is a little more complicated, as I like to shoot it in black & white with available light only.

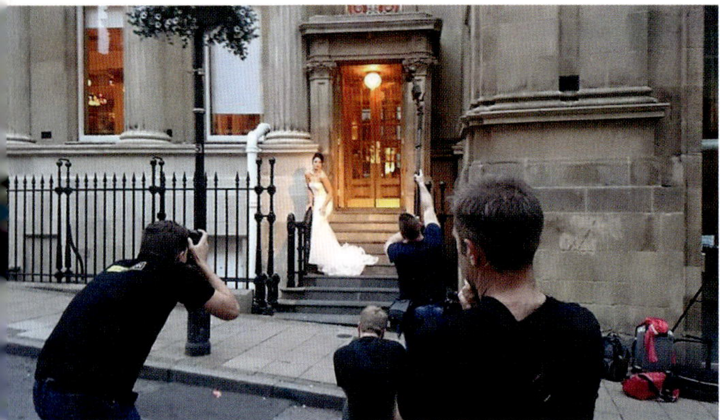

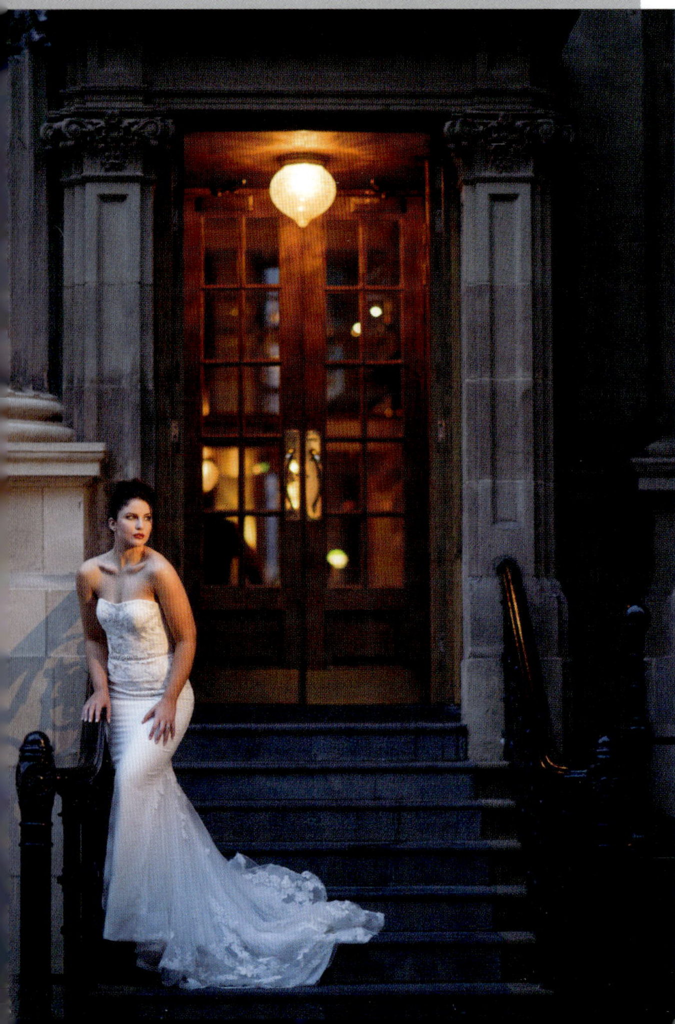

Images I–1 and I–2. I am fortunate to work with some great brands, including Enzoani gowns. These images are from a campaign I shot for them on the streets of Birmingham, in the UK. I loved combining the existing ambient light with the Lowel GL1. As you can see from the behind-the-scenes image, I had the GL1 mounted on a monopod and elevated to give a very theatrical spotlight feel. This light can be focused, and here I opted to have a narrow beam isolating the model. As a tungsten-balanced light source, it tied in very well with the light bulb that was in the doorway behind her (more on color balance in chapter 4). It wasn't intentional, but I like the shadow of the person inside the room; it adds a narrative to the image and gives us the impression that the bride is taking a moment for herself out of the reception—time to reflect on the events of the day. *Tech Specs:* Nikon D4s, 800 ISO, Lens: 85mm f/1.4, Aperture: f/1.4, Shutter speed: 1/100 second, Mode: M.

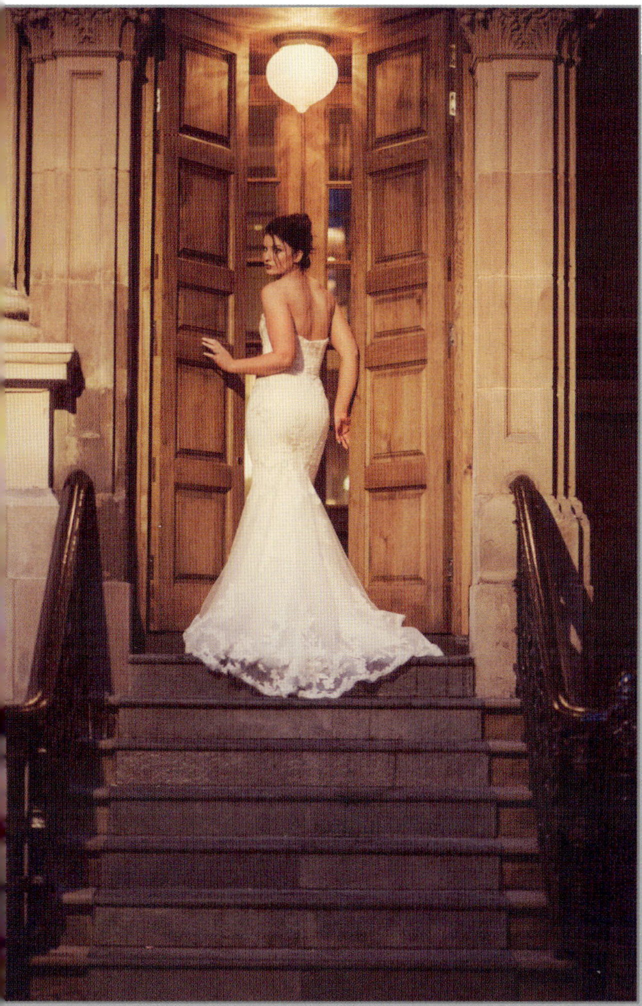

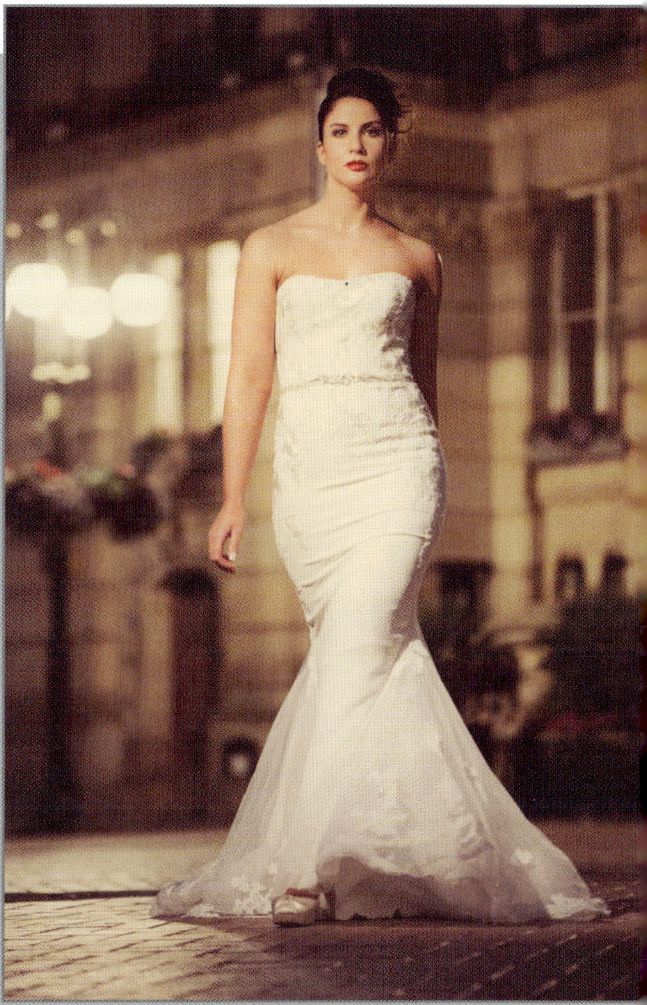

Images I–3 and I–4. For these images, created during the same session, I decided to spread out the beam from the Lowel GL1 in order to illuminate the gowns. I also used a different postproduction technique to give myself more options. *Tech Specs:* Nikon D4s, 800 ISO, Lens: 85mm f/1.4, Aperture: f/1.4, Shutter speed: 1/100 second, Mode: M.

However, using ISO 400 film means I battle with slow shutter speeds. As films use a chemical process to develop, I can push it 2 stops (technically underexposing it, but recovering the image in processing). The grain in the resulting images does make them resemble a form of sand art—but, hey, it's art! I would also need to remember to let the lab know *which* roll I would like pushed and by how many stops. This would involve tricks like tearing off the lid of the box containing the roll of film, putting that particular roll in a separate place in the camera bag, or making a strong mental note as to which is which . . .

Oh my word—I get exhausted just remembering the rigamarole I had to go through!

Image I–5. An engagement session is a great opportunity to show off your lighting and photographic skills. I shot this image in a hotel room against a large mirror. The bride, Naailah, was illuminated with a pocket flashlight, and I really like how the light bounces off the mirror to light up the back of her dress in the reflection. The flare from the reflection of the flashlight also created an interesting flare above her hair, which added to the atmosphere of the image. The harsh light accentuated her high cheekbones and beautiful jawline. *Tech Specs:* Nikon D4, 320 ISO, Lens: 85mm f/1.4, Aperture: f/1.4, Shutter speed: 1/60 second, Mode: M.

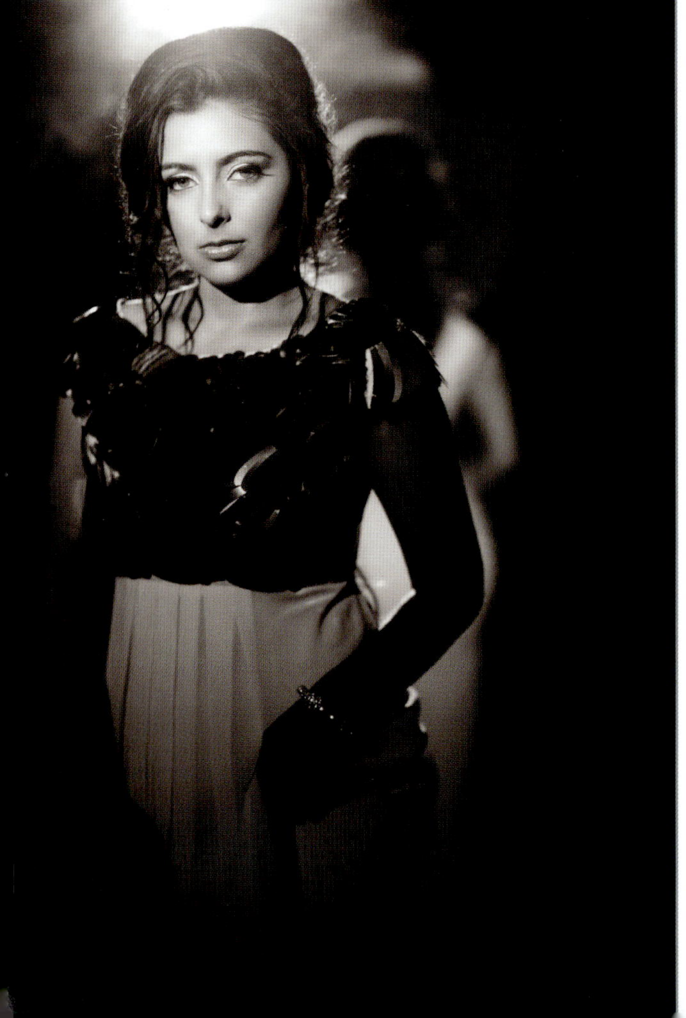

Shooting film was physically and mentally tiring. I am so grateful for the digital revolution that has, amongst many other things, enabled us to shoot a different ISO simply by changing a camera setting—in mere seconds! Aside from no longer having to carry dozens of different rolls of film, with their limited capabilities, we now have the ability to literally shoot in the dark! The hardware available to us these days is so advanced that it has opened a whole new avenue for us to express our creativity. Not only have the cameras advanced but new lighting solutions have also emerged, with costs that are not beyond the reach of most photographers.

As a result, I'm no longer afraid of the dark. In fact, I embrace it and use the opportunity to create images for my clients that they never dreamed were possible. These are not only my wedding clients, but also my commercial, fashion, and portrait clients. Once you learn to trust your camera's capabilities—which may take a while, since the concept of shooting smooth images at 12,800 ISO or higher seemed totally unfathomable just a few years ago—you will find infinite ways to express yourself.

“Once you learn to trust your camera's capabilities, you will find infinite ways to express yourself.”

1. Equipment and Exposure Basics

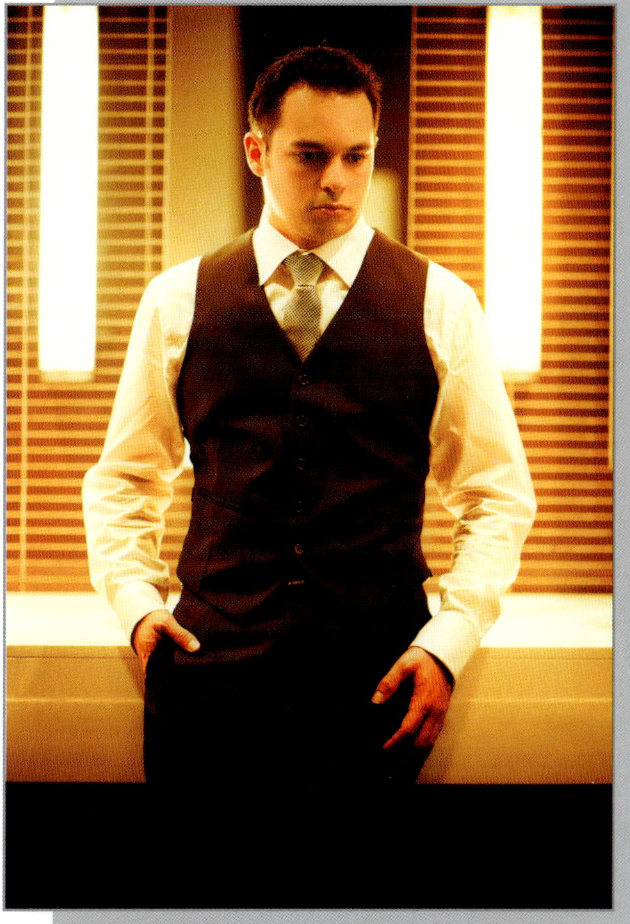

ISO and Noise

The light sensitivity of the camera's sensor is described numerically with an ISO number (ISO is an abbreviation for the "International Standardization Organization"). The higher the ISO number, the more reactive to light the sensor will be. The ISO setting is of particular concern to low-light

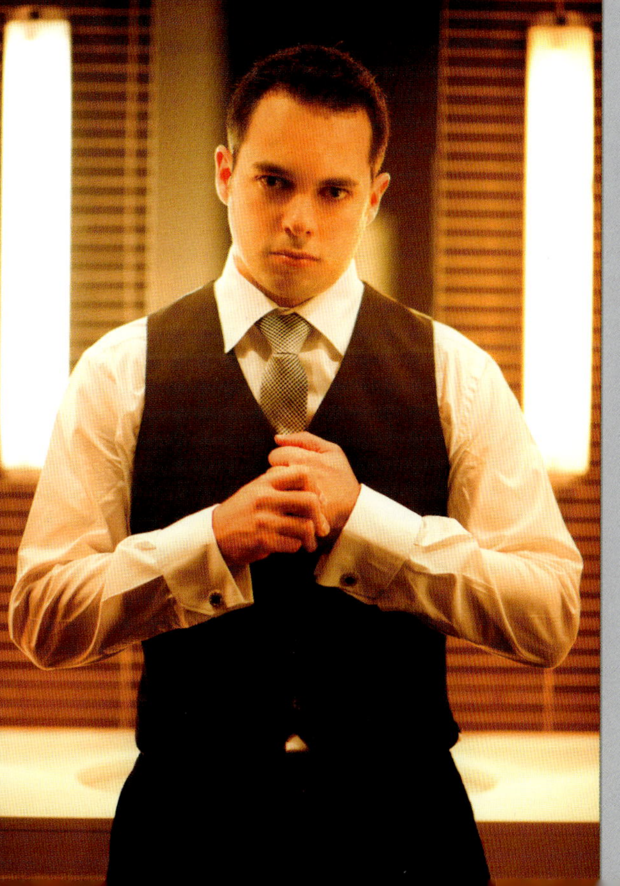

Images 1–1 and 1–2. High-end hotels and event venues often pay a lot of attention to the decor and feel of the restrooms. This means they can be very visually appealing—and sometimes make for great and unexpected images. These images were shot at a country club where the groom was preparing for the wedding. I went into the restroom to wash my hands and loved the light. (Always be observant regarding light and locations; you will be amazed at how a seemingly common location can facilitate interesting images!) No additional lighting was used here—only the ambient lighting in the room. *Tech Specs:* Nikon D3s, 4000 ISO, Lens: 85mm f/1.4, Aperture: f/1.4, Shutter speed: 1/500 second, Mode: A.

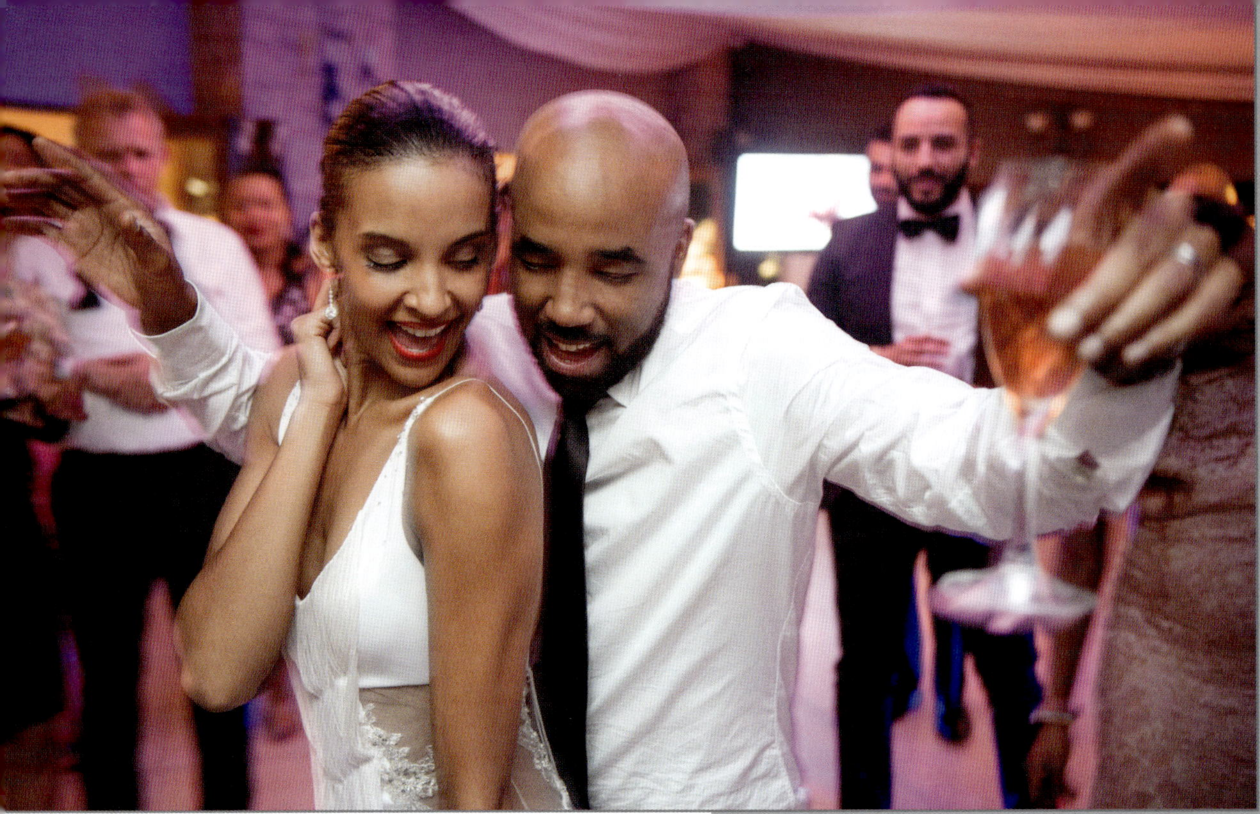

Image 1–3. Capturing the mood and atmosphere that the bride and groom have constructed is imperative to the success of a wedding photographer. This image of a very happy bride and groom dancing at their reception not only captures their love and intimacy, but also the vibe of the wedding. In the past, when the maximum ISO available to us was around 400, the background didn't feature as prominently because the flash "killed" it. Now, the flash acts as a fill light to complement the ambient light. *Tech Specs:* Nikon D750, 2500 ISO, Lens: 24–70mm f/2.8, Aperture: f/2.8, Shutter speed: 1/15 second, Mode: M.

photographers because, along with aperture and shutter speed, it is one of the settings used to control exposure. In low-light conditions, we want to maximize the light entering the camera—but our aperture settings are limited by our lenses (we can only open up so much), and our shutter speeds can only get so long before camera shake and motion blur become serious issues. Therefore, enabling the camera's image sensor to record more of the limited amount of light entering the camera is a crucial factor.

However, setting a higher ISO comes at its own price: noise. Noise, sometimes called "digital noise," refers to random, image-degrading speckles that appear that become especially pronounced when a high ISO setting is selected. For example, images created at 8000 ISO will have more noise than images created on the same camera at 100 ISO. Noise also tends to be most obvious in the shadow areas, the tonal range that is integral to low-light images. The appearance of noise can also vary according to your shutter speed, the ambient temperature where you are shooting, and the camera model you are using.

In the next section, I'll walk you through a test sequence that will help you evaluate the level of noise your gear produces at various ISO settings.

Equipment

It's a simple fact that some cameras and lenses perform better under lower light conditions than others. If you are shooting weddings and other social functions where low-light photography will be an everyday part of your work, it will make sense to invest in equipment that lets you make the most of these situations.

Cameras

One of the easiest ways to reduce the noise in your images is to invest in a newer camera. Film produced "grainy" images at ISO 800, and the early digital cameras couldn't do much better than that. In the last two to three years, however, great advances have been made in sensor technology, resulting in cameras that can produce relatively noise-free images when shooting at 12,800 and even 25,600 ISO. For wedding, portrait, fashion, event, and some landscape photographers, this technology has made it possible to capture great images in lighting conditions that, even a few years ago, would have been extremely problematic. Studio photographers, on the other hand, generally shoot at lower ISO settings and wouldn't really get that excited about lower noise technology. (*Note:* You may also notice that your camera has a noise reduction feature available in its file settings. It's not a setting I activate for my low-light wedding and portrait photography. It tends to be used more often in long-exposure scenarios like those described in chapter 6.)

ISO Test

Many photographers feel that their cameras have difficultly capturing images at higher ISO settings, so I fully understand their hesitance to shoot in low light. If you are reluctant to try high ISO shooting, I suggest you go out and really test how far your camera will allow you to go. You will then at least have a definitive guideline as to the capabilities of your particular camera.

The tests that I did with my own camera are presented in the next image sequence. I started by choosing a low-light scene with a consistent overall light level. Then, I set my camera to aperture priority at f/1.4 (any consistent aperture

"I suggest you go out and really test how far your camera will allow you to go."

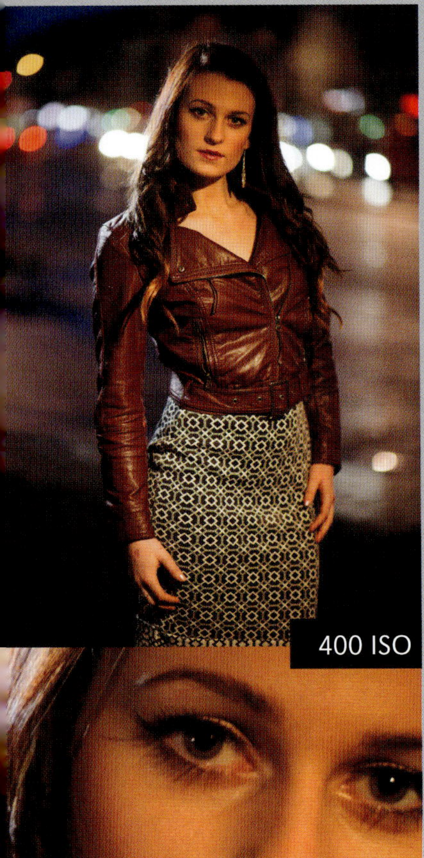

Image 1–4. *Tech Specs:* Nikon D4s, 400 ISO, Lens: 85mm f/1.4, Aperture: f/1.4, Shutter speed: 1/60 second, Mode: A.

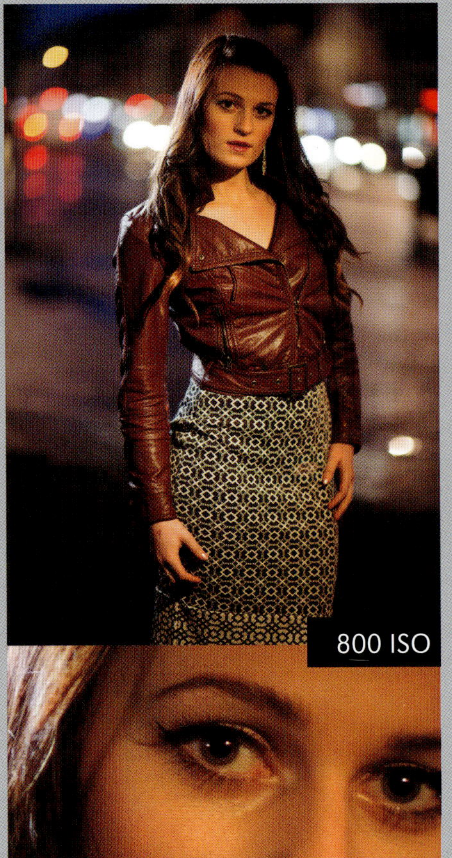

Image 1–5. *Tech Specs:* Nikon D4s, 800 ISO, Lens: 85mm f/1.4, Aperture: f/1.4, Shutter speed: 1/100 second, Mode: A.

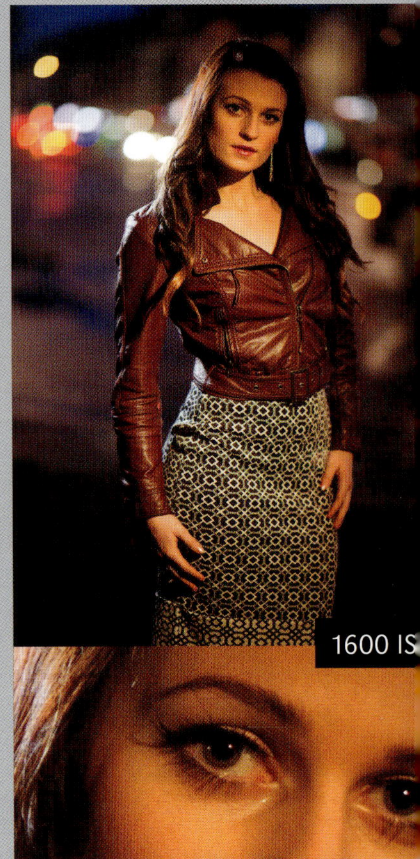

Image 1–6. *Tech Specs:* Nikon D4s, 1600 ISO, Lens: 85mm f/1.4, Aperture: f/1.4, Shutter speed: 1/200 second, Mode: A.

will do; if the maximum aperture of your lens is f/4, shoot at that—more on lenses and aperture in the next section). With the camera at 400 ISO, I shot one frame. Then, without moving the camera, I adjusted the ISO up one stop and took another shot. I repeated this process until I reached the upper limit of my camera's available ISO settings (20,000 ISO). Because I had the aperture setting locked down, this produced a consistent sequence of exposures (**images 1–4** through **1–10**). For each shot, the enlargement gives you a closer look at the noise formation and image detail. Looking at the specs for the images, you can see that the shutter speed automatically got shorter in reaction to each increase of the ISO.

Once you've shot your own sequence of images like this, go through them one by one and assess the limitations—or, indeed, the *capabilities*—of your camera. At what point does the noise level become objectionable to your eye?

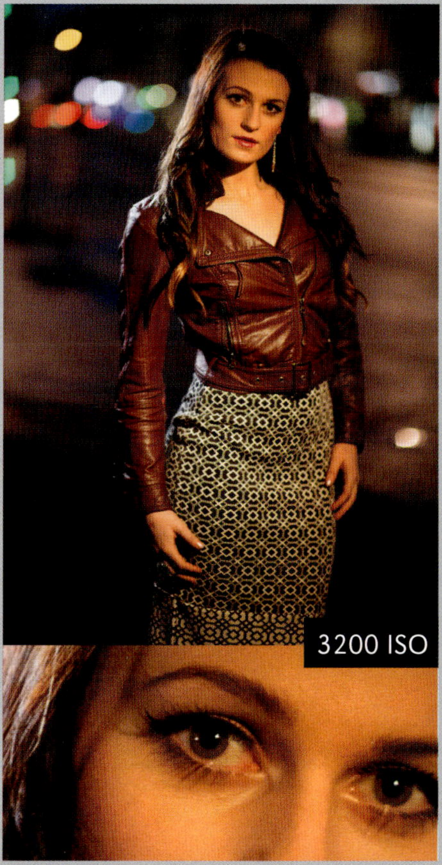

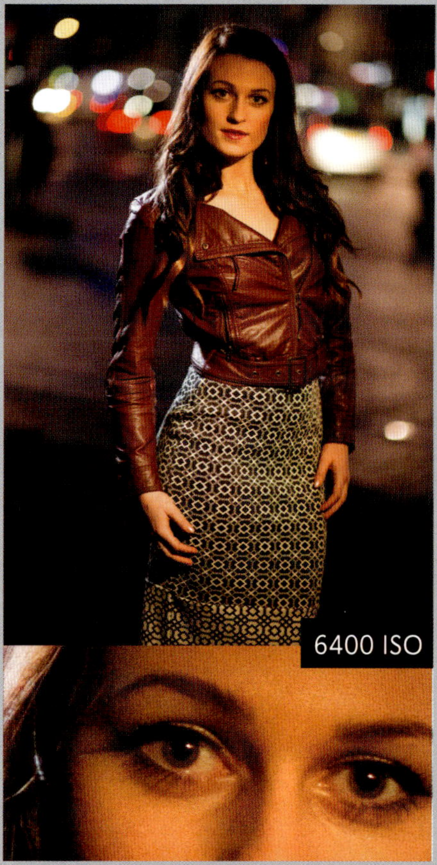

Image 1–7 (left). *Tech Specs:* Nikon D4s, 3200 ISO, Lens: 85mm f/1.4, Aperture: f/1.4, Shutter speed: 1/400 second, Mode: A.

Image 1–8 (right). *Tech Specs:* Nikon D4s, 6400 ISO, Lens: 85mm f/1.4, Aperture: f/1.4, Shutter speed: 1/1000 second, Mode: A.

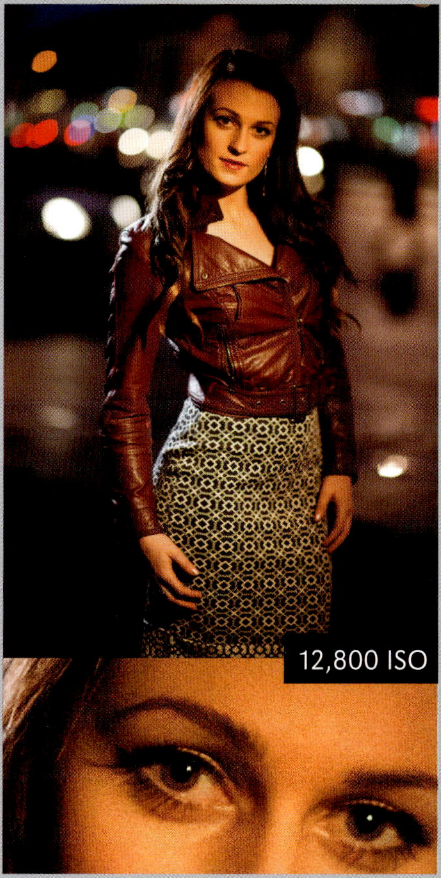

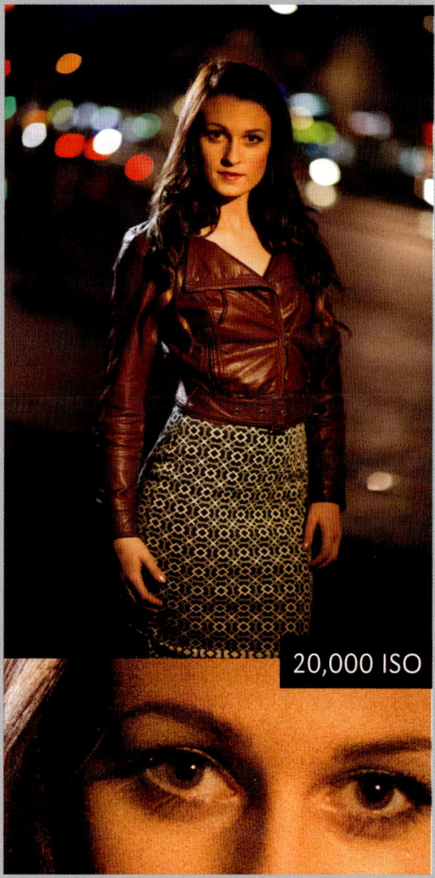

Image 1–9 (left). *Tech Specs:* Nikon D4s, 12,800 ISO, Lens: 85mm f/1.4, Aperture: f/1.4, Shutter speed: 1/2000 second, Mode: A.

Image 1–10 (right). *Tech Specs:* Nikon D4s, 20,000 ISO, Lens: 85mm f/1.4, Aperture: f/1.4, Shutter speed: 1/4000 second, Mode: A.

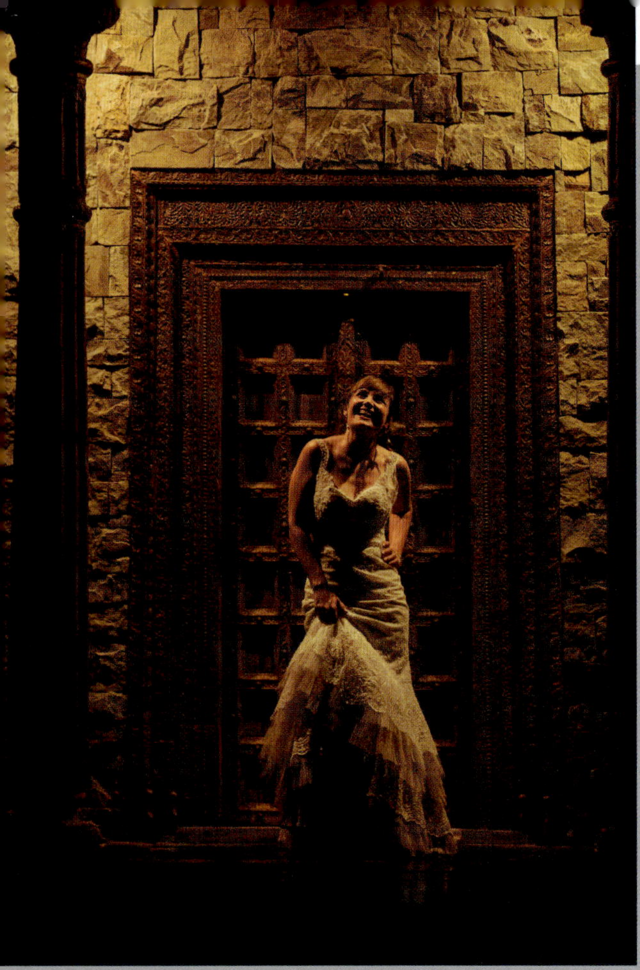

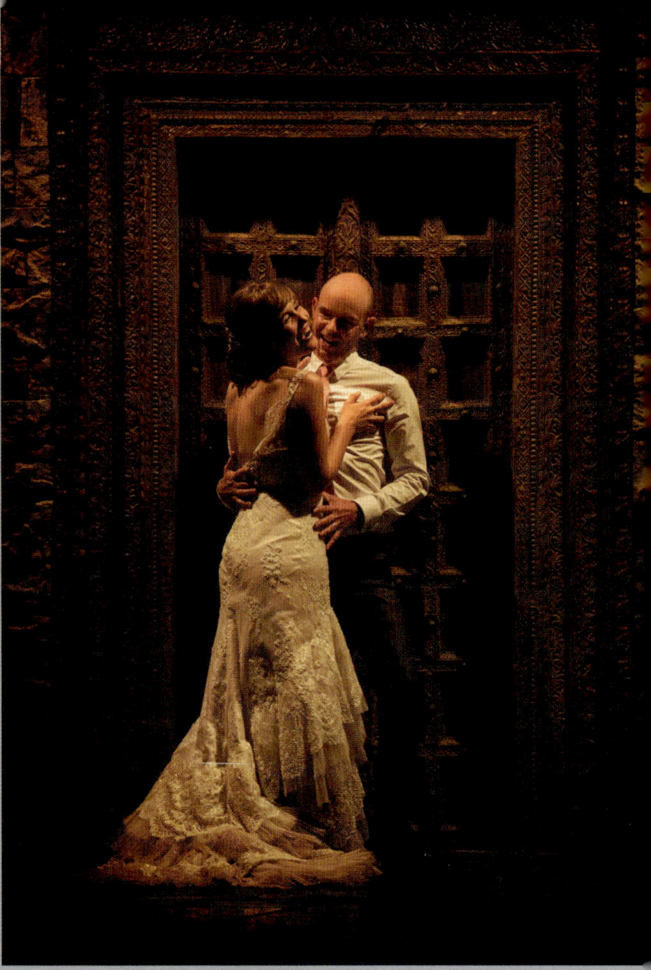

Images 1–11 and 1–12. These images were created at Harford House, an exquisite boutique hotel in the KwaZulu-Natal Midlands in South Africa. The décor has a Balinese influence and when I saw these doors that were so beautifully lit by tungsten down-lighters, I had to shoot there. With directional lighting from above, it's important to keep your subjects' faces up toward the light. That will give you the most flattering results. Notice how the directional lighting really accentuates the texture in the dress, showcasing the wonderful lace work, as well as the carpentry in the door and stone work. You will see that the shutter speed is quite low. In retrospect, I could have gone to 4000 ISO and a 1/100 second shutter speed, but I am pretty stable when I hold my camera—maybe that's an advantage of my military training on how to hold a firearm. *Tech Specs:* Nikon D4, 2500 ISO, Lens: 70–200mm f/2.8, Aperture: f/2.8, Shutter speed: 1/60 second, Mode: M.

Lenses

Since both high ISOs and long shutter speeds tend to exacerbate noise problems, it makes sense that low-light photographers would favor other ways of maximizing the light recorded in their low-light exposures. This means shooting at wide apertures. Accordingly, fast lenses (lenses with very wide maximum aperture settings) are especially desirable for night and low-light shooting. A lens like the 85mm f/1.4 or f/1.8 will work really well.

A happy side effect is that shooting at a wide aperture also enhances the chance of creating an image with interesting bokeh. This term comes from the Japanese word *boke*, meaning "blur" or "haze." In photographic terms, it is the aesthetic result of the blur created by the lens in the out-of-focus (out of the depth of field) parts of an image. It produces especially smooth and dreamy effects on the background when shooting at very wide apertures. (More on bokeh in chapter 6.)

Getting Great Exposures

When it comes to metering exposure in low-light conditions, it is a slightly different ball game to metering in bright ambient lighting situations. The principles are intrinsically the same, but there are a few challenges that may present themselves.

Basics

A good basic guideline to keep in mind when handholding the camera (as you will for most event photography) is to choose an ISO that will give you a shutter speed that is the same or higher than the focal length of the lens that you are using. For example, if you are shooting with the previously mentioned 85mm lens, you'd want your shutter speed set at no less than 1⁄85 second—or the closest equivalent (usually 1⁄125 or 1⁄100 second). This will reduce the amount of motion blur caused by any small camera movement during the shot. Of course, if you expressly *want* to have that motion in your image, you can choose as long a shutter speed as you need to achieve the desired degree of blurring. The beauty of being in a creative field is that you are able to interpret and express things in your own way.

Histograms

Whether you're shooting in bright light or low ambient light, one of the most important pieces of exposure advice I can give you is to learn how to use your camera's histogram. The histogram is available for viewing on your camera's LCD during image playback, but it does not always appear when using the default settings. If that's the case on your camera, check the manual and make sure you know how to find it.

> "During playback, it's important to learn how to evaluate what the histogram is telling you about your image."

During playback, it's important to learn how to evaluate what the histogram is telling you about your image. The histogram is a graphical representation of the distribution of pixels within your image. These pixels are graphed on a scale that extends from dark/black on the left

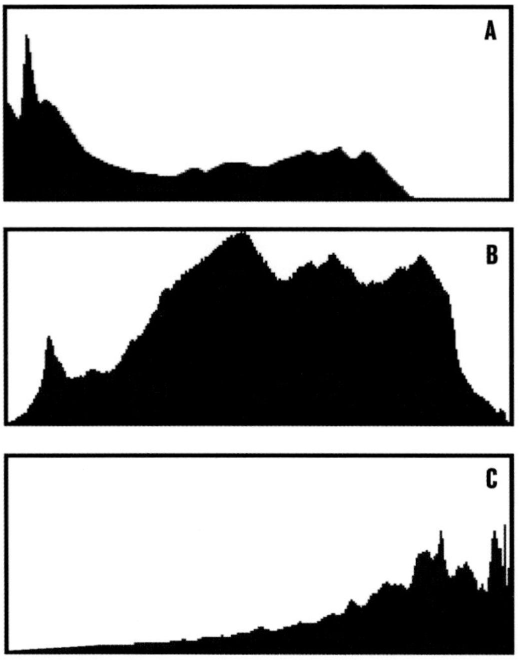

Image 1–13. When the histogram data presses against the left edge of the graph (A), the image may be underexposed. When the data bunches up at the right edge of the histogram (C), the image may be overexposed. When the histogram data tapers down to the left and right edges (B), the captured tones should contain all the available detail.

(numerically represented by 0) to light/white on the right (numerically represented by 255). Pixels that fall within the bounds of this graph represent tones that will be depicted with detail in the final image. If you see that a lot of pixels are bunched up at the left edge of the histogram, this can indicate underexposure or shadow clipping (areas of black with no detail). Conversely, if a lot of pixels are bunched up at the right edge of the histogram, this can indicate overexposure or highlight clipping (areas of white with no detail).

It's important to remember that histograms are image-specific, so scenes that contain a lot of dark tones will naturally tend to have more data toward the left edge of the histogram. Likewise, the pixels in a very light or bright scene will tend to fall more toward the right edge. You have to interpret the histogram based on your intent for the scene. In most cases, however, seeing data that is blocked up at the far right or far left edge deserves consideration; it is a good indicator that some exposure adjustment may be needed.

You may also find that your camera can display the data for each RGB color channel on the histogram, revealing the color distribution of the pixels. This is useful when you need to ensure great color rendition, however it may be a little too much information for most photographers to process on the fly. I personally stick to using the luminosity (grayscale) histogram on my camera's LCD. I use the white balance presets or a gray card to ensure good color; more on these techniques in chapter 4. At the end of the chapter, we'll take another look at histograms.

Shooting Modes

If you understand exposure and control your exposure in manual mode, then you shouldn't have too many problems transitioning from bright light shooting to working in low ambient light situations. However, if you are a photographer who shoots in one of the preset modes (either the program, shutter priority, or aperture priority modes), then you are going to need to alter your conventional way of achieving good exposure.

Exposure Metering and Compensation

During bright ambient light conditions, we often find ourselves shooting with backlighting—a look that has romantic and flattering connotations. When shooting in one of the preset modes, this tends to mean using the EV (exposure value) button to dial in an exposure compensation adjustment to compensate for the backlighting. Since the camera's metering system will tend to see the bright backlighting and underexpose the scene, we'll usually be increasing the exposure value by whatever the scene dictates. This lets us push the histogram to the right (creating brighter values)—but just to the point where we don't sacrifice detail in the highlights of the important parts of the image.

Image 1–14. Shooting first dances can create spectacular images. However there are often challenges encountered. Sparklers seem like a great idea and can create dramatic results, but you need to be aware of the contrast between the ambient light and the bright light of the sparklers. You could get lucky and coincidentally have a situation where the ambient light is bright enough. However, if you find that the sparklers are correctly exposed and your subjects are really dark, then you will need to introduce additional artificial light. Having a dimmable light is very beneficial in this instance, as you can communicate to your assistant to increase or decrease the intensity as needed. *Tech Specs:* Nikon D3s, 4000 ISO, Lens: 70–200mm f/2.8, Aperture: f/4, Shutter speed: 1/80 second, Mode: M.

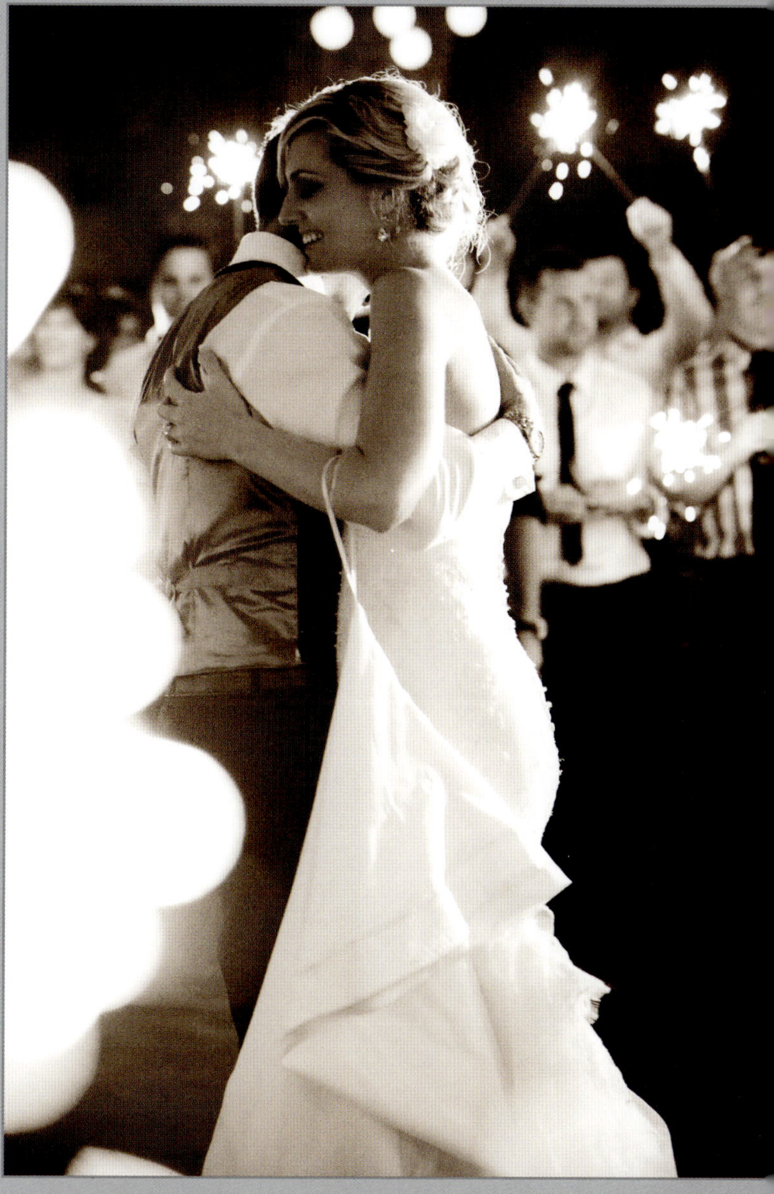

When shooting in low-light conditions, introducing an artificial light source or shooting in a pool of brighter ambient light produces a situation where the background is substantially darker that your subject. If you are shooting in the program, aperture priority, or shutter priority modes, the camera will detect a darker scene and compensate—either by opening the shutter for longer, or by opening the aperture wider, or perhaps a combination of both adjustments.

This is the opposite of the backlighting scenario. With backlighting, if you don't know how to control your exposure correctly, you can very easily end up with a silhouette—an image with the background correctly exposed but very little detail on your underexposed subject. In low light, the automatic metering often allows for

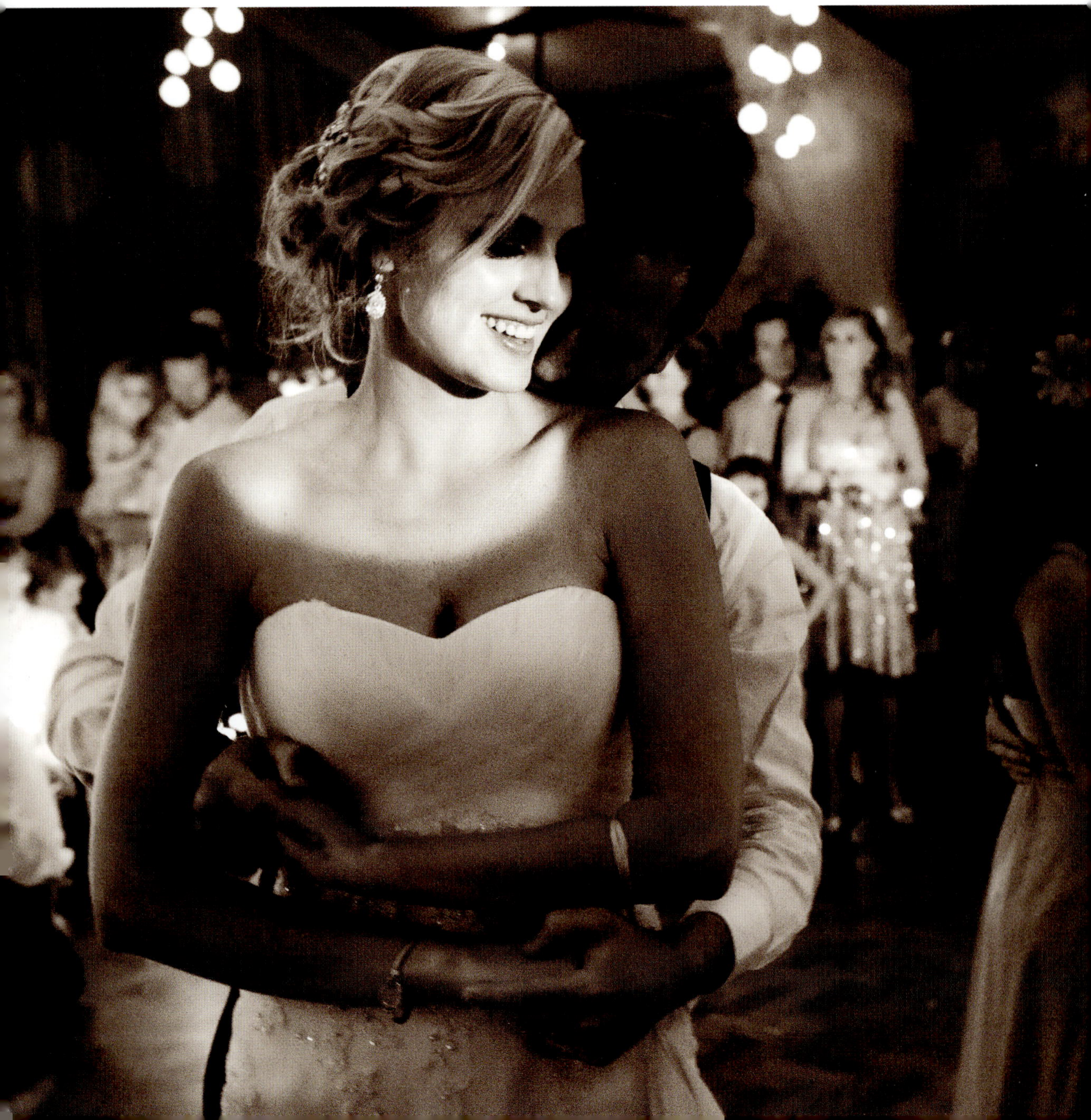

too much light on your subject. They may appear blown out, and the darker background may also record as lighter than it should.

Both of these metering problems occur because the camera is built to properly expose an 18 percent gray subject. When your subject is not 18 percent gray—especially if it's much lighter or much darker—the automatic exposure modes make it *appear* gray. This will happen when photographing a black wall: 18 percent gray. It will happen when photographing a white wall: 18 percent gray. To get a correct exposure that accurately depicts a subject that is *not* 18 percent gray, you will have to intervene and override the settings suggested by the metering system.

If you have a scene where the background is darker than the light landing on your subject, you will need to decrease the exposure by however many stops is required to obtain the correct exposure on your subject. In the manual mode, this is a simple matter of reducing the shutter speed, aperture setting, and/or ISO to cut the required amount of light. In the automated modes, you can use the exposure compensation settings to bring down the exposure to the right level.

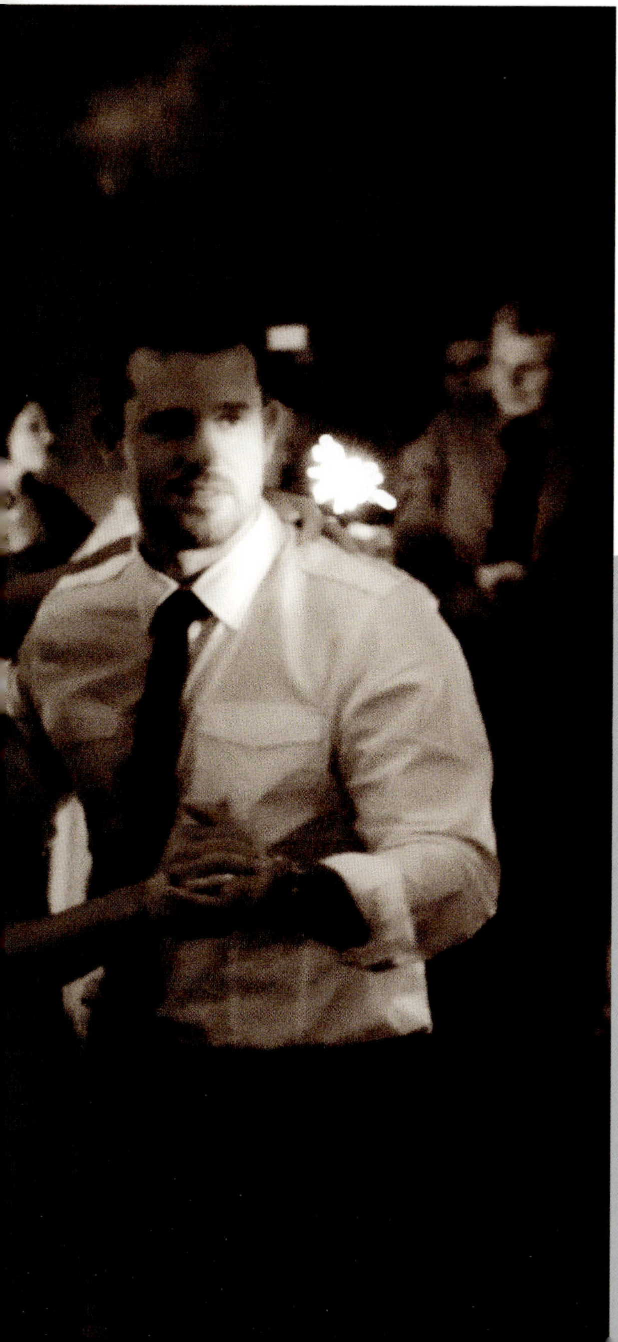

Image 1–15. Often, the DJ brings lights to use during the dancing. These may include revolving lighting or lasers. To be safe, I always try to shoot the dancers with their backs to the lights—so that I don't get dots of light or hot spots on them. That isn't always easy when you are shooting photojournalistically and can't really control the position of the subjects. In this shot, I just got lucky with my timing. The light passed by at the split second I fired the shutter and captured the bride's spontaneous smile while dancing with her husband. *Tech Specs:* Nikon D3s, 4000 ISO, Lens: 24–70mm f/2.8, Aperture: f/4, Shutter speed: $^1/_{50}$ second, Mode: A.

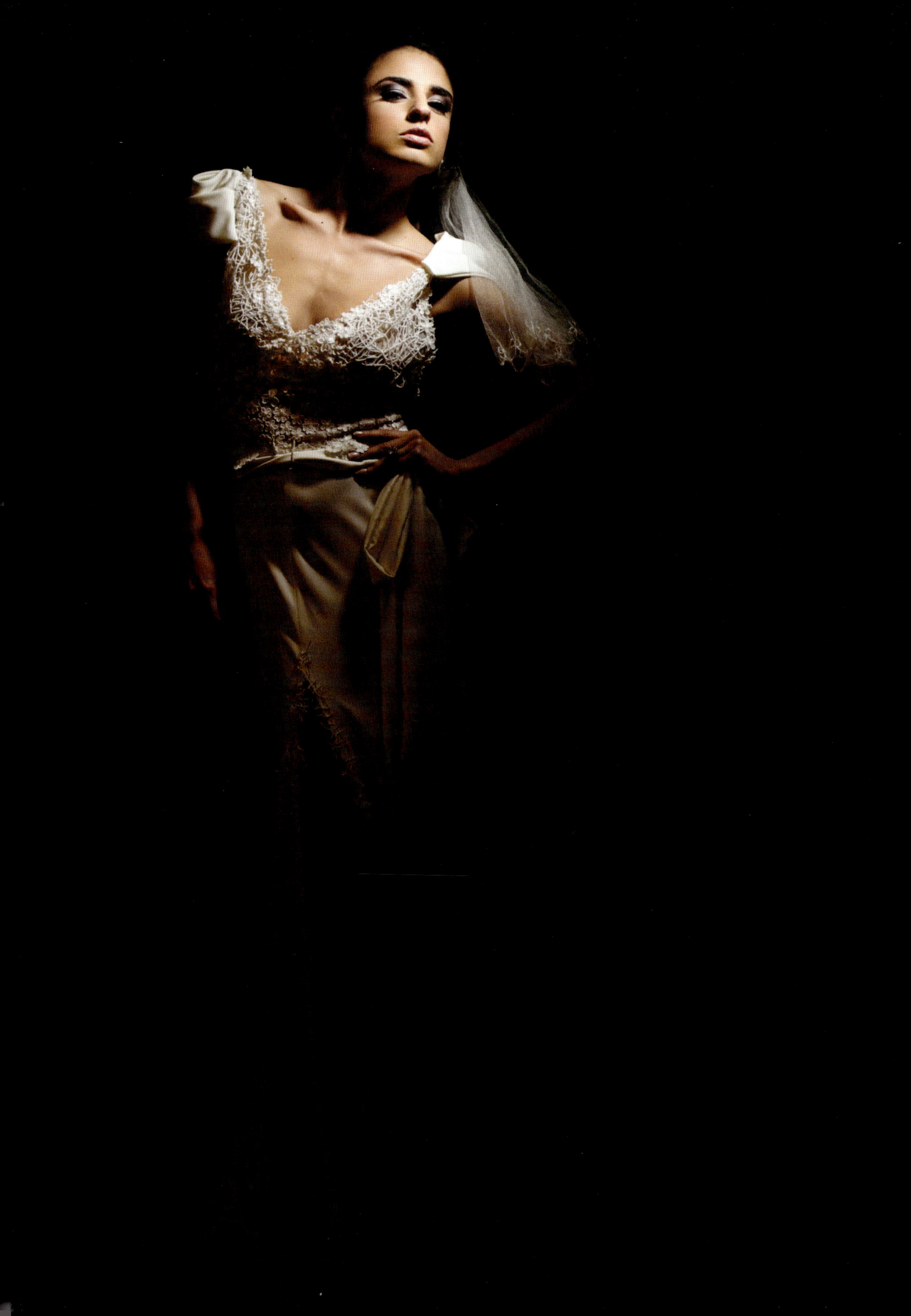

Balancing the Subject and Background Exposure

This brings us to an important point for low-light photography: the difference in the light levels on your subject and your backgrounds. Just as in any other photographic situation where your subject will be recorded at a consistent exposure level, you can indirectly control the ambient light exposure of the *background* by adjusting the level of the light on the *subject*. If you add more light on the subject, you'll need to stop down (using the ISO, aperture, or shutter speed) to maintain the desired exposure level on their skin tones; this, in turn, will result in a comparatively darker exposure on the ambient-lit background. Conversely, you could make the ambient-lit background record as lighter (again, relative to the subject) by reducing the light on the subject and opening up to maintain that skin tone exposure level.

Image 1–16 (facing page). You can allow ambient light from the background to be present in your images—but you can also eliminate it, if you like. By increasing the intensity of the artificial light on the subject and exposing for that, you are—in effect—overpowering the ambient light. Here, I wanted to create a dramatic portrait that showcased the texture of the dress. By exposing for the bright main light I added to do this, I completely eliminated the background. It wasn't a terrible background (just a flight of stairs) but I wanted to demonstrate that you can darken the background considerably if you want to. *Tech Specs:* Nikon D4, 400 ISO, Lens: 70–200mm f/2.8, Aperture: f/2.8, Shutter speed: 1/125 second, -1.7EV exposure compensation, Mode: A.

During the daylight hours, this approach to manipulating the background brightness of your image is not all that easy; powerful strobes will be required to compete with and overpower the bright sunlight. In low-light conditions, you don't need nearly as much light to combat the darkness. If you are using any continuous light source, you can control the amount of light landing on your subject in two ways. First, you can simply increase or decease the power output of the light source. Second, you can move the light source closer to or further away from your subject. From there, compensating for this shift in light levels by changing your ISO, shutter speed, or exposure compensation will enable you to control the exposure of the entire image and get to the point where you want to be. My advice is to start with the desired *background* exposure. Get to that point first—before illuminating your subject. Personally, I have found that is a faster way of getting the desired effect.

Practical Examples

Stick with what you know—if you are accustomed to using the exposure compensation method, or spot metering, or manual exposure, the principles stay the same. However, some techniques and concerns are reversed for low-light shooting. For example, rather than concentrating on avoiding a loss of detail due to blown-out highlights (a major

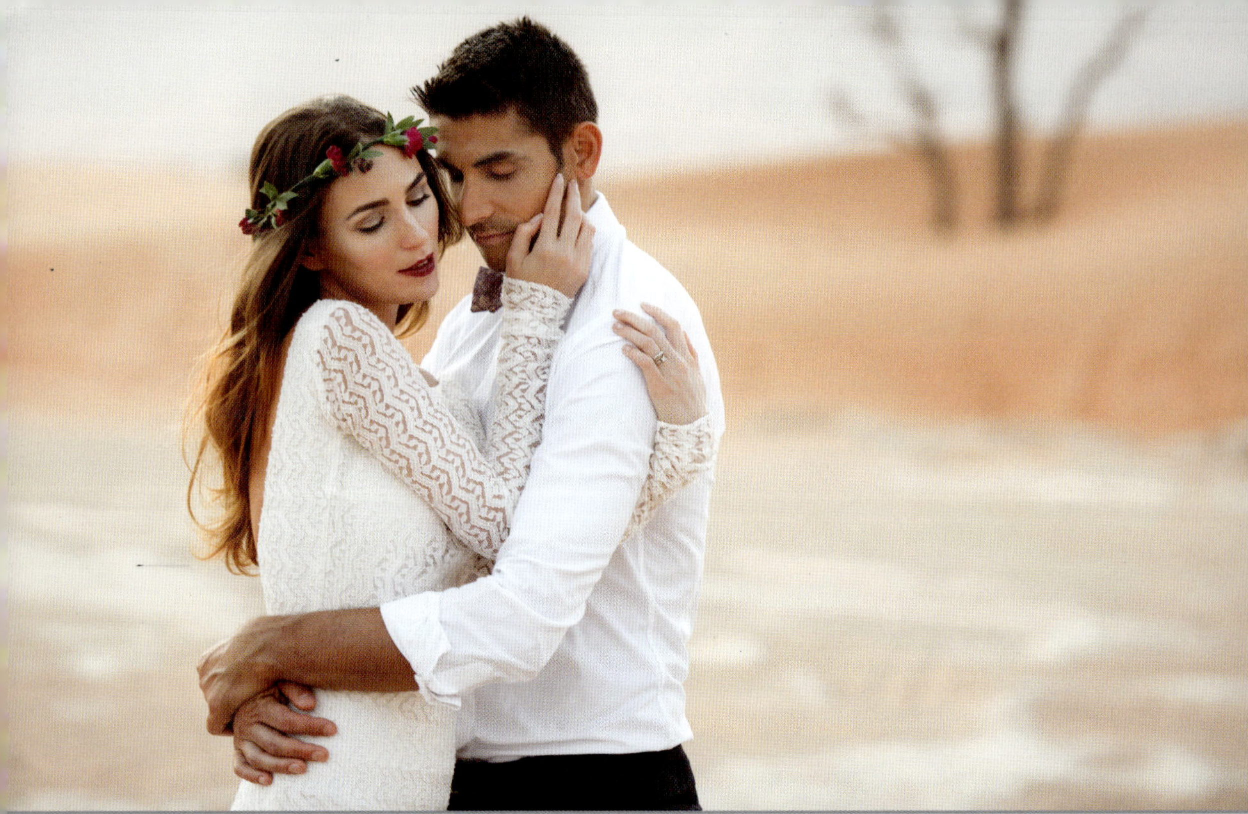

Images 1–17 (above) and 1–18 (right). Lighter tones prevail in this backlit, daylight image. Accordingly, the histogram data is shifted to the right—but the exposure was not allowed to become so bright that important detail was clipped in the highlights. *Tech Specs:* Nikon D750, 1000 ISO, Lens: 70–200mm f/2.8, Aperture: f/2.8, Shutter speed: 1/100 second, Mode: A.

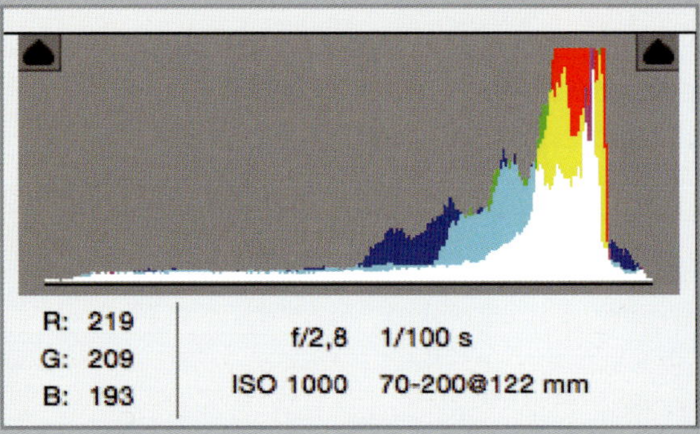

concern in bright conditions), low-light photographers need to be alert for loss of detail in the shadow areas. Let's look at a couple of examples.

A Daylight Portrait

In this typical backlit image (**image 1–17**), I shot in the aperture priority mode using matrix metering. To capture my subjects accurately, I had to increase the exposure to 1⅓ stops over the metering reading. If I had not compensated for the very bright tones and backlighting that dominated the frame, the camera's metering would have led to an image where the subjects were underexposed. Looking at the histogram (**image 1–18**), you can see that the majority of the pixels are gathered between the midtone and highlight exposure areas. I was careful to ensure that the exposure

Images 1–19 (below) and 1–20 (right). Darker tones prevail in this night portrait. As you can see, the histogram data is also shifted to the left—but the exposure was not allowed to become so dark that important detail was clipped in the shadows. *Tech Specs:* Nikon D4s, 6400 ISO, Lens: 70–200mm f/2.8, Aperture: f/2.8, Shutter speed: 1/80 second, Mode: A.

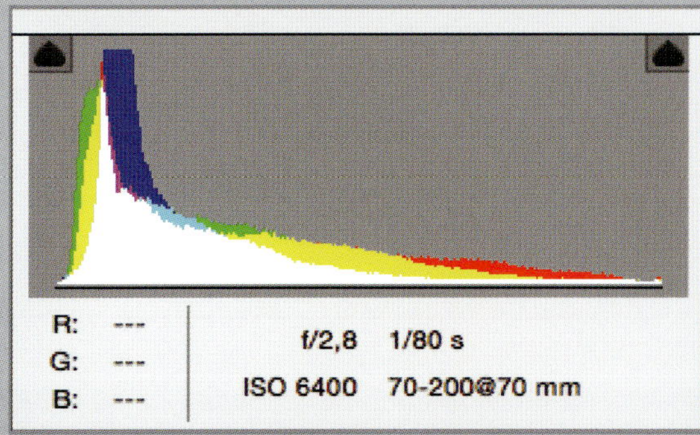

of my subject wasn't influenced by the brightness of the background.

A Night Portrait

In this low-light shot (**image 1–19**), you can see that the majority of the image is darker than the subject. In this case, I was shooting in the manual mode. If I had chosen an automatic mode, I would have had to compensate by decreasing the exposure by 2/3 stop. Otherwise, the subject would have been too bright and I would have lost the detail in the dress. Notice that the histogram (**image 1–20**) is totally different from the one accompanying the bright light shoot; the majority of the pixels are between the midtone and shadow exposure areas. Understanding the information your histogram displays is critical to producing a well-exposed image.

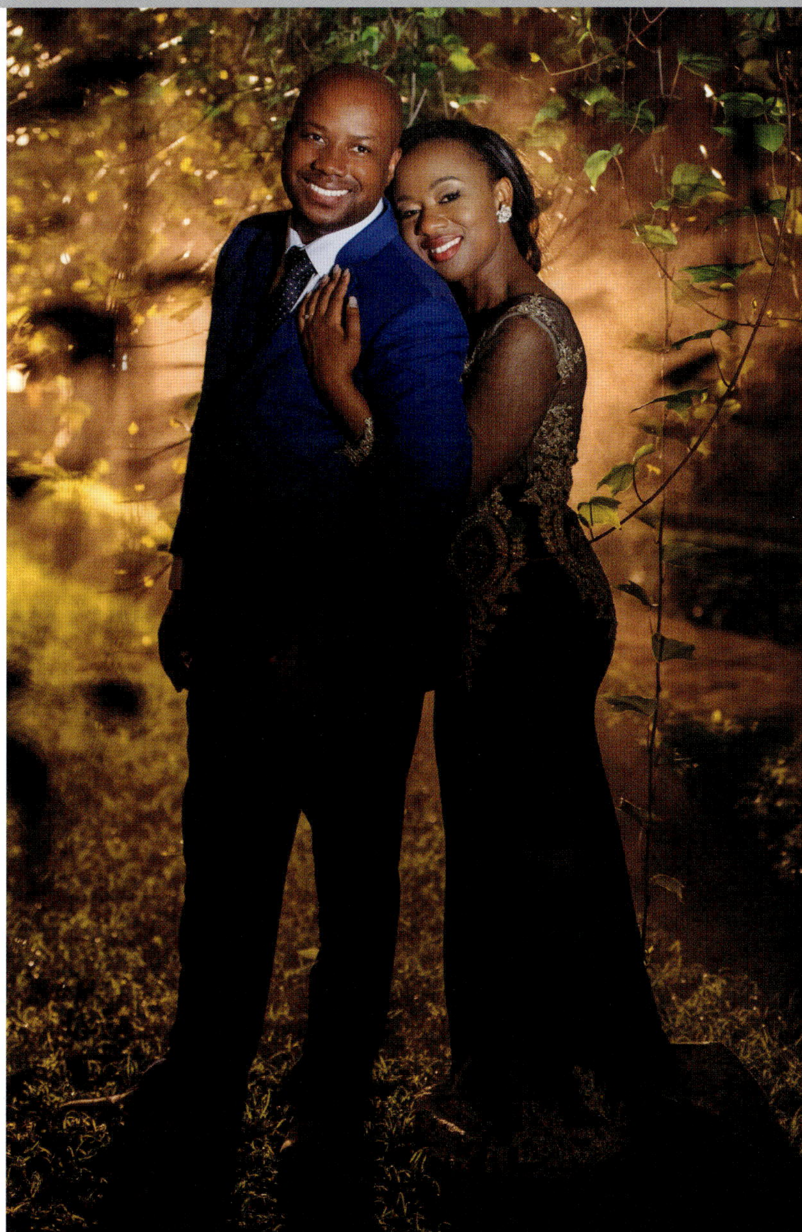

2. Playing with Light

Now that we've covered the basic principles of low-light photography, let's look at the different ways it can be used—and practical examples of the tools you can use to fine-tune your images.

Images 2–1 and 2–2. Shot with only artificial lighting, these late-night images were created during a wedding workshop that I was presenting. The décor company that designed this incredible flower wall had utilized spotlights with pink and red gels to illuminate the blooms and create the atmosphere intended by the team. I used a Lowel GL1 LED (tungsten balanced) to light the models. I really like the dramatic, theatrical effect this produced. *Tech Specs:* Nikon D4s, 1000 ISO, Lens: 85mm f/1.4, Aperture: f/2, Shutter speed: 1/250 second, Mode: M.

The Importance of Playing

As photographers, I think we need to play and experiment more often—especially when we're looking to adopt new techniques. Knowing that we have accomplished a desired look or style in previous shoots instills confidence in our

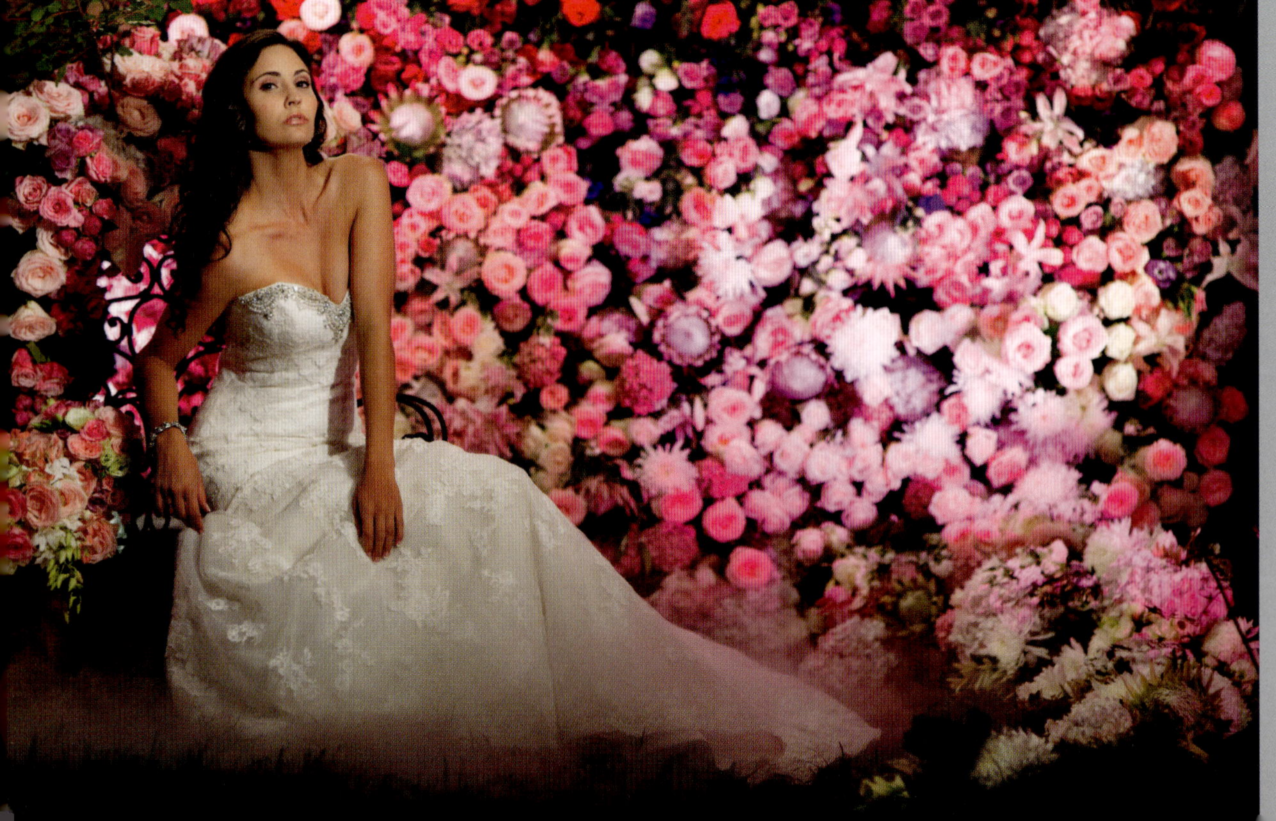

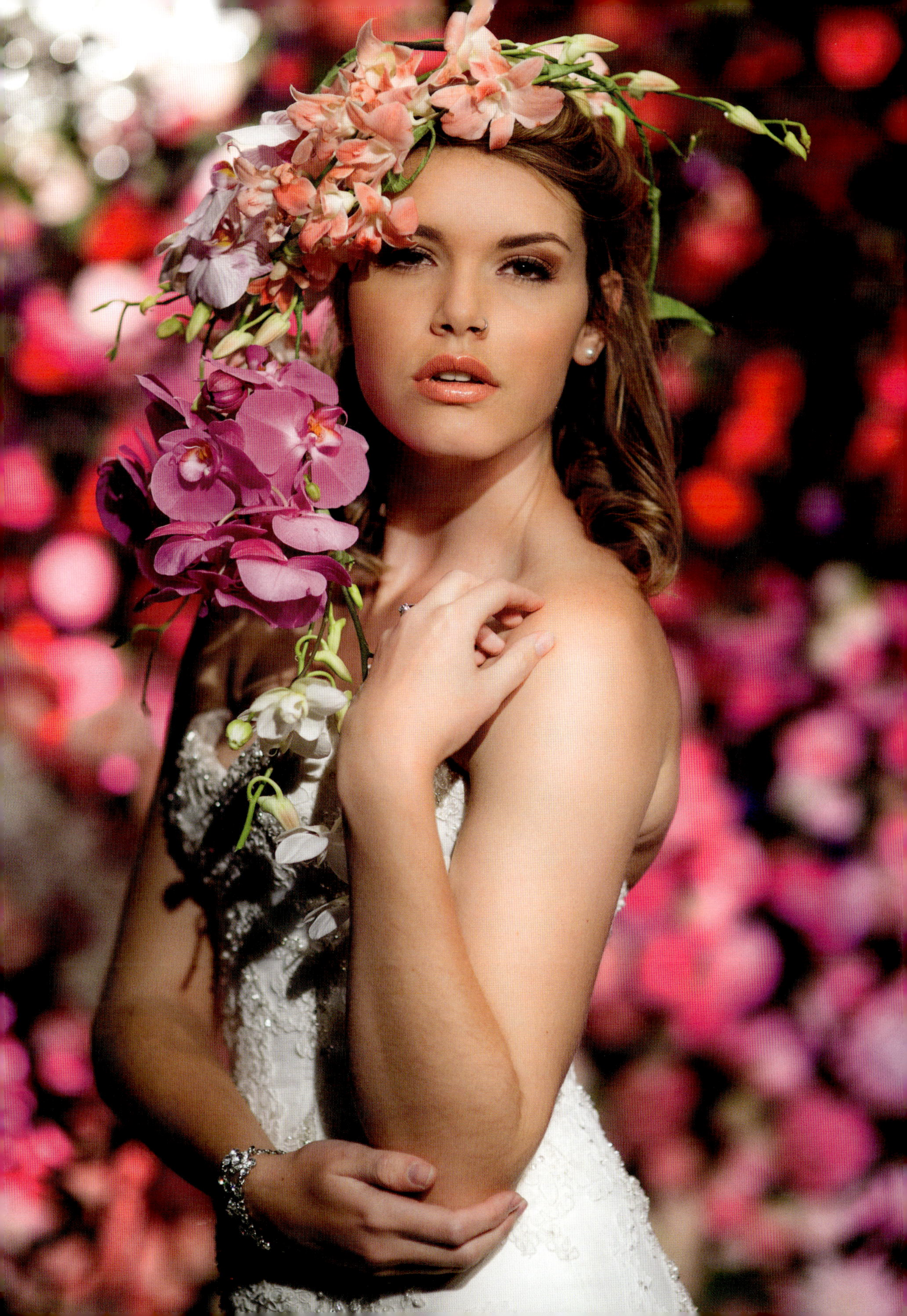

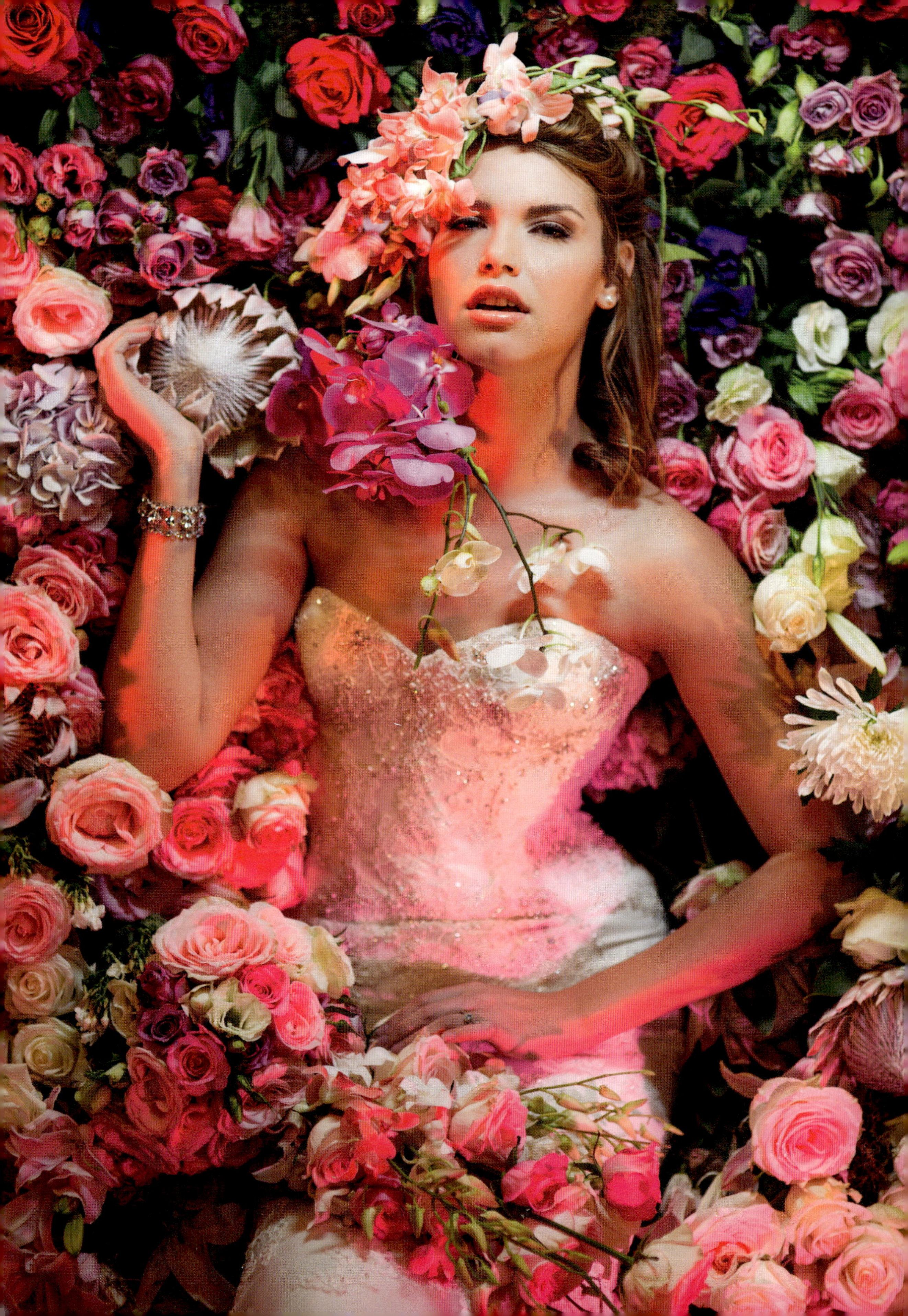

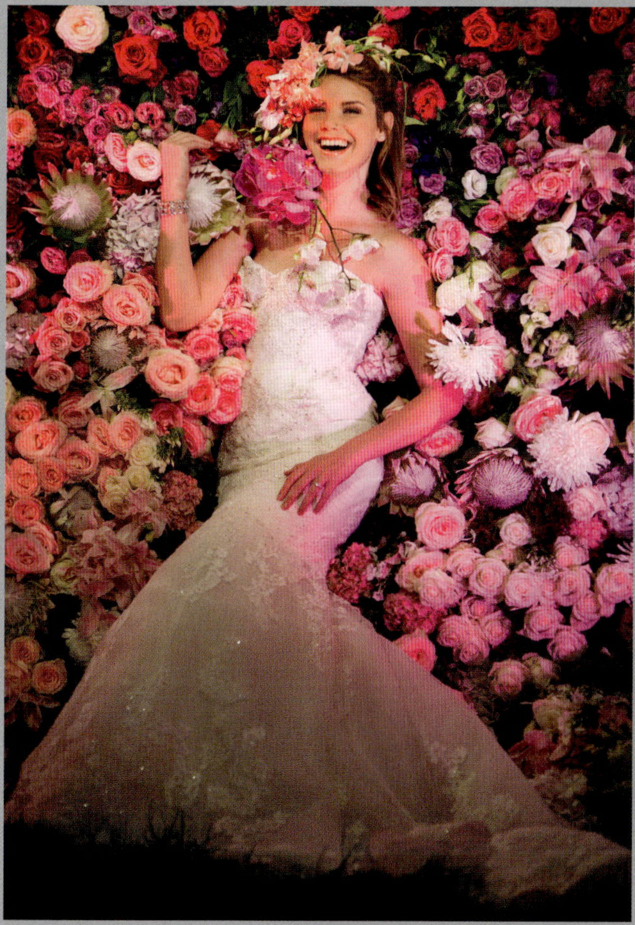

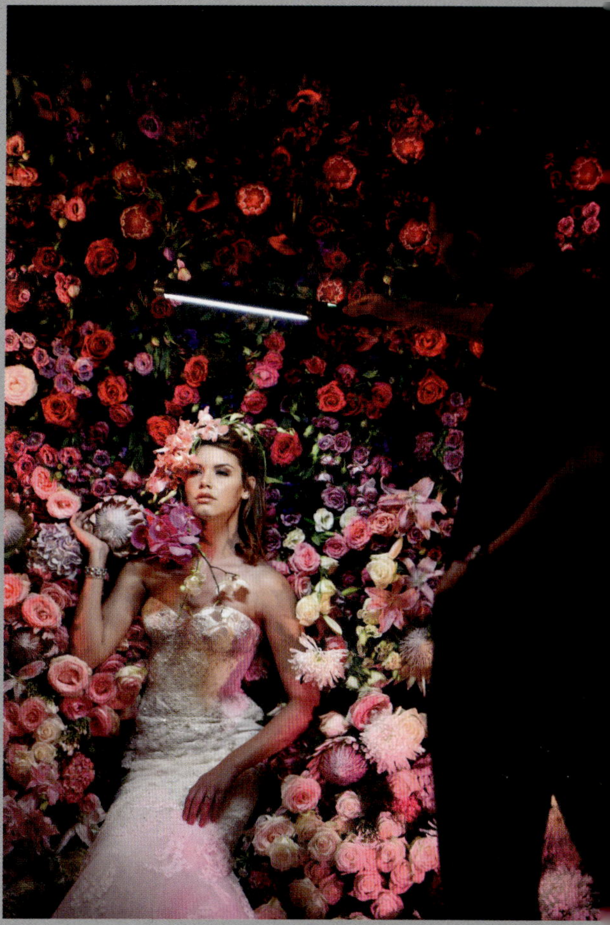

Images 2–3, 2–4, and 2–5 (above and facing page). These images are obviously from the same scene as images 2-1 and 2-2, but this time I used an Ice Light on the model. You can see that this produced a window-light look with softer shadows. Which style is right totally depends on the effect you are looking to achieve—and that will determine the type of light source you choose to use. *Tech Specs:* Nikon D4s, 1000 ISO, Lens: 85mm f/1.4, Aperture: f/2, Shutter speed: 1/320 second, Mode: M.

ability to re-create those same looks amidst the stresses and demands of a session or event. The possibilities and combinations you can explore are as diverse as the countless different styles photographers possess. This is fantastic, because it means that you can create images that personally resonate with you and your carefully nurtured brand.

The Emotional Language of Light

The trick to playing with light is getting to know the different properties of each light source and the emotions they evoke. For example, the Ice Light from Westcott is a soft light source that emulates window light. The Manfrotto LED panel produces light that is a little harder—almost like a beauty dish on a strobe. An LED torch

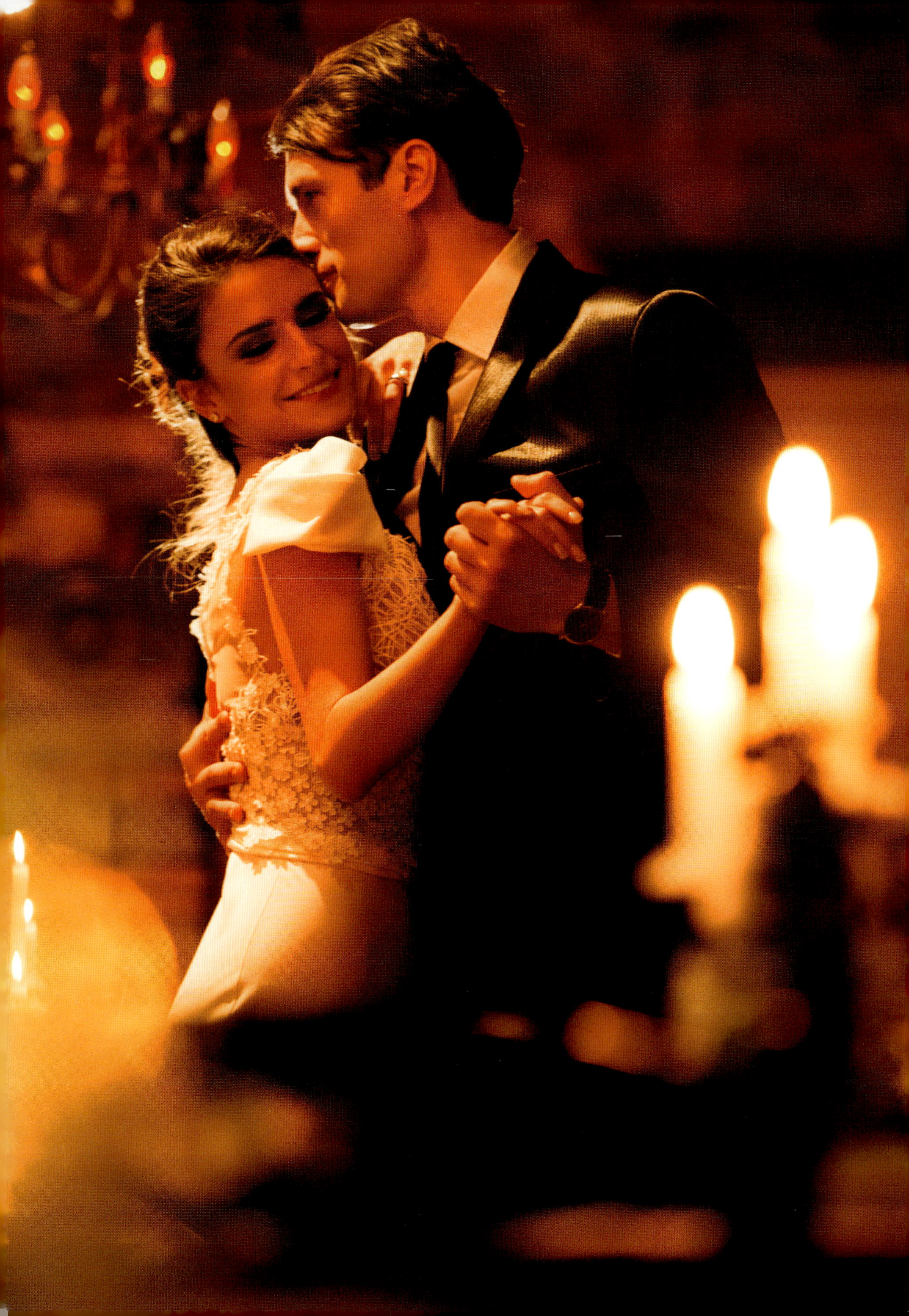

(flashlight), such as the Fenix, is essentially designed for domestic use but can be repurposed for photography to create a rather harsh lighting effect that emulates the look of a bare bulb strobe; it produces razor-sharp shadows that yield a distinctly editorial feel.

Once you've selected a source, don't overlook the myriad ways you might modify it or the look of your image. You can use gels to color the light source and create a very specific mood for your image. You could try shooting through a transparent object (like a prism or a wine glass) to create interesting foreground textures in your images. And we haven't even begun to explore the potential of using some combination of speedlights or off-camera strobes and dragging the shutter to allow ambient light onto the sensor! All of these creative controls can enhance the emotion and visual appeal of your low-light photography.

Image 2–6 (facing page). Photographing through objects on the table can increase the foreground interest. Here, the candelabra and wine glasses improved the sense of depth in the image. The ambient light in the room was very warm and I kept it that way in the postproduction. The rim light behind the couple was created with an Manfrotto LED. This was equipped with a warming gel to maintain the warm glow. *Tech Specs:* Nikon D4, 8000 ISO, Lens: 70–200mm f/2.8, Aperture: f/2.8, Shutter speed: $^{1}/_{125}$ second, +.33EV exposure compensation, Mode: A.

Find the Right Location

The key to low-light or night shooting is to find a location that has some ambient light around—ambient light that would be interesting when out of focus. As you can imagine, this means areas that might not necessarily look good during the daylight can be perfect settings for night and low-light photography. There are so many creative possibilities; the only limit is your imagination.

Collaborate

Once you've set aside a night or two to experiment and create, my advice would be to collaborate on the shoot with a hair and makeup artist, as well as a clothing designer. This will be mutually beneficial. Offer images to the participants in return for their contribution. Approach the shoot as a collaborative partnership, rather than as "your" shoot. This will be more attractive to the other contributors, which in turn will elevate the chances of a successful shoot. The following images were produced during just a few hours of playing.

Practical Example: Tests with a New Camera

I recently acquired a new Nikon DSLR, an incredible piece of technology that can produce astonishingly high-quality images at very high ISO settings. I channeled my enthusiasm for my new acquisition into testing the camera (as well as various light sources) to see what an array of different and striking images I could create.

Test 1: Ambient Light Only

Image 2–7 is the first image I shot during my experiment with my new camera. I started by looking for a background that had some interesting ambient light. In this case, that happened to be a restaurant at a local square. The lines in the background on the bottom half of the image are the railings of a staircase. Shooting only with the available light, I exposed for the ambient light landing on Catherine and fired off a few frames. You will notice that there are multiple catchlights in her eyes, these were from an office building behind me. Those same multiple light sources also caused the various shadows on her chest. The light falling on her is flat and doesn't create much form, however it is still flattering light that yields a pleasing result.

Test 2: Manfrotto LED

Image 2–8 was lit with a Manfrotto LED panel as the main light. You can see that the light from the LED has dominated the ambient light, revealing only one catchlight in her eyes and one shadow on her chest. The shadow is relatively sharp and, as you can see from the contour on her cheek, it is shape revealing. Because of the increased amount of light falling onto the subject, I was able to reduce the ISO setting on my camera. This created an image with a darker background because

Image 2–7. *Tech Specs:* Nikon D4s, 10,000 ISO, Lens: 85mm f/1.4, Aperture: f/1.4, Shutter speed: 1/125 second, Mode: A.

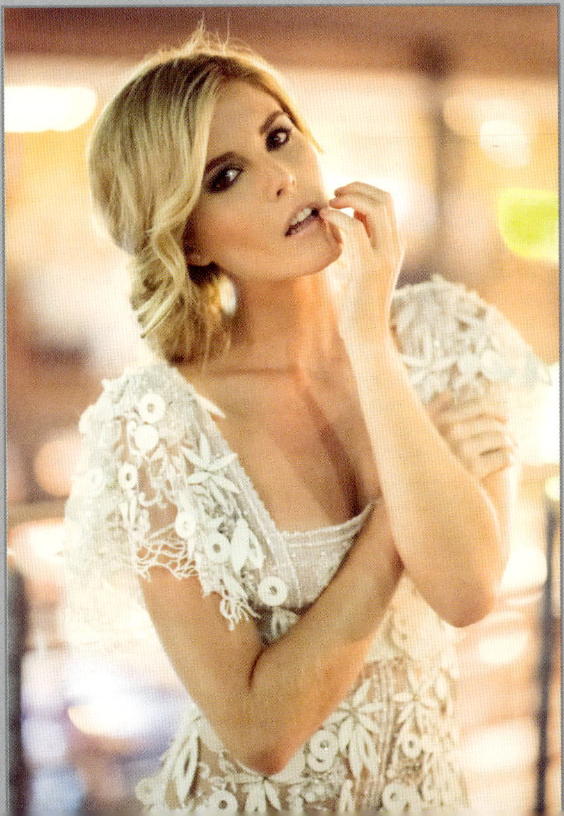

Image 2–8. *Tech Specs:* Nikon D4s, 2000 ISO, Lens: 85mm f/1.4, Aperture: f/1.4, Shutter speed: 1/200 second, Mode: A.

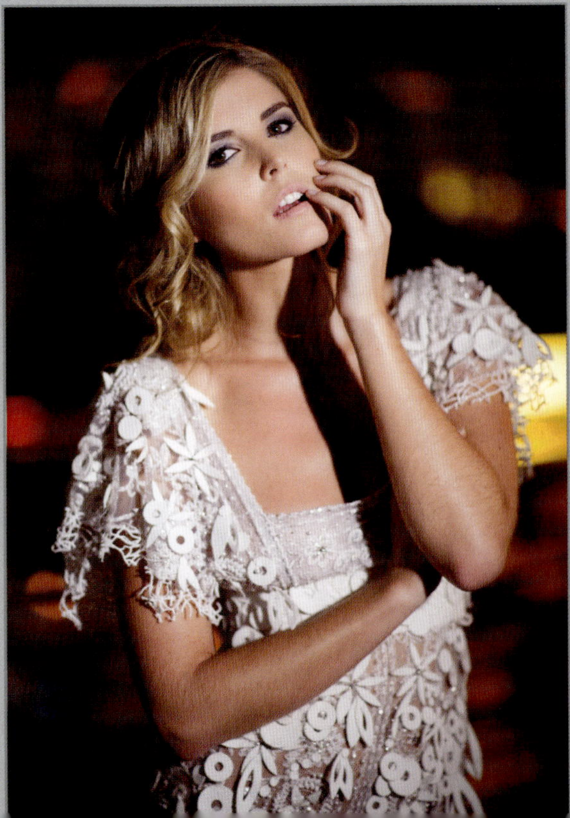

the LED was illuminating only the model, not the background.

Test 3: Adding a Hair Light

Image 2–9 was also shot with a Manfrotto LED panel as the main light. If you compare this to the previous shot, you can see the similarities in the shapes of the shadows and the cheek contouring. For this image, I also added a second Manfrotto LED panel as a hair light. This created separation between the subject and the background, making the image appear more three-dimensional. If you check out the tech specs, you'll notice that my shutter speed on this shot was a little slower than in the previous image. My assistant must have been holding the main light a little farther away from the subject here; the matrix light metering system picked that up and adjusted accordingly—by reducing the shutter speed. This allowed more of the background ambient light in, making it appear lighter than in the image without the hair light.

Test 4: Blue Gel on the Hair Light

By covering the hair light with a blue gel, I added some color and created a more interesting result in **image 2–10**. I have noticed lately that many photographers are having fun with colors in their images used for perfume advertising and I took my inspiration from that style.

Image 2–9. *Tech Specs:* Nikon D4s, 2000 ISO, Lens: 85mm f/1.4, Aperture: f/1.4, Shutter speed: 1/125 second, Mode: A.

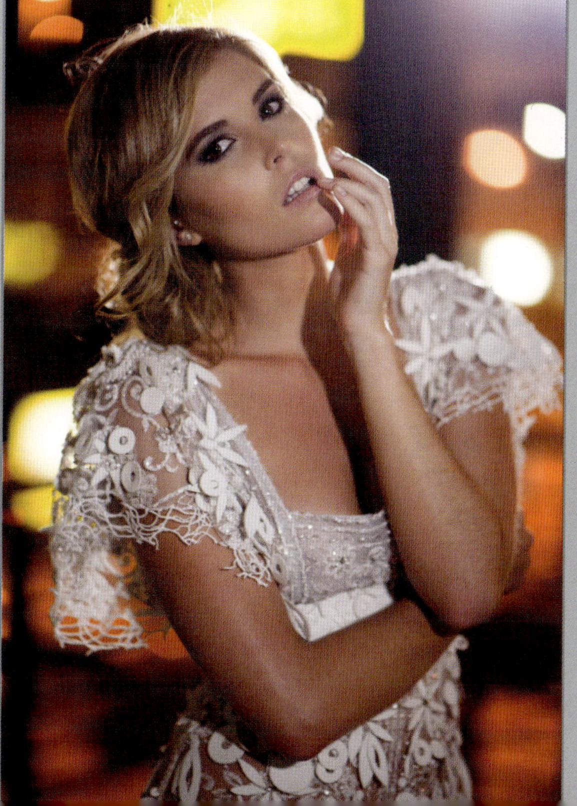

Image 2–10. *Tech Specs:* Nikon D4s, 4000 ISO, Lens: 85mm f/1.4, Aperture: f/1.4, Shutter speed: 1/100 second, Mode: A.

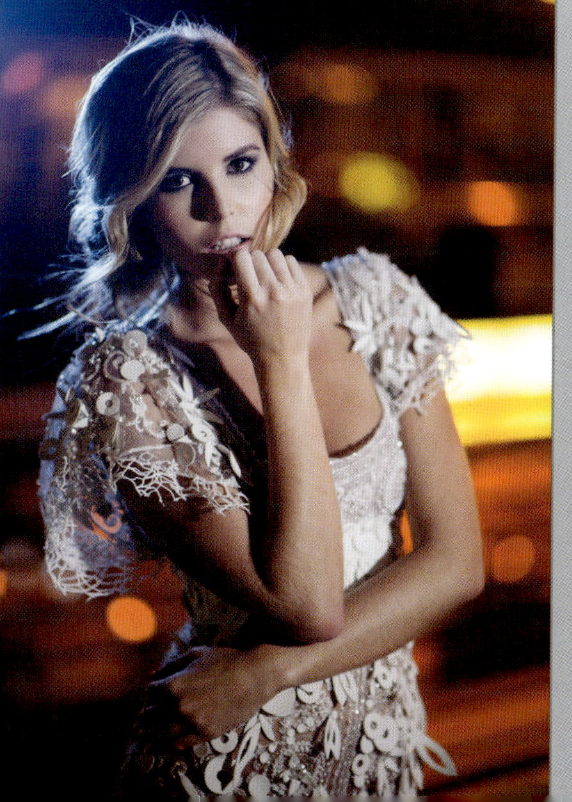

Test 5: Lower Output, Reduced Distance

For **image 2–11**, the main light was still the Manfrotto LED, but I reduced the output and moved it closer to Catherine. The shadows have softened on her chest and the ambient light is more prevalent. Due to the lower output of the light source, the shutter speed dropped. This created a lighter background. I also decided to include some flare from the hair light. With the softer shadows, this created a more whimsical, ethereal result.

Test 6: Trying a Red Gel

Now you can clearly see that I am experimenting with a variety of options—just to see what happens. **Image 2–12** has the Manfrotto LED covered with a red gel. Really, it's just a different option. I also increased the output of the primary light source, the red-gelled Manfrotto LED. This resulted in a higher shutter speed, which in turn reduced the influence of the blue-gelled hair light.

Image 2–11. *Tech Specs:* Nikon D4s, 4000 ISO, Lens: 85mm f/1.4, Aperture: f/1.4, Shutter speed: 1/80 second, Mode: A.

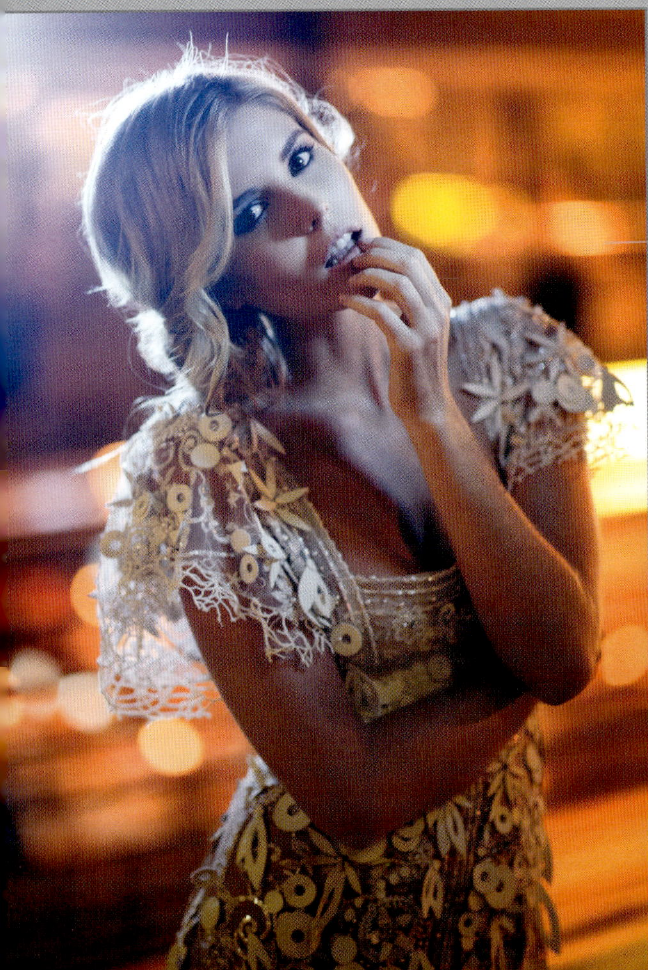

Image 2–12. *Tech Specs:* Nikon D4s, 4000 ISO, Lens: 85mm f/1.4, Aperture: f/1.4, Shutter speed: 1/320 second, Mode: A.

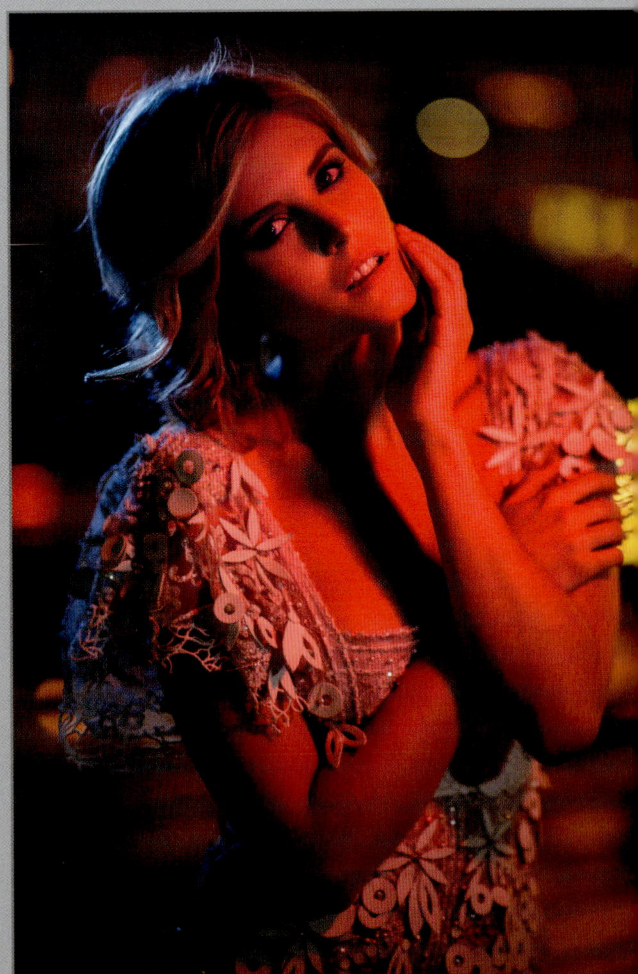

Test 7: Westcott Ice Light

For **image 2–13**, I switched to a Westcott Ice Light for the main light. This produced a softer, window-light effect, similar to a softbox on a studio strobe. I had my assistant hold the light rather close to Catherine, creating a very pleasing result with great form and soft shadows. I hadn't noticed how bright the main light was and that my shutter speed had shot up. If I'd noticed, I could have dropped the ISO to reduce the potential for problematic noise in my image. However, you can see that—even at this high ISO—the image is very smooth.

Test 8: Blue-Gelled Monfrotto LED

With the introduction of a blue-gelled Manfrotto LED panel as the hair light (**image 2–14**), I was able to combine the soft window-light qualities of the Ice Light with the sharper effect of the Manfrotto LED. This resulted in an image with more depth and interest.

Image 2–13. *Tech Specs:* Nikon D4s, 4000 ISO, Lens: 85mm f/1.4, Aperture: f/1.4, Shutter speed: 1/640 second, Mode: A.

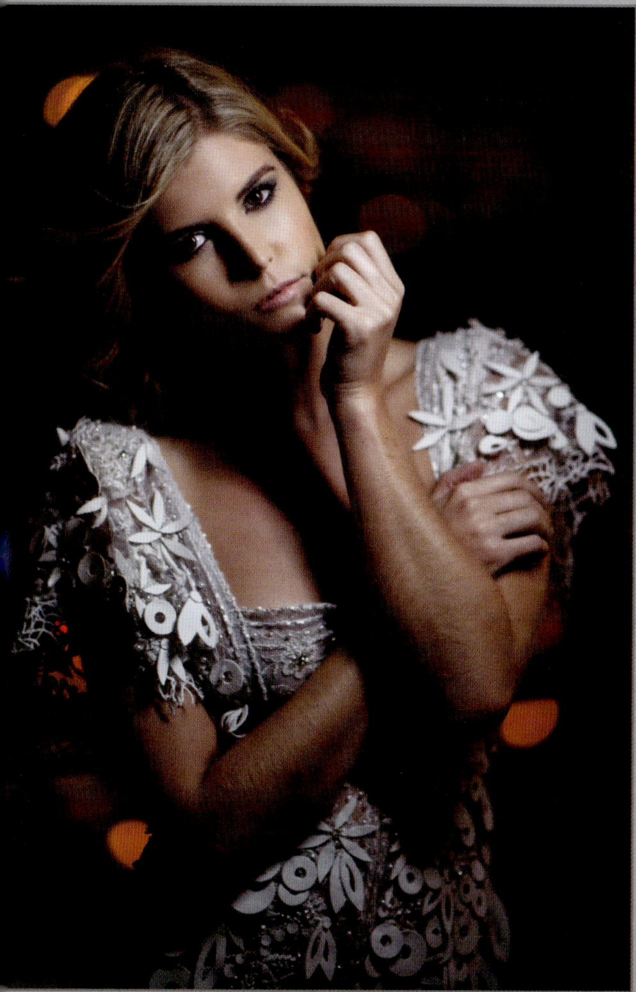

Image 2–14. *Tech Specs:* Nikon D4s, 4000 ISO, Lens: 85mm f/1.4, Aperture: f/1.4, Shutter speed: 1/640 second, Mode: A.

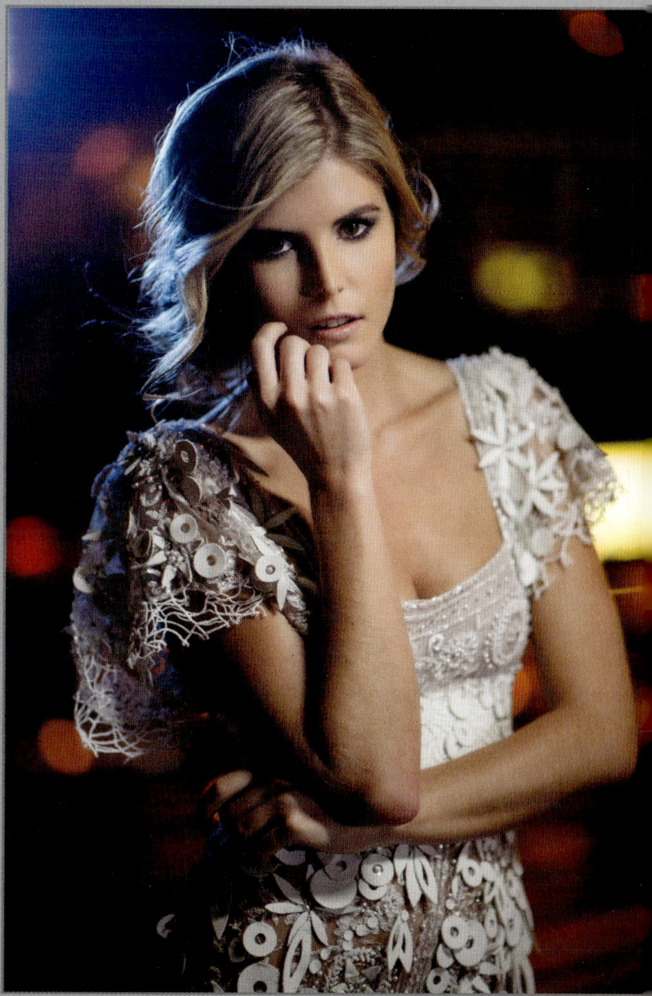

Test 9: Adding a Blue-Gelled Ice Light

For **image 2–15**, the Ice Light was covered with a blue gel. I also kept the blue gel in place on the Manfrotto LED hair light, resulting in an image infused with an eerie "science fiction" feel.

Test 10: Fenix LED Flashlight

For a change of pace, I switched the main light to a Fenix PD35 LED. This flashlight is designed for sporting activities, but it works really well as a light source and is handy in your camera bag. The light has very small surface area, so the shadows are razor sharp—a more expected style in high-fashion photography. In **image 2–16**, look at the sharpness in the shadow created by Catherine's hair across her face. When using a very small light source like this, positioning the source is especially critical; the wrong angle may reveal texture and emphasize contours in a way that is not flattering to the subject.

Test 11: A Three-Light Setup

For **image 2–17**, I switched to a three-light setup. I kept the Fenix LED flashlight as the main light, then added two Manfrotto LED panels (one covered in a red gel) as hair lights. This yielded a multi-dimensional image, illustrating that you can make use of many light sources to achieve whatever effect you desire in your night and low-light images.

Test 12: A Fashion Look

Image 2–18 was created with a diffuser over the flashlight. This was the main

Image 2–15. *Tech Specs:* Nikon D4s, 640 ISO, Lens: 85mm f/1.4, Aperture: f/1.4, Shutter speed: 1/80 second, Mode: A.

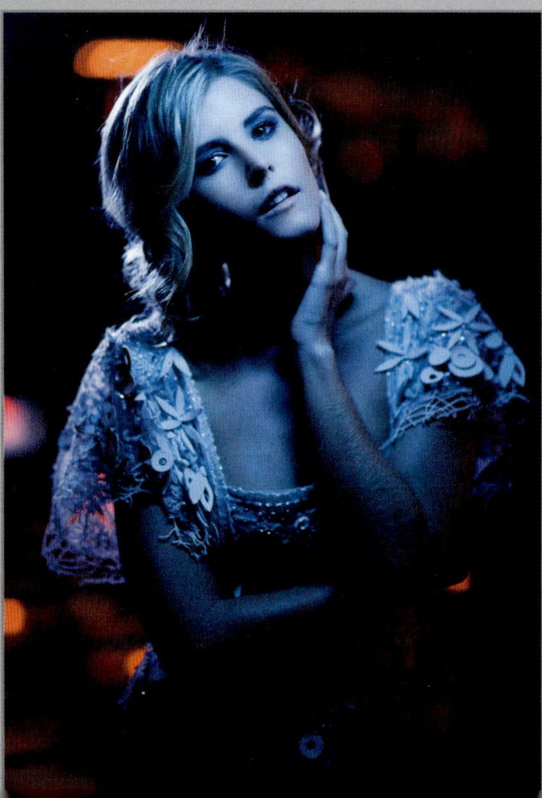

Image 2–16. *Tech Specs:* Nikon D4s, 4000 ISO, Lens: 85mm f/1.4, Aperture: f/1.4, Shutter speed: 1/320 second, Mode: A.

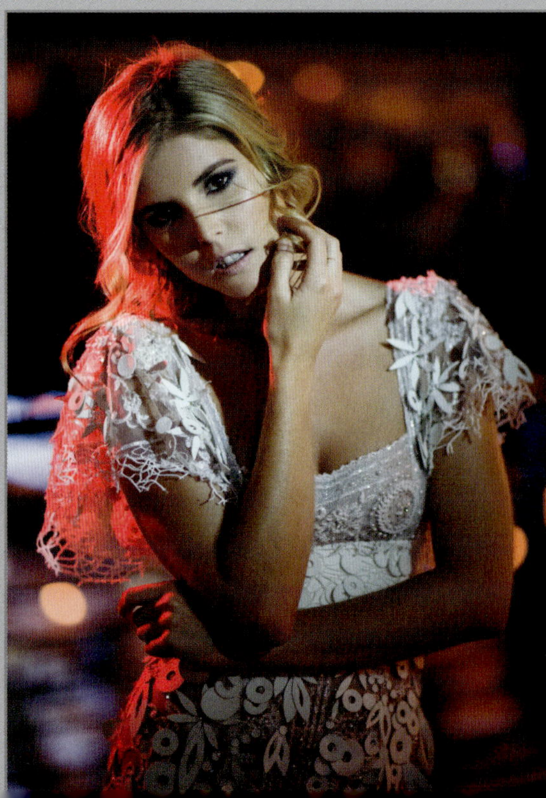

light, illuminating Catherine from a frontal angle. A second Manfrotto LED panel was positioned as a hair light. The dramatic, resolute pose and lighting join forces to produce a striking look that is reminiscent of the high-fashion images found in glossy magazines.

Test 13: Rembrandt Lighting

Image 2–19 is one of my favorites from the session. It was lit with a blue gel covering the Ice Light, which was positioned for a wonderful Rembrandt lighting effect (a pattern characterized by the illuminated triangle under the subject's eye on the shadow side of the

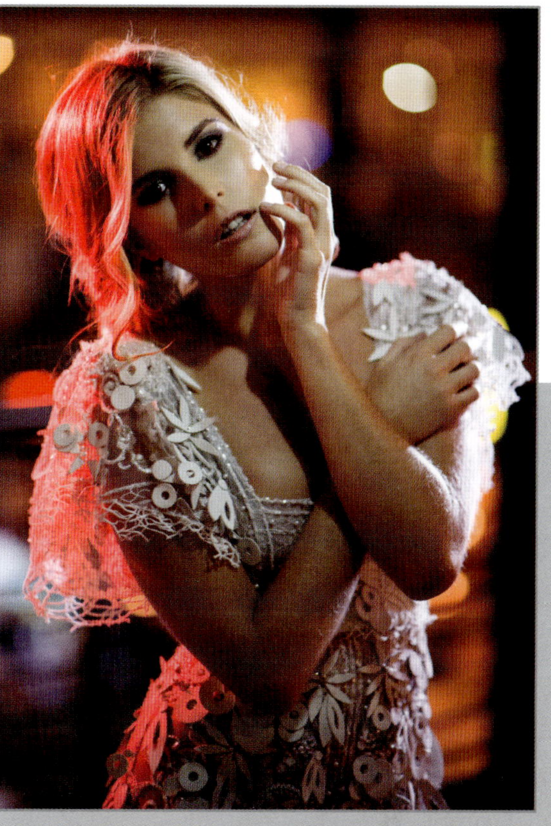

Image 2–17 (right). *Tech Specs:* Nikon D4s, 4000 ISO, Lens: 85mm f/1.4, Aperture: f/1.4, Shutter speed: 1/200 second, Mode: A.

Image 2–18 (bottom left). *Tech Specs:* Nikon D4s, 1600 ISO, Lens: 85mm f/1.4, Aperture: f/1.4, Shutter speed: 1/320 second, Mode: A.

Image 2–19 (bottom right). *Tech Specs:* Nikon Df, 1600 ISO, Lens: 85mm f/1.4, Aperture: f/1.4, Shutter speed: 1/160 second, Mode: A.

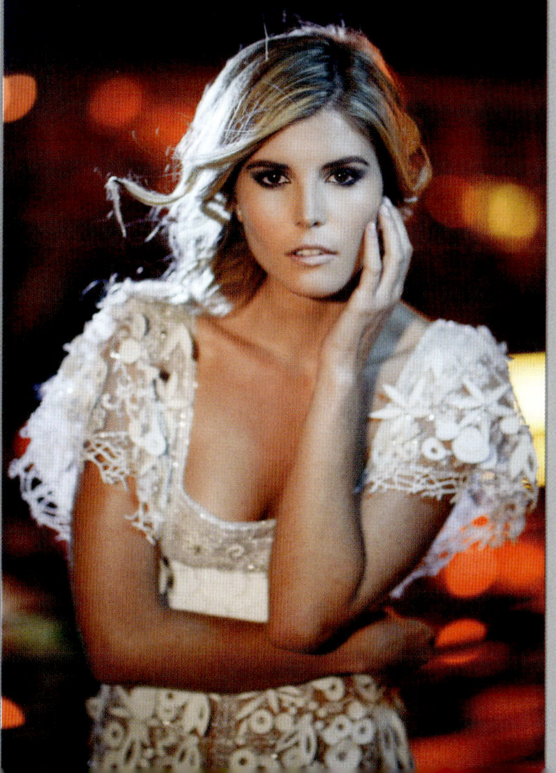

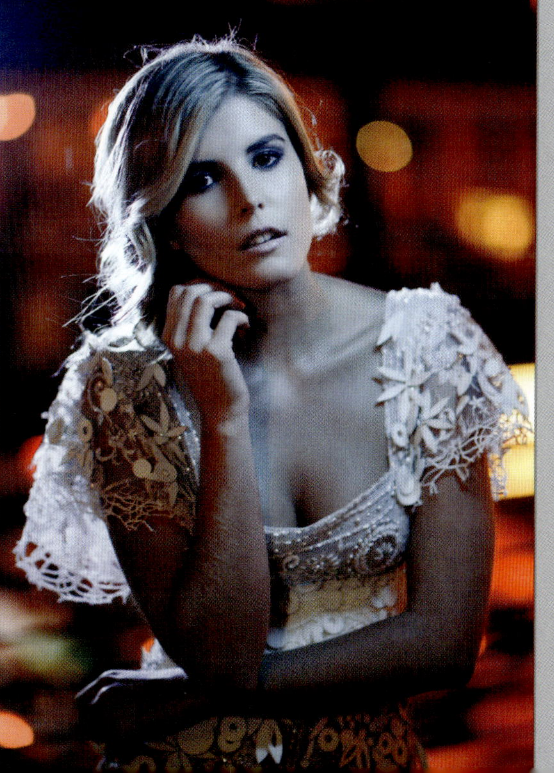

face). The Manfrotto LED I added as a hair-light was also fitted with a blue gel. In postproduction, I reduced the heavy blue cast by adjusting the white balance in Adobe Camera Raw. This "reddened" the background to create an image that really resonates with me.

Test 14: Storefront Windows

Shooting with light emanating from storefront windows can be quite effective. **Image 2–20** was created with only the available light at the location. You will be surprised at what you can create if you know what to look for.

Test 15: Storefront Windows Plus Blue-Gelled Ice Light

Combining the ambient light with a blue-gelled Ice Light created the great mood and a high-fashion feel in **image 2–21**. The side-lighting enhanced the texture in the fabric, but the look is still soft enough to maintain the femininity of the image.

Image 2–20. *Tech Specs:* Nikon D4s, 4000 ISO, Lens: 85mm f/1.4, Aperture: f/1.4, Shutter speed: 1/250 second, Mode: A.

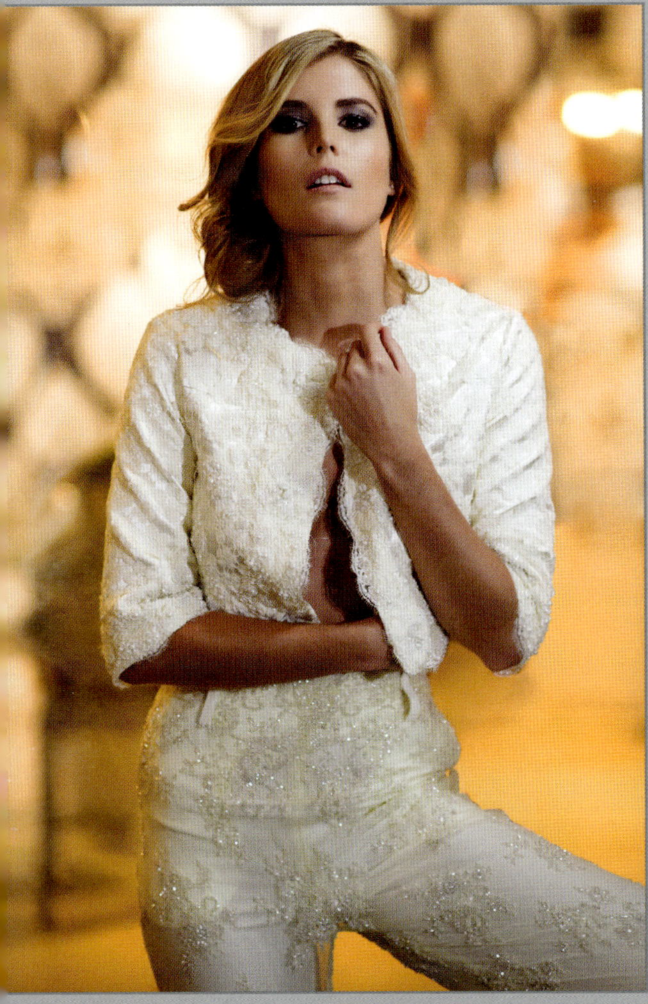

Image 2–21. *Tech Specs:* Nikon D4s, 4000 ISO, Lens: 85mm f/1.4, Aperture: f/1.4, Shutter speed: 1/200 second, Mode: A.

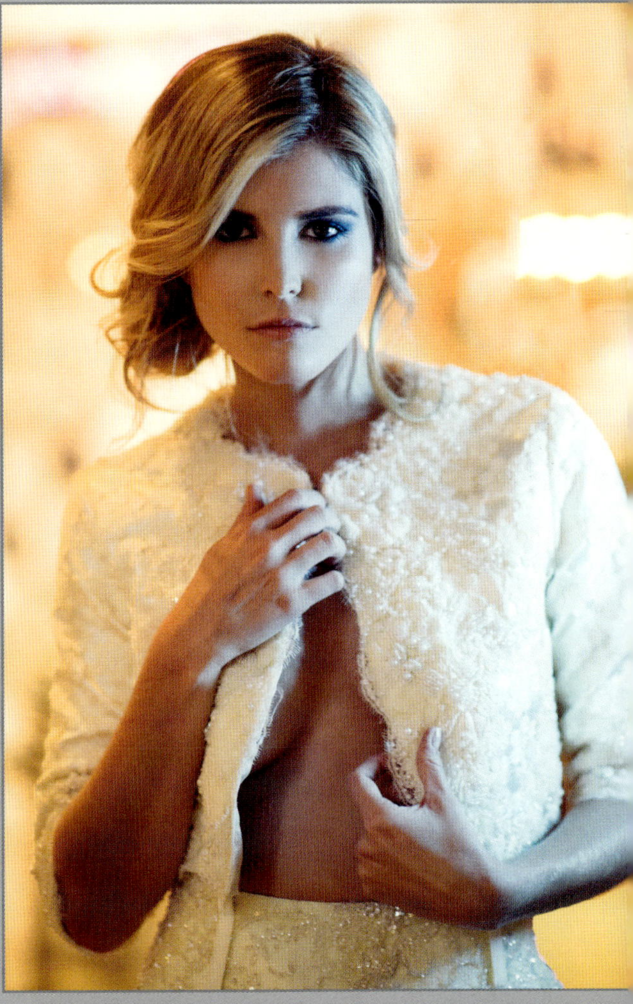

3. Focus in the Dark

Focusing in the dark is a particular challenge for most photographers. The modern camera's autofocus system adjusts the camera lens intelligently to ensure that a subject is correctly in focus. This is, of course, critical to a successful image. To the uninformed, this may seem like a simple task. In fact, it's far from simple. The camera is a piece of machinery without a subjective thought process; it has no idea of what the operator is trying to achieve. That makes focusing a very complicated process for the camera—and a huge amount of technology goes into ensuring that our results are crisp.

This section of the book aims to educate you with regard to how the camera's autofocus functions. It will teach you how to take advantage of the technology and systems the camera uses. It will also explain how to avoid situations where you battle to focus because of the technology's shortcomings. This discussion will be broken down according to the two basic focusing strategies used by today's photography equipment: passive autofocus and active autofocus. Modern cameras have many focusing options (single point, group focusing, and 3D tracking to name a few), but I am going to talk primarily about single shot (AFS) and single point focus. This is where there is one focal point in the viewfinder. At the end of the chapter, I'll discuss continuous focus (AFC) techniques.

> "Passive autofocus relies on the camera's built-in contrast sensors to achieve accurate focus."

Passive Autofocus

Passive autofocus relies on the camera's built-in contrast sensors to achieve accurate focus. The contrast sensors are laid out in various formations across the camera's field of view. Each one of these sensors calculates the relative focus by assessing the changes in contrast and identifying where there is maximum contrast. It then calculates that point to maximum sharpness. In a split second, the autofocus processor (AFP) initiates a change in the focusing distance, then reassesses the contrast level and determines whether further adjustments need to be made. If so, it will adjust and repeat these steps until it determines a satisfactory level of focus has been achieved. Sometimes, this happens almost instantly—however you may find, in certain conditions, that the camera spends a while focusing or keeps "hunting" for focus. That's not great for photographers who require split-second timing. This particularly affects event and sports photographers.

"If the subject is walking toward you (advancing), you may want to pre-focus on the point where you are anticipating taking the shot."

There are basically three factors that can contribute to frustrating focusing. It could be that 1) the subject is moving, 2) there is very little contrast in the subject area of the frame, and/or 3) the ambient light levels are too low.

Moving Subjects

A subject in motion can challenge the AFP, which will battle to assess and reassess focus (especially if there's also little light). If the subject is walking toward you (advancing), you may want to pre-focus on the point where you are anticipating taking the shot. Look for an area of contrast or even place a marker on the floor over which your subject will walk. Focus on that spot and hold the focus either by maintaining the pressure on your shutter release button, or (if you have mastered the back button focus technique) by holding the focus with your thumb. Then, trigger the shutter when the subject is directly over the spot where you focused. (Later in the chapter, we'll also look

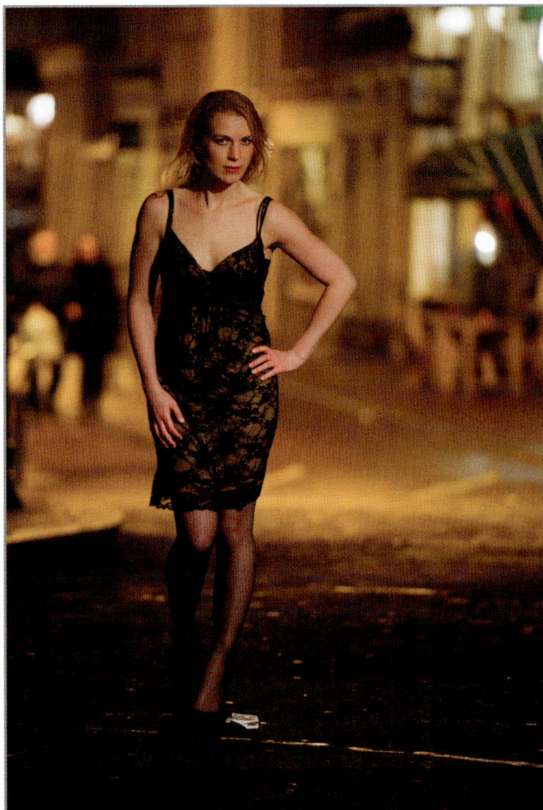

Image 3–1 and 3–2 (above and facing page). I used a small white box to "pre-focus" my camera. As my model, Ineke, reached the box, I pressed the shutter and she was therefore in focus. As you can see in the final image, I simply removed the box in postproduction. *Tech Specs:* Nikon D4s, 6400 ISO, Lens: 70–200mm f/2.8, Aperture: f/2.8, Shutter speed: 1/125 second, Mode: M.

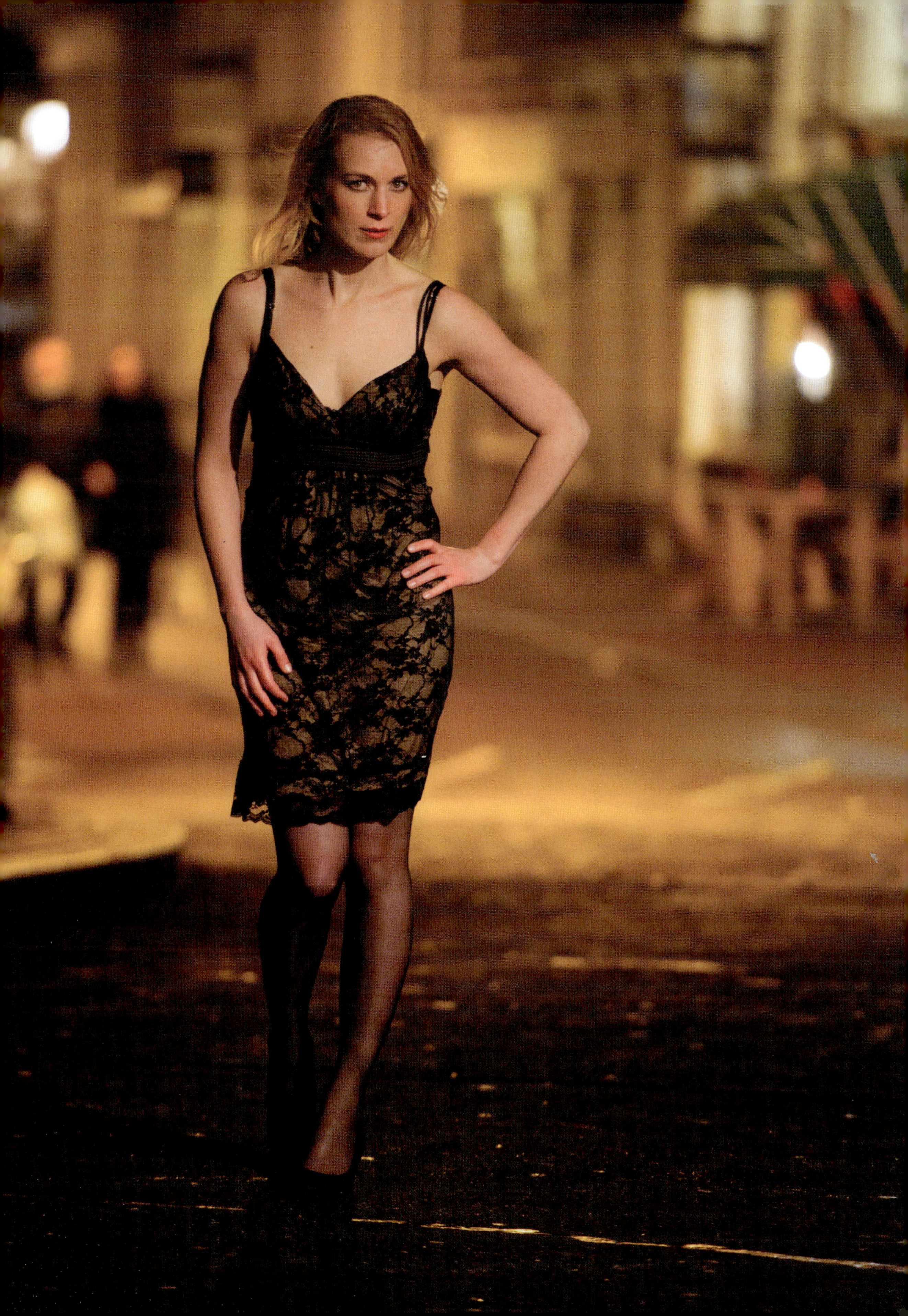

at another approach to photographing moving subjects: the use of focus tracking for continuous shooting.)

Low Subject Contrast

Low contrast on the subject is another factor that can trip up your camera's passive autofocus. Imagine trying to focus on a blank white wall—there is no contrast. This will result in the AFP not being able to make any realistic assessment of contrast and, therefore, proper focus.

Likewise, if your subject is wearing a top that has no pattern on it or is a very even color, the AFP will find it very difficult to focus on that area. Instead, try moving the autofocus point in your viewfinder to the area of your subject with the most contrast. Places where the sleeves or neckline end are always good options. If your subject is in a well-lit area, this will help; in low light, however, it may not always be a viable option.

Low Light

Low light levels on the subject are the source of many focusing issues. One solution is to carry a small flashlight to illuminate the subject and help achieve focus, then hold or lock your focus and switch the flashlight off before shooting. This may not always be logistically possible, but it does make things a little easier. (Read on to learn about active autofocus, which uses essentially the same approach.)

Image 3-3 (facing page). Here, I focused in the dark with the assistance of my speedlight's infrared focusing beam, but without the flash firing (we'll look at this technique later in the chapter). I had my assistant behind the couple with a Manfrotto LED light and the light from above was the DJ's stage lighting—it created great flare. *Tech Specs:* Nikon D3s, 2000 ISO, Lens: 70–200mm f/2.8, Aperture: f/2.8, Shutter speed: 1/80 second, Mode: M.

> "If your subject is wearing a top that has no pattern on it or is a very even color, the AFP will find it very difficult to focus on that area."

Now that you know how passive autofocus works, you can implement that knowledge and help make focusing in difficult situations a little bit easier. Basically, you need to find or create an area of contrast on or near your subject.

Active Autofocus

Most DSLR cameras come with a built-in autofocus-assist beam. This is the real core of active autofocus. The continuous beam of light is initiated whenever the camera senses that there is not enough light on the subject for the AFP to achieve sharp, accurate focus. Unfortunately, this method only really addresses *one* of the issues (insufficient light) that contribute

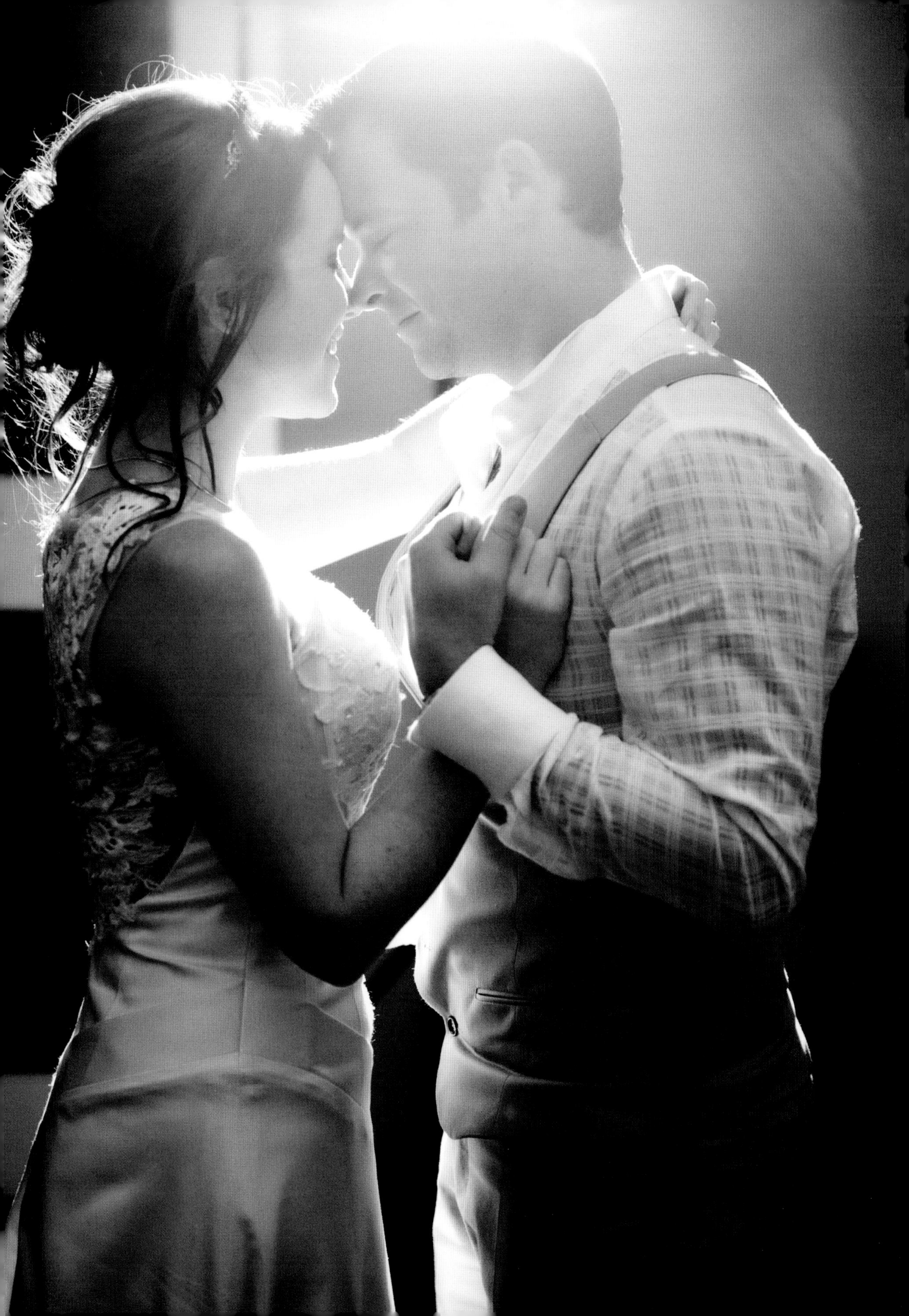

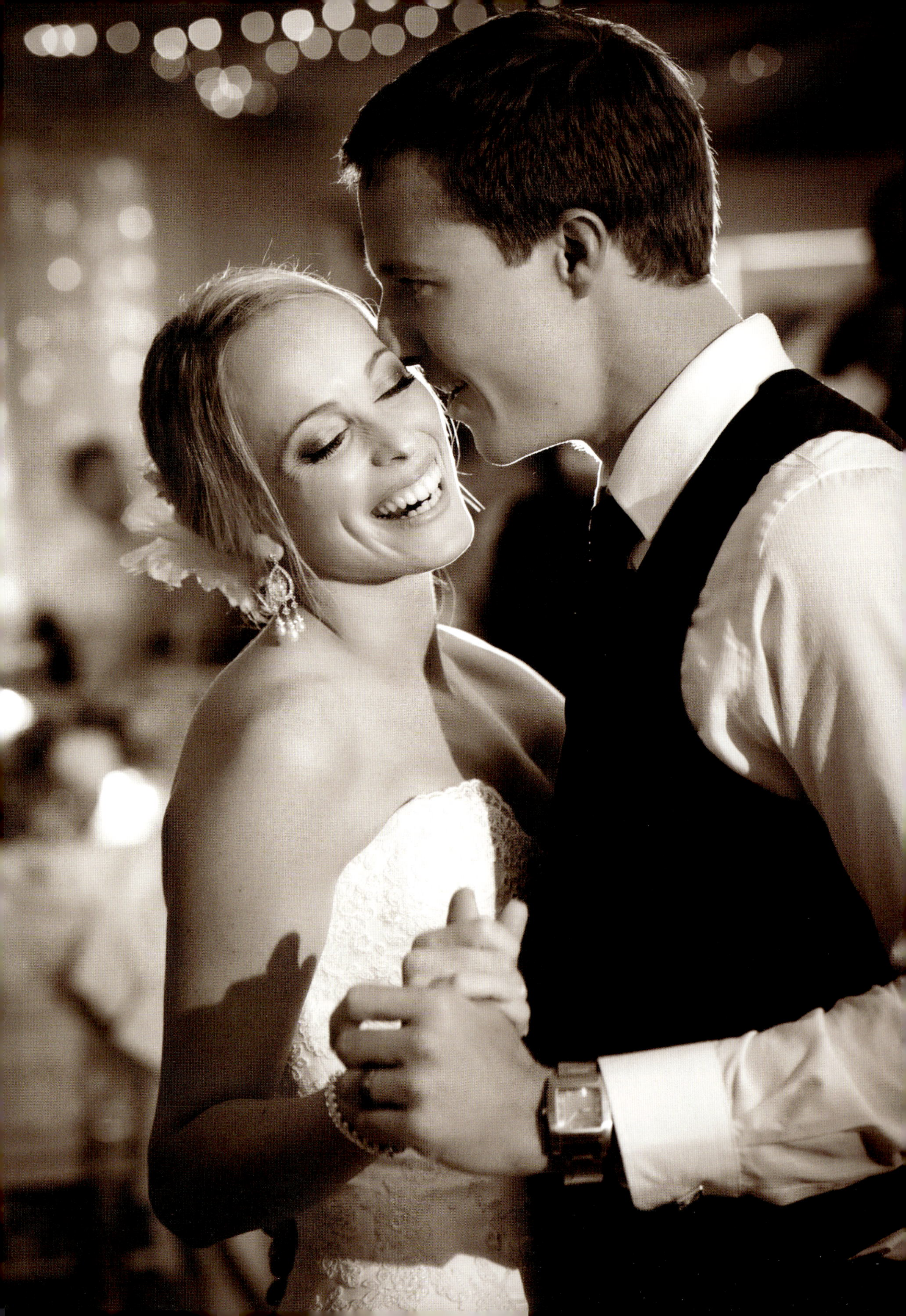

to the difficulties we face when trying to focus. The autofocus assist beam can be effective in certain conditions; however, it is not ideal and can be quite slow. Because it is a small source, it also works best when the subject is relatively close to the photographer. To an amateur, the sluggish focusing that results may not be too frustrating. For a paid professional who must be able to achieve sharp focus quickly under difficult circumstances, it's more than an inconvenience.

Enter the Speedlight

The autofocus-assist function built into some speedlights is much more effective than the one in your DSLR because it employs an infrared grid that produces contrast and allows the AFP to focus more accurately. In conjunction with this, the system's sensors collect data regarding the distance of the subject in relation to the camera. The infrared beam also intelligently follows the focus point that you determine in the viewfinder, whereas the camera's autofocus-assist beam generally illuminates only the center of the image.

Image 3–4 (facing page). This is one of my favorite first dance images—everything just came together perfectly. I had my assistant behind the couple with the Manfrotto LED, creating the rim light. I was fortunate to know one of the guests at the wedding who was a keen amateur photographer and volunteered his services to hold a second Manfrotto LED and illuminate the couple from the front. I used my speedlight (set not to fire; more on this later in the chapter) to assist in focusing—and I love the moment of pure contentment. *Tech Specs:* Nikon D4, 4000 ISO, Lens: 70–200mm f/2.8, Aperture: f/3.5, Shutter speed: 1/125 second, Mode: A.

“The autofocus-assist function built into some speedlights is much more effective than the one in your DSLR.”

Now, that may sound very effective—and it is—but some of you may be thinking, “But this autofocus system only works when I have the speedlight on.” That's true. So what happens if you want to shoot in difficult focusing conditions *without* firing your speedlight? Happily, camera manufacturers have realized that the flash's infrared focusing system is very effective, accurate, and relatively fast, so they've devised a way to do this.

I will start with the Nikon system and a method to utilize this fantastic technology. On the Nikon SB910 and SB900, you will need to go into the menu on the back of the speedlight. Toggle down until you get to a symbol that looks like a speedlight with broken lines emanating from the area below where the flash fires. Press OK to go to a submenu where you will have three options: ON, OFF and, AF-ILL ONLY. The option you will need to select is AF-ILL ONLY. Press Exit and you will now

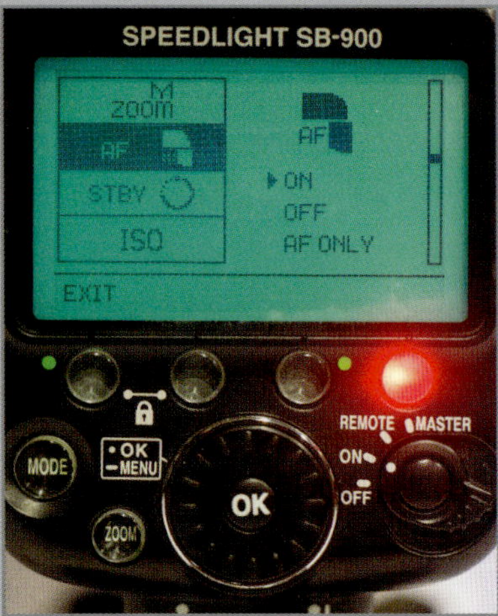

Image 3–5. In the Nikon SB900 Speedlight's AF menu, the ON setting activates the autofocus-assist beam. In this mode, the flash can also fire.

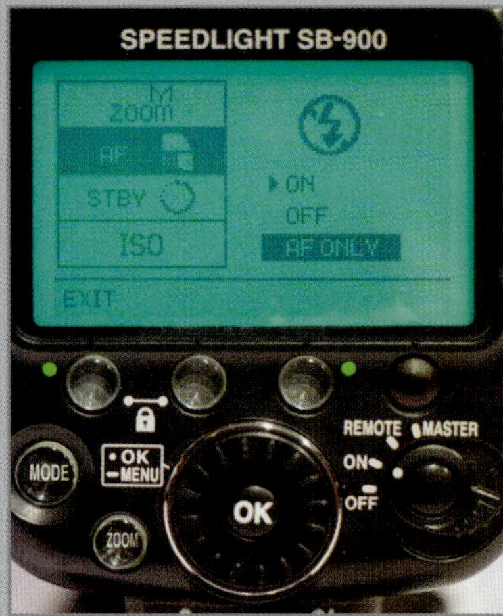

Image 3–6. Switching to the AF-ILL ONLY mode allows you to use the autofocus-assist beam, but prevents the flash from firing.

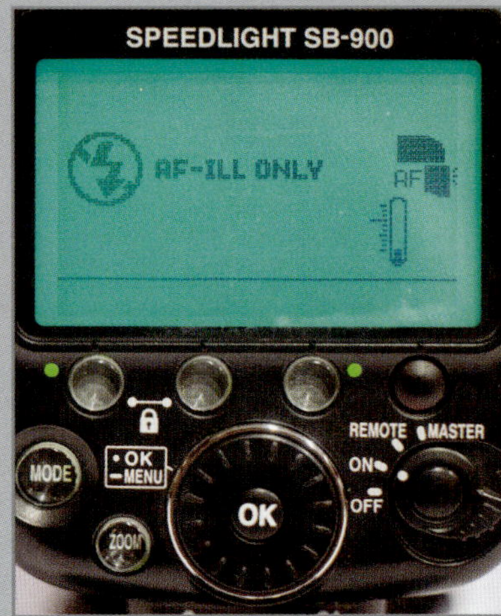

Image 3–7. When the AF-ILL ONLY feature is active, a crossed-out flash icon appears on the Speedlight's LCD panel.

notice that there is a symbol on the back of the speedlight resembling a crossed-out flash. This indicates that you will now be able to access the infrared focus-assist without your speedlight firing. (*Note:* This only works for single focus {AFS] shooting, not continuous focus [AFC] shooting.)

For Canon users, you need to have your speedlight attached to your camera in order to access the menu that controls the flash functions. Navigate to the submenu entitled External Speedlight Control. Under Flash Firing, choose the Disable option. You will then be able to use the infrared facility without your speedlight firing. This technique will only work on AFS and not AFC (continuous). A word of caution to Canon users: When you're done, be sure to switch the Flash Firing setting back to Enable. This system essentially does everything *except* fire the flash (by not sending an electrical impulse to the speedlight) when the shutter is released. When you go into the studio or are using triggers to fire your off-camera strobes, the camera will neglect to send that pulse through to your trigger. This can be very frustrating—and you'll probably assume that there is something wrong with your triggering system or camera. I've known of photographers who spent good money sending in their gear to be repaired, when the flash was just mistakenly disabled!

Continuous Focus (AFC)

Now, let's look at the AFC mode—the continuous focusing mode designed for photographing moving subjects. (As noted above, with this mode you won't be able to implement the AF-ILL ONLY technique; the system doesn't allow it.) What I do to overcome the moving subject dilemma is switch to AFC and then choose either the Group or 3D tracking option. There needs to be some contrast on your subject for your camera to be able to focus on them. I have set my camera to fire *only* when the subject is in focus, thereby increasing my "strike rate" of sharp images. I also switch the camera to burst mode (CH) to capture more images per second.

The portraits of Sadie that appear below and on the next two pages (**images 3–8** through **3–29**) were created during one of my workshops and shot using AFC-3D tracking. As you can see from the various options we have from just one walk toward the camera, it is a reliable method of capturing a series. This approach gives the photographer more options when it comes to choosing images to show the client.

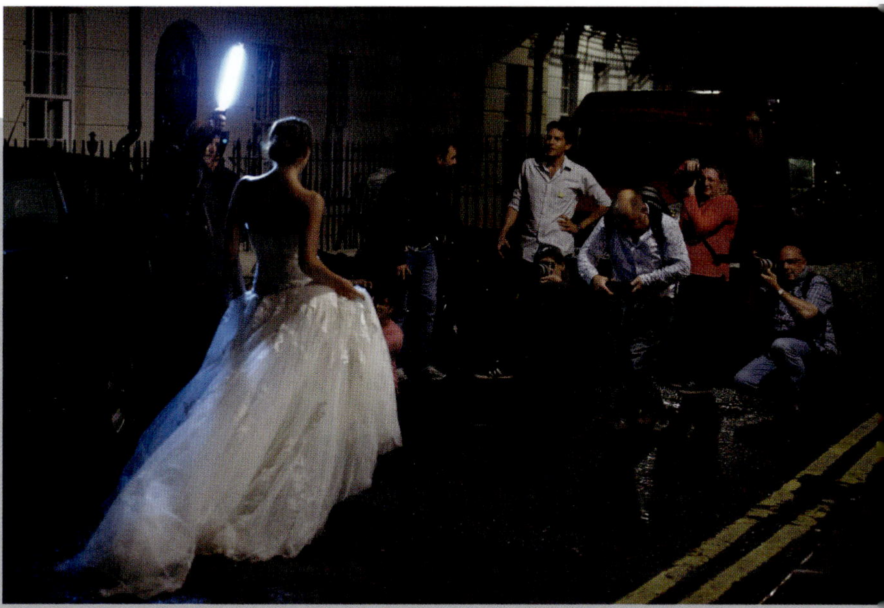

Image 3–8 (right). Behind the scenes of the shoot.

Images 3–9 through 3–29 (below and next two pages). I photographed Sadie's walk using AFC-3D tracking. *Tech Specs:* Nikon D4s, 10,000 ISO, Lens: 70–200mm f/2.8, Aperture: f/2.8, Shutter speed: 1⁄400 second, Mode: A.

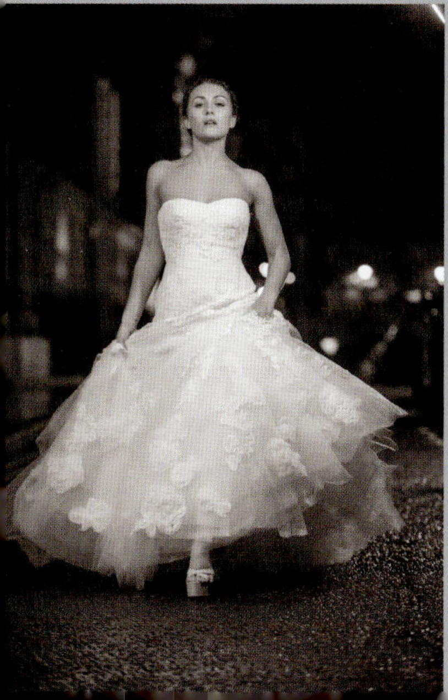

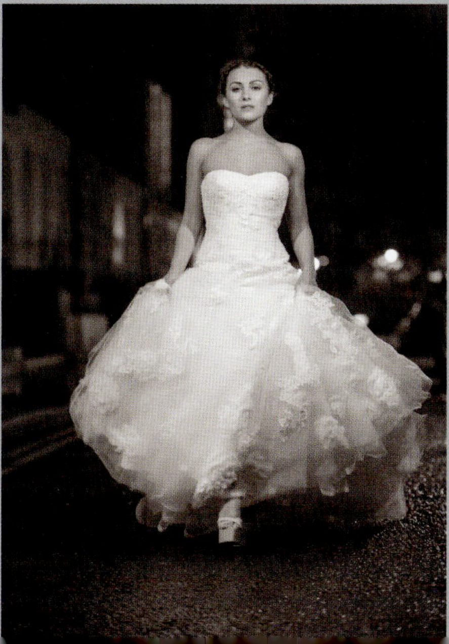

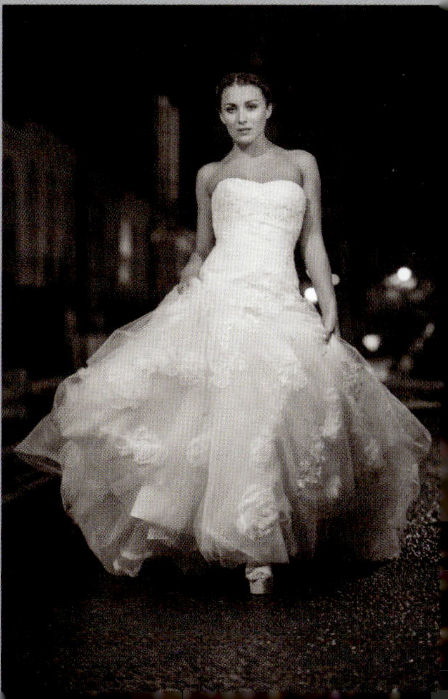

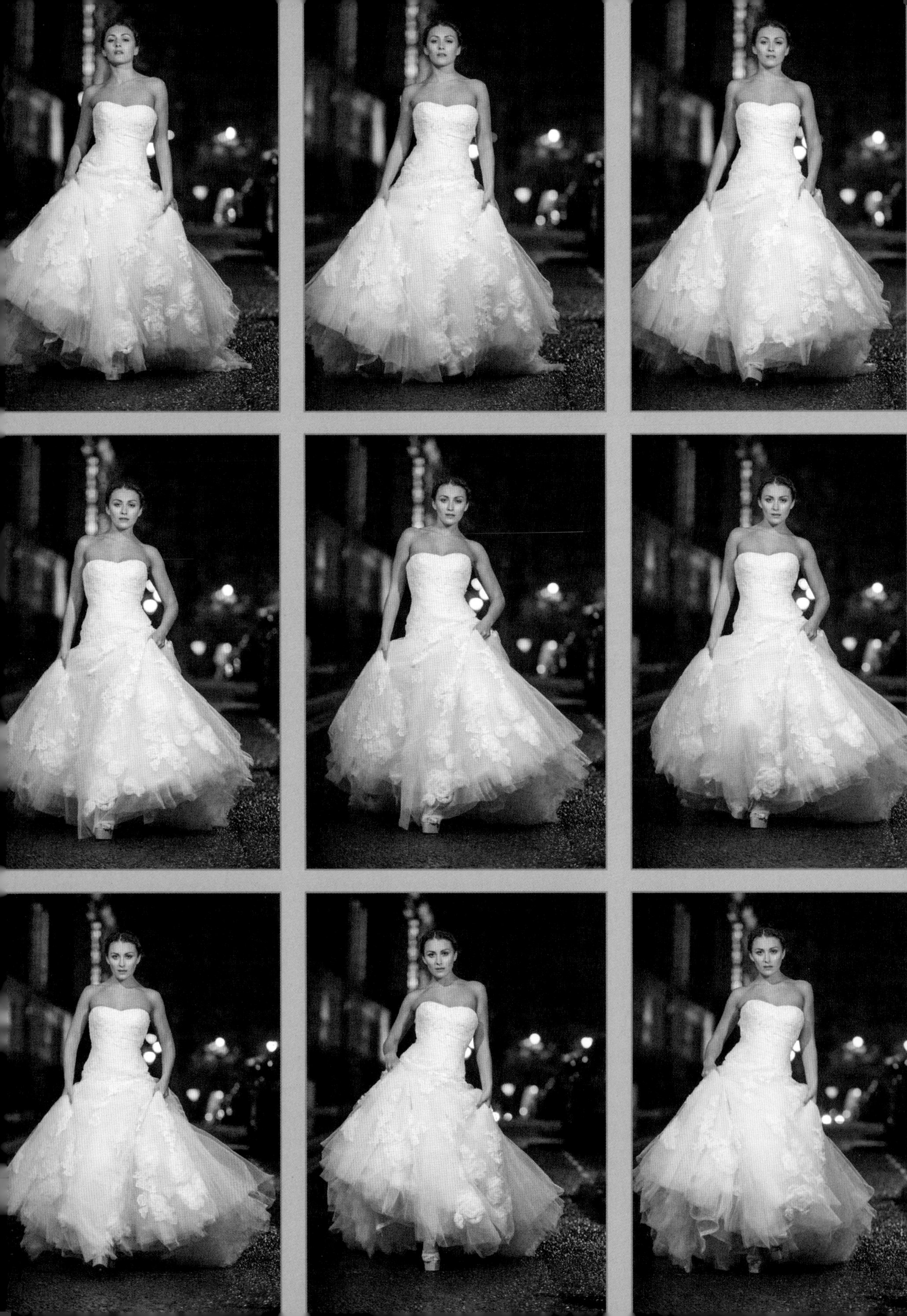

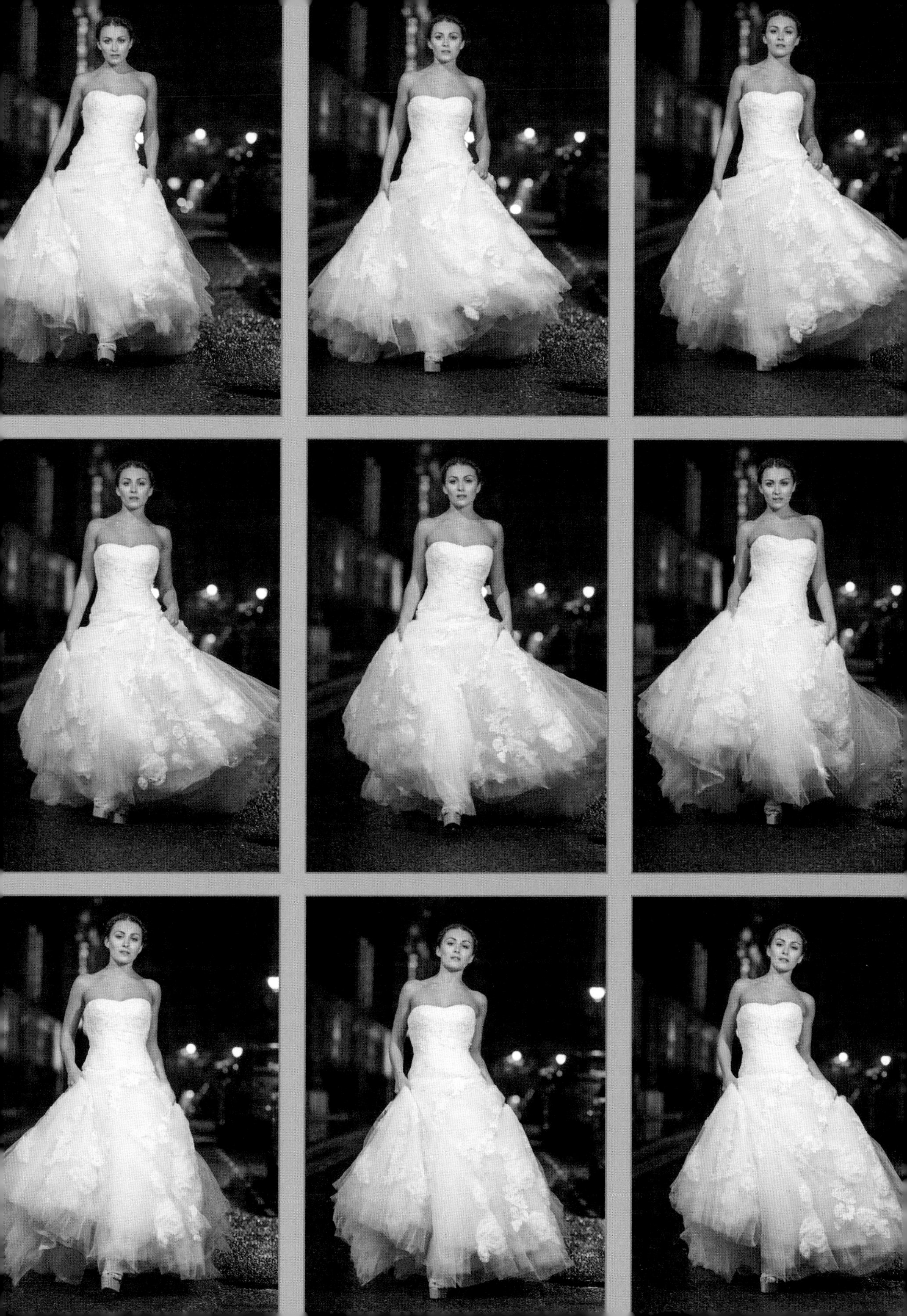

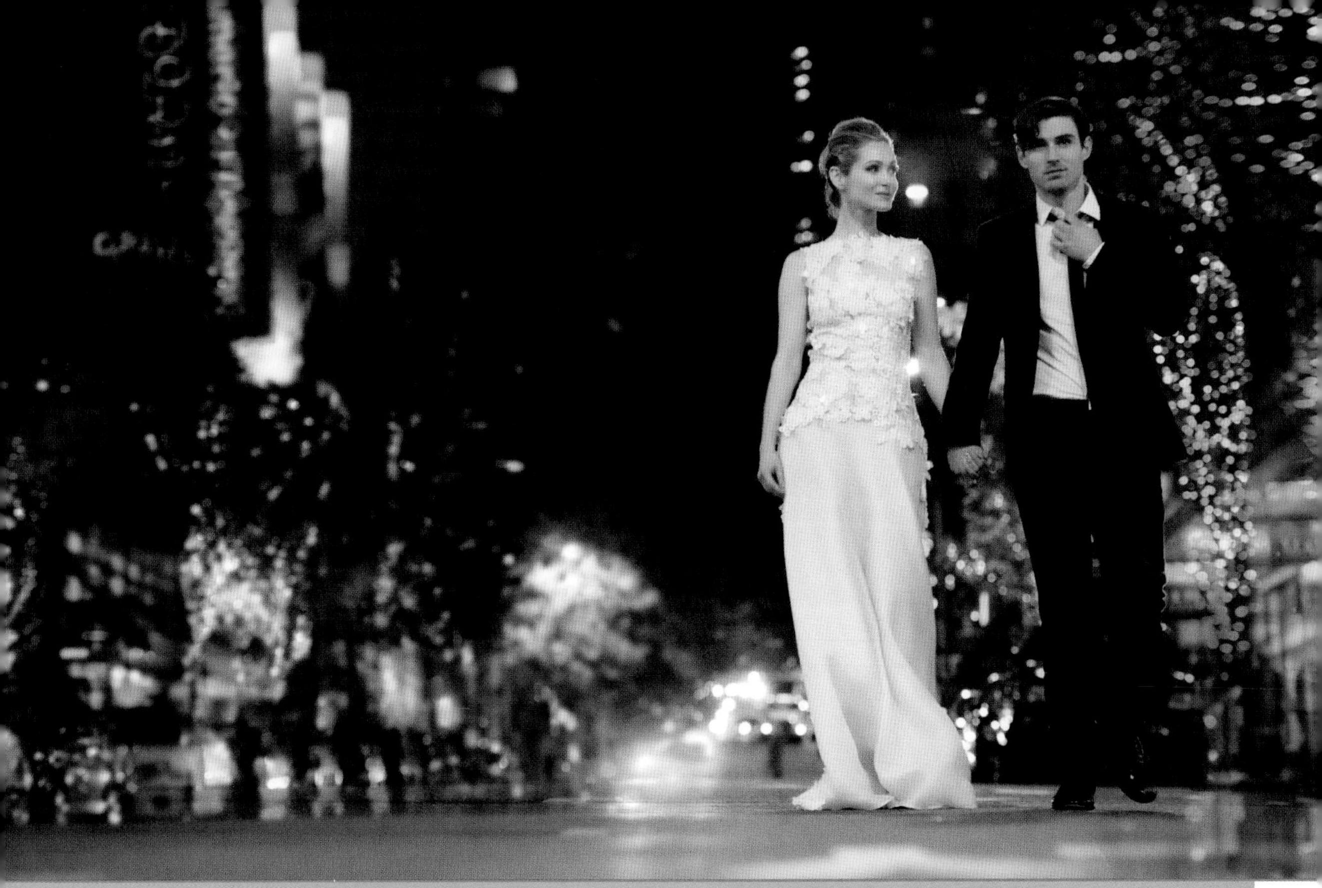

Image 3–30. Shot with AFC-3D tracking while shooting on the streets of Seattle. *Tech Specs:* Nikon D4s, 4000 ISO, Lens: 70–200mm f/2.8, Aperture: f/2.8, Shutter speed: 1/160 second, Mode: M.

Image 3–30 was also created using AFC-3D tracking—this time on the streets of Seattle. It may look a little dangerous for your subjects; however, if you get the timing correct between the red traffic lights, you need only to have the couple walk once and you will have a variety of options to choose from!

Lens Selection

If I am shooting a stationary subject, I like the Nikkor 85mm f/1.4 for its very wide aperture. For moving subjects, I prefer the Nikkor 70–200mm f/2.8 lens, which gives me the flexibility to use various focal lengths and go quickly from a full-length to a three-quarter crop in no time at all.

Images 3–31 through 3–34. Shooting with the 70–200mm zoom lens lets me quickly change the crop length of my images. *Tech Specs:* Nikon D4s, 4000 ISO, Lens: 70–200mm f/2.8, Aperture: f/2.8, Shutter speed: 1/160 second, Mode: M.

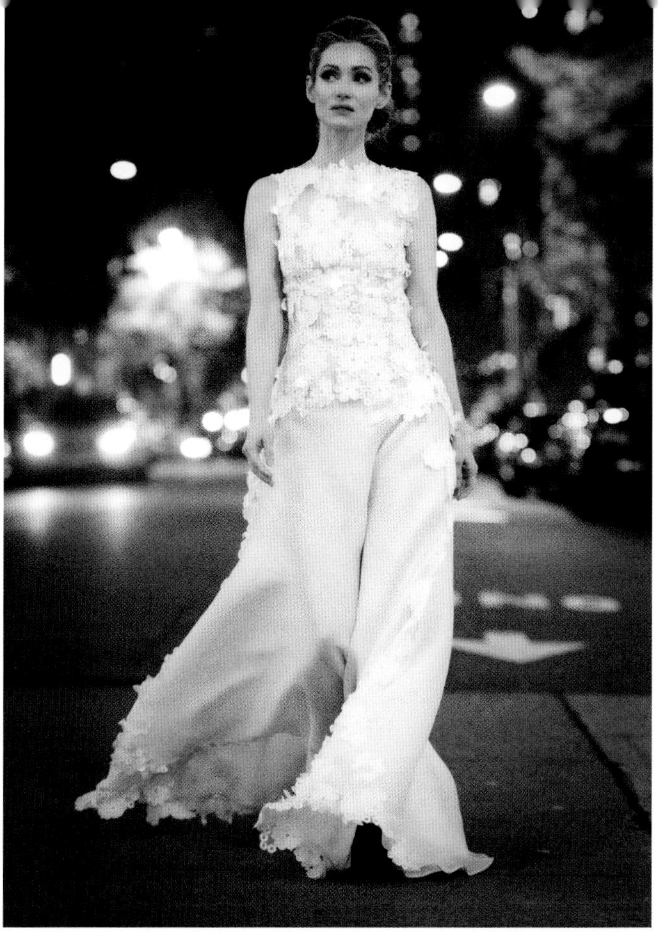
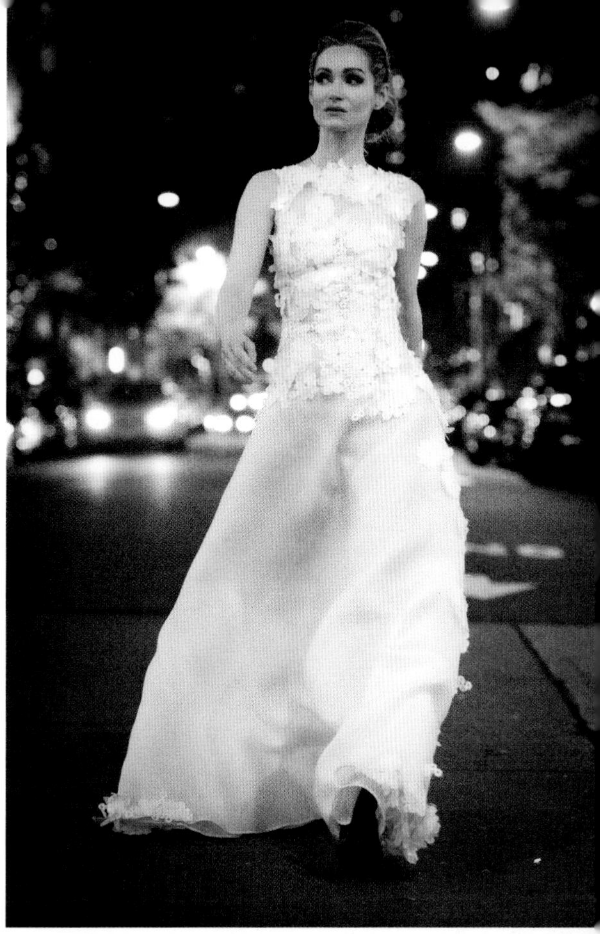
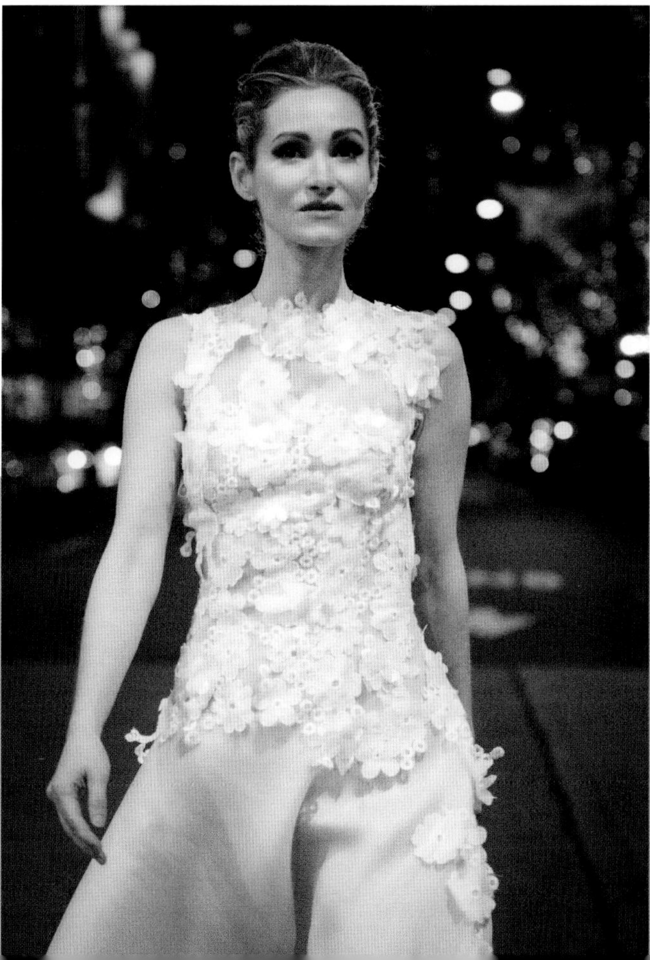
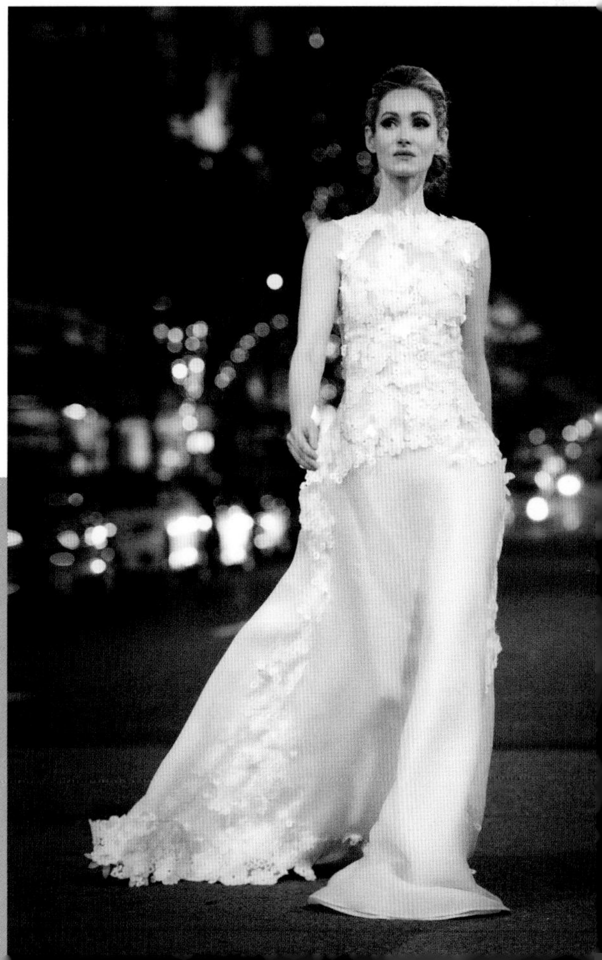

4. The Right Color Balance

Color Temperature

All light sources emit light with a particular color cast. We refer to this shift in color output as the color temperature of the light source and use a unit of measurement called a Kelvin (K) to describe it in numerical terms. The scale ranges from 1000K to 10,000K—from very warm (reddish) colors to very cool (bluish) colors. The table shown in **image 4–1** is a rule-of-thumb guide to the color temperature of some common light sources.

COLOR TEMPERATURE	LIGHT SOURCE
1000–2000K	Candlelight
2500–3500K	Tungsten Bulb
3000–4000K	Sunrise/Sunset
4000–5000K	Fluorescent Lamps
5000–5500K	Flash/Strobes
5000–6500K	Daylight with Clear Sky
6500–8000K	Partly Cloudy Sky
9000–10,000K	Shade or Completely Overcast Sky

Image 4–1. Common light sources and their corresponding color temperatures

Why does the color temperature of the light source matter to photographers? Unless we compensate for it, the same color shifts present in the lighting itself will be visible on our subjects, resulting in color inconsistencies or inaccuracies in our images.

Image 4–2 (facing page). This image was shot in Florence, Italy, where we had access to a rooftop terrace with a view of a beautifully lit building. We couldn't miss the opportunity to capture the ambiance and romance! I pushed a table up against the wall of the terrace and had the bride stand on it. Then, I had my assistant attach the Manfrotto LED to a monopod to get it to the height I needed. I had a CTO (color temperature orange) gel on the LED to match the warmth of the light that illuminated the building behind her. *Tech Specs:* Nikon D4s, 800 ISO, Lens: 70–200mm f/2.84, Aperture: f/2.8, Shutter speed: 1/100 second, Mode: M.

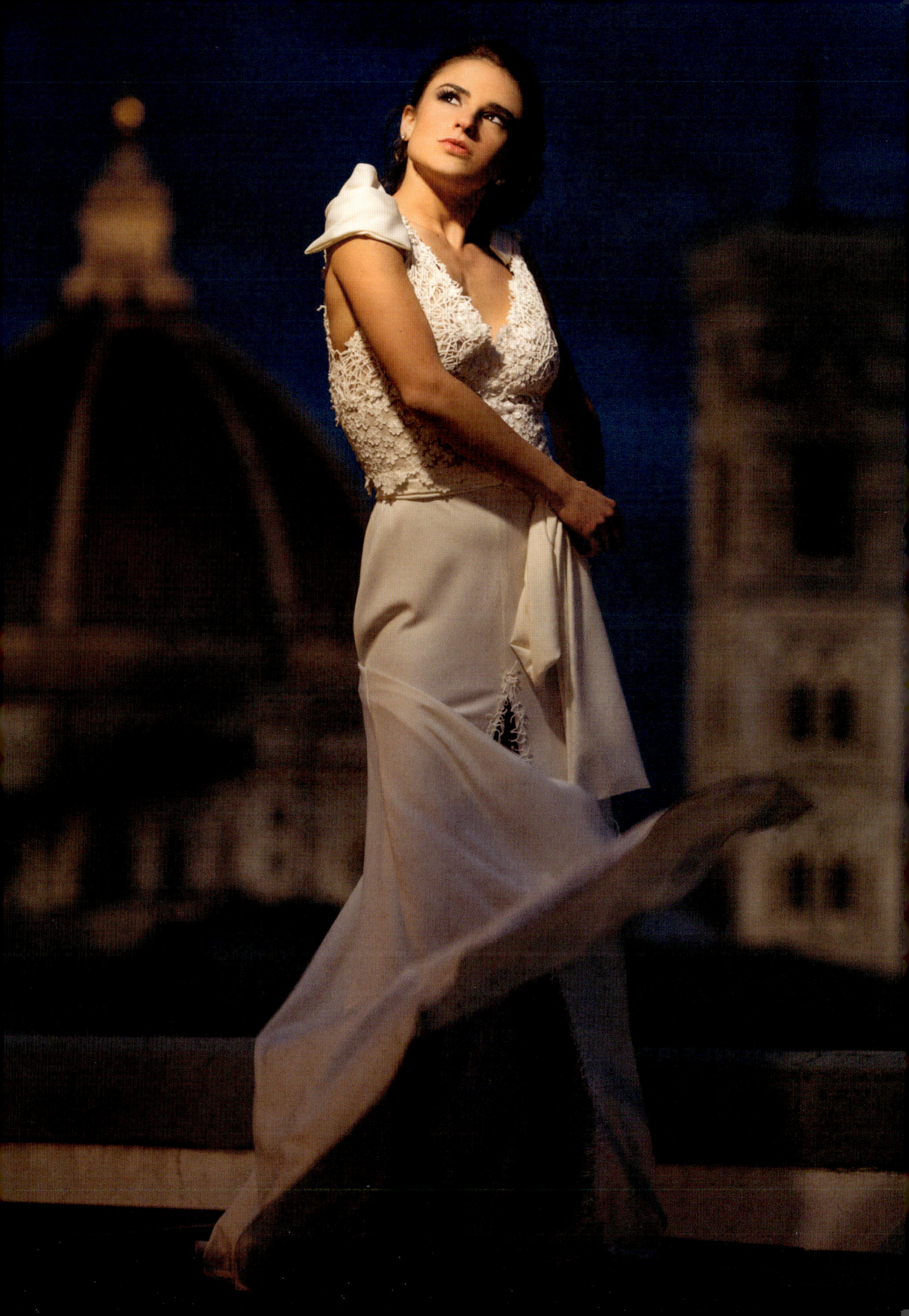

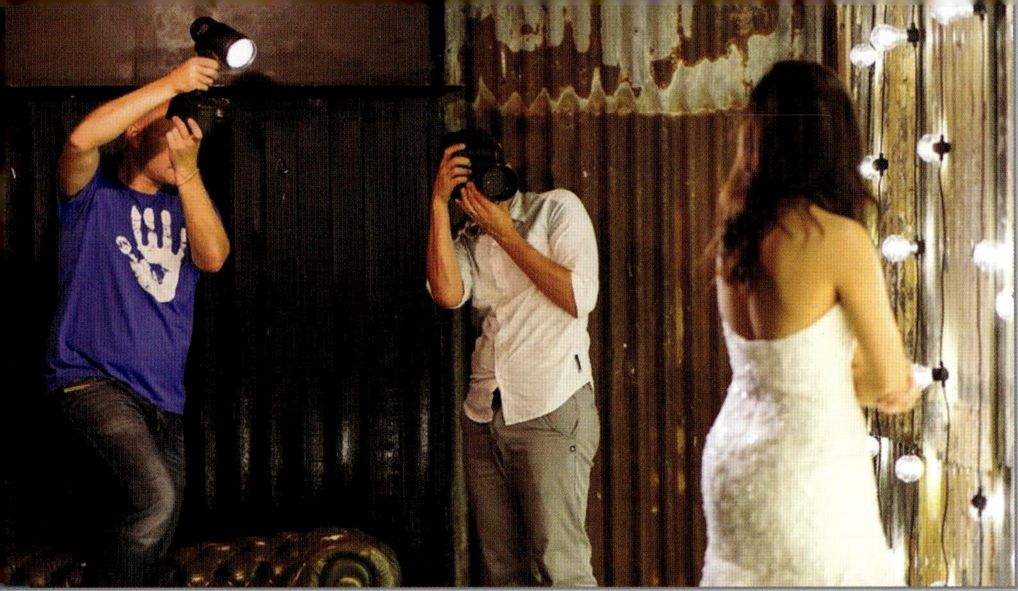

Images 4–3, 4–4, 4–5, and 4–6 (this page and top of facing page). At a wedding workshop conducted in London, the stylist created a wall of hanging light bulbs as a backdrop. I used the Lowel GL1 as a dramatic light source, as well as for a color balance that matched the tungsten light bulbs perfectly. In the behind-the-scenes image, you can see how easy it is to use; the assistant can control the intensity of the light by adjusting the pressure of their finger on the trigger. For a simple variation, I also added a triangular prism in front of the lens (more on that technique in chapter 6). The color variations in the images (which were all lit identically) were created in postproduction. *Tech Specs:* Nikon D4s, 800 ISO, Lens: 85mm f/1.4, Aperture: f/1.4, Shutter speed: 1/160 second, Mode: M.

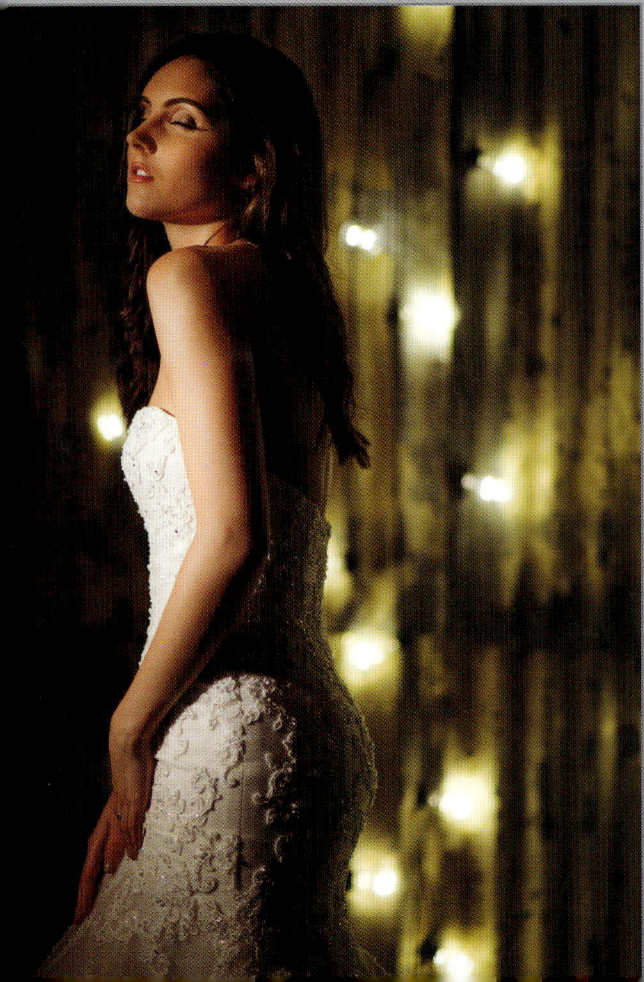

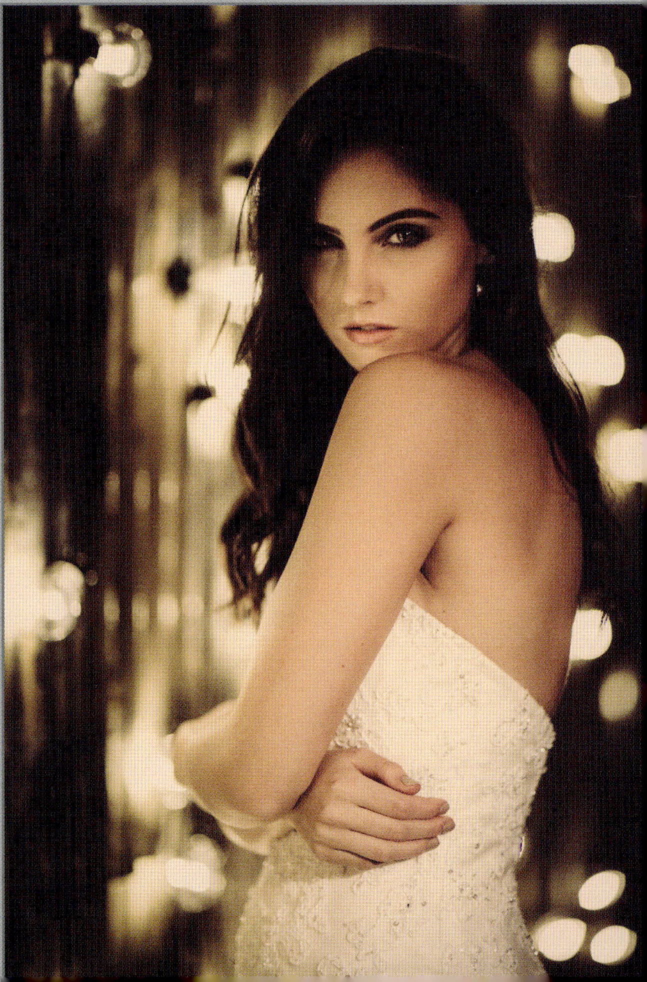

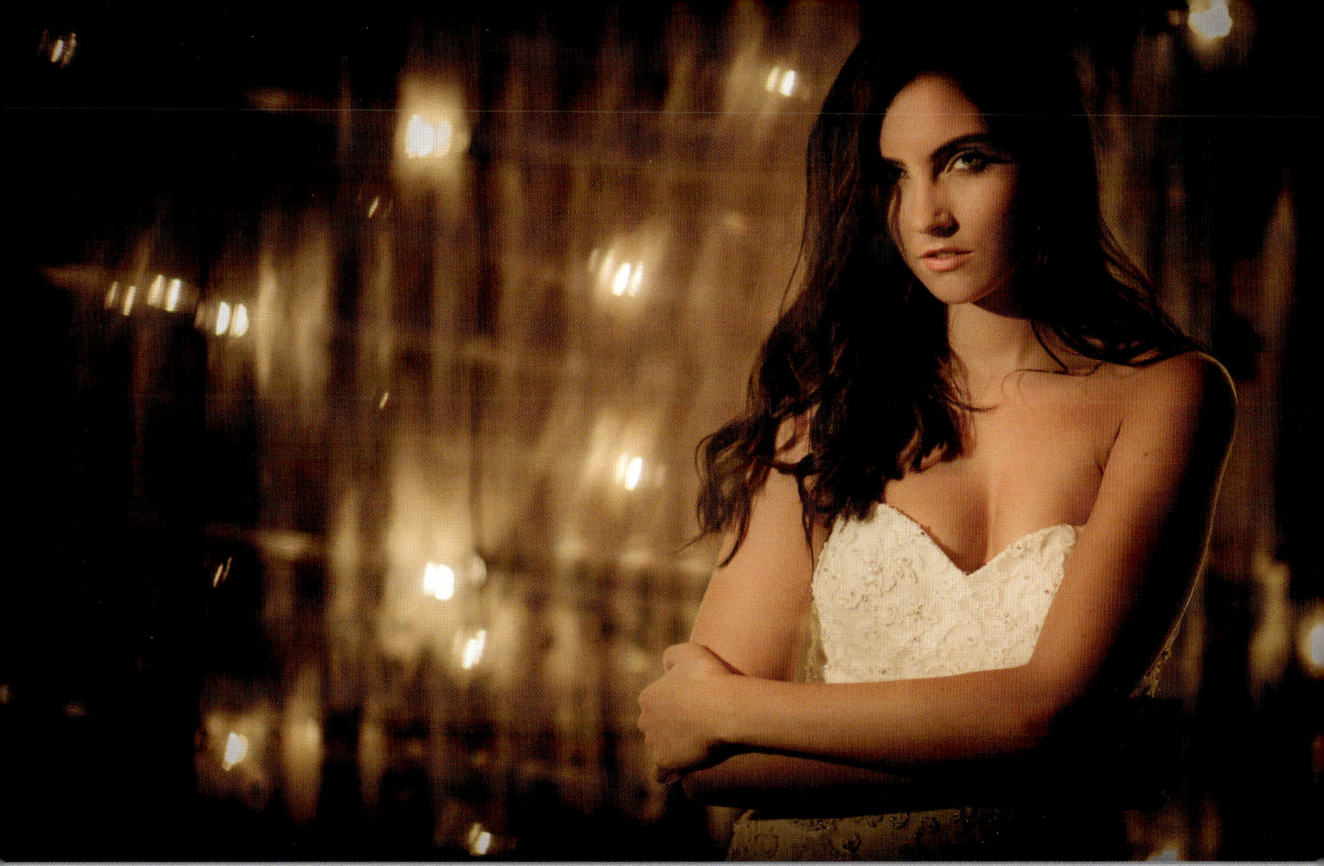

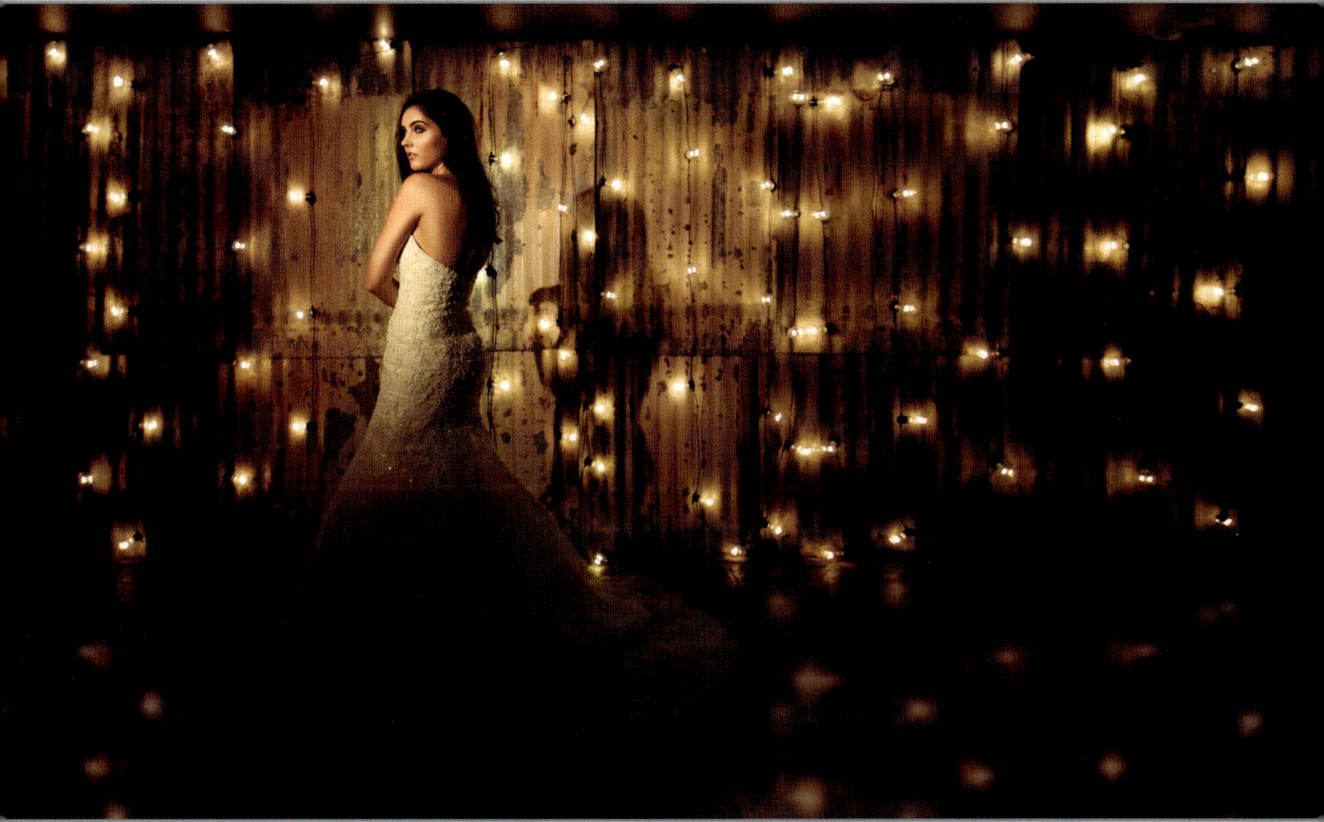

Image 4-7 (above). This bridal portrait was shot by Zane Colquhoun—a good friend of mine and my former full-time assistant. I love what he did in the processing and the way he interpreted the scene. I wish I had shot this image!

White Balance Settings

To compensate for all the different color temperatures of light photographers may encounter, digital cameras use a system of built-in color filters (called the white balance setting) to neutralize the color of the brightest tones in the image. Neutralizing the white tones also shifts the colors throughout the spectrum and, hopefully, produces an accurate overall rendition of the scene as our eyes perceived it. Take a look at the color wheel illustration (**image 4–8**) to see exactly how this works.

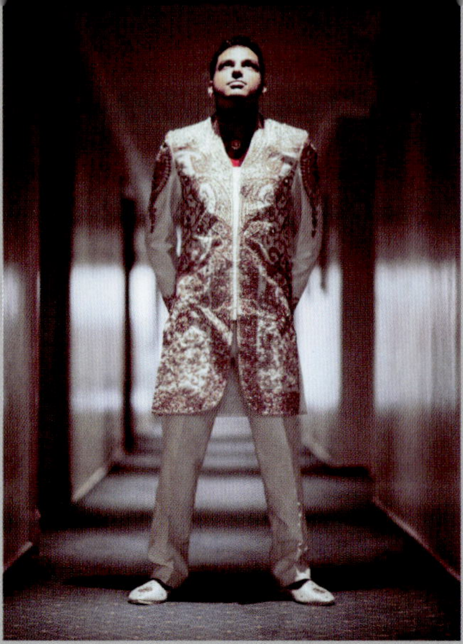

Images 4–9 and 4–10 (above and facing page). The color doesn't have to be neutral to be "right." I used the hotel's down-lights (lights that usually create unsightly hotspots) to design a dramatic, regal image. The very warm tungsten lighting further enhanced the gold embroidery on the groom's garment. Had I set the white balance to neutralize the tungsten lighting (as seen in the smaller image), the shot wouldn't have worked. Sometimes, it's not beneficial to go the purist route to ensure "correct" color rendition. *Tech Specs:* Nikon D4, 400 ISO, Lens: 85mm f/1.4, Aperture: f/1.6, Shutter speed: 1/125 second, Mode: M.

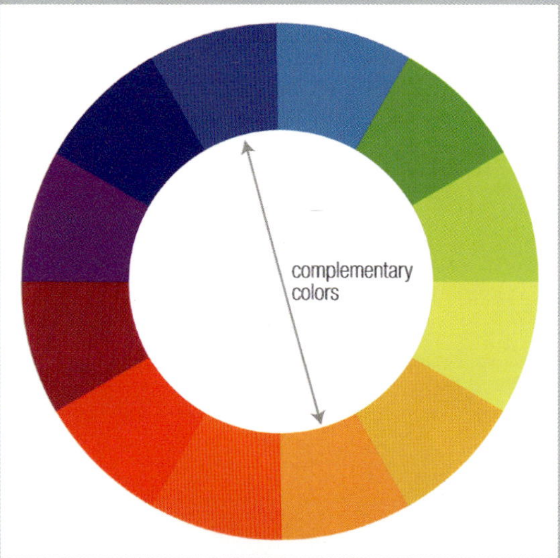

Image 4–8. All of the primary colors are arrayed around a color wheel. The colors opposite each other are considered "complementary," meaning one tends to neutralize the other. Digital white balance systems all rely on this fundamental concept. For example, if an image or light source has a yellowish color cast, adding blue (the complement of yellow) tends to neutralize it. Likewise, If you're shooting in the cool light of a shady area (blue/cyan), the white balance function tried to neutralize that color cast by adding warmth (red/yellow) to the capture.

White Balance Presets

Most digital cameras come with a range of scene-specific white balance presets designed to coordinate with a variety of lighting scenarios (sunlight, cloudy sky, shade, tungsten, flash, and more). I suggest using these presets, as they have been engineered by the camera's manufacturer based on complicated

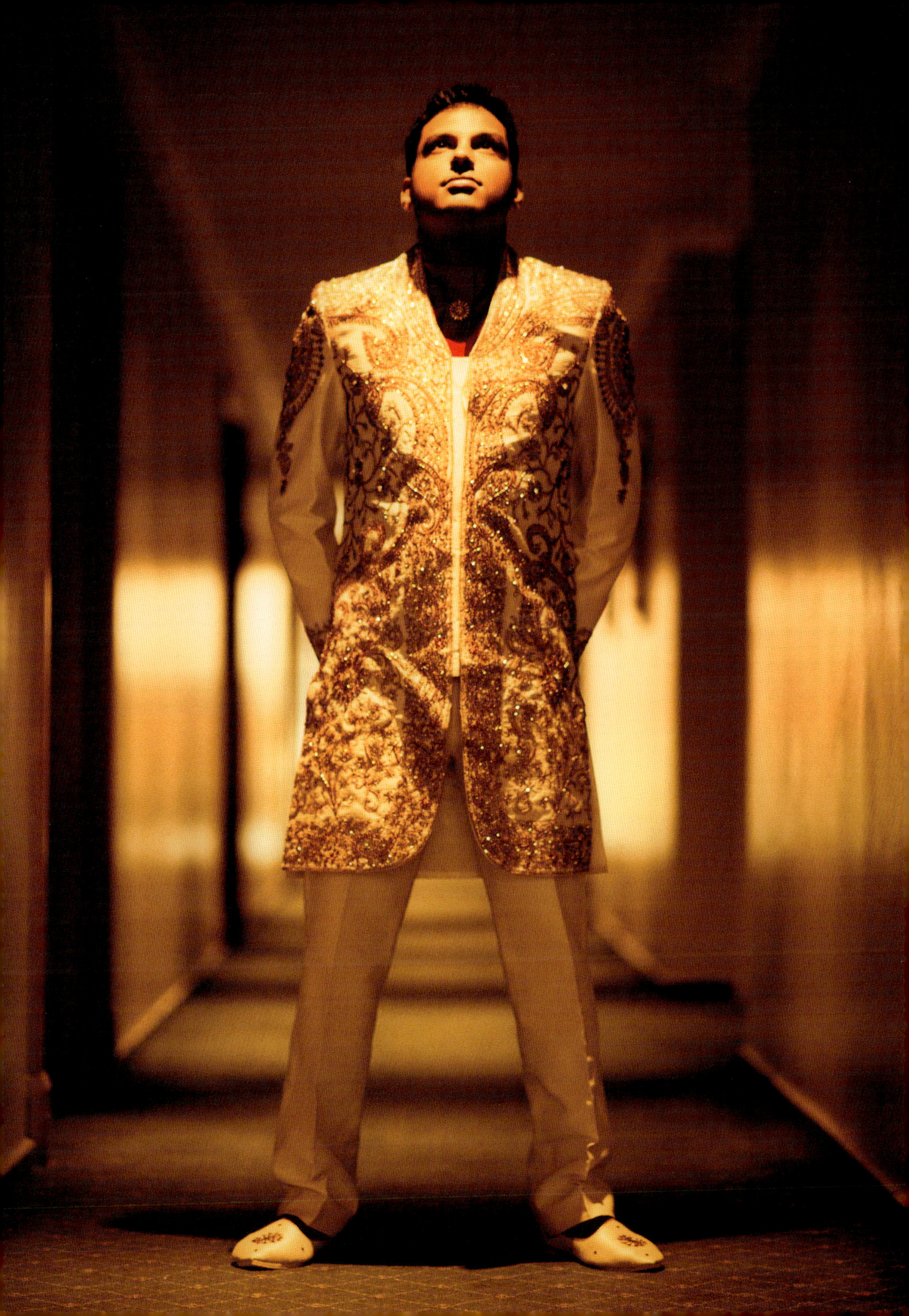

algorithms that were developed to render the most accurate colors under the specific lighting scenarios.

Automatic White Balance

Another option is the automatic white balance setting. In this mode, the camera assesses the light entering the lens and, again, applies a complicated algorithm designed to record the image in a way that should produce natural, realistic colors.

I say "should," because the automatic white balance is not *always* an accurate way of attaining realistic color capture. As we know, the camera is a mechanical device and relies on technology to assess what lands on the sensor; it can't adapt as readily or subjectively as our eyes, and it can sometimes be tricked. In fact, there some very common issues that can result in the color not being recorded accurately.

For example, the automatic white balance can struggle in mixed lighting—situations where light sources with different color temperatures are present in one image. Imagine you have cool daylight coming in through a window, illuminating the subject on one side of their face, but tungsten light (warmer light) illuminating the other side of the face. The camera, without cognitive thought, will assess the lighting conditions and apply the coordinating programmed algorithm. This may result in an image that doesn't reflect the true colors in the part of the image that is important to the photographer.

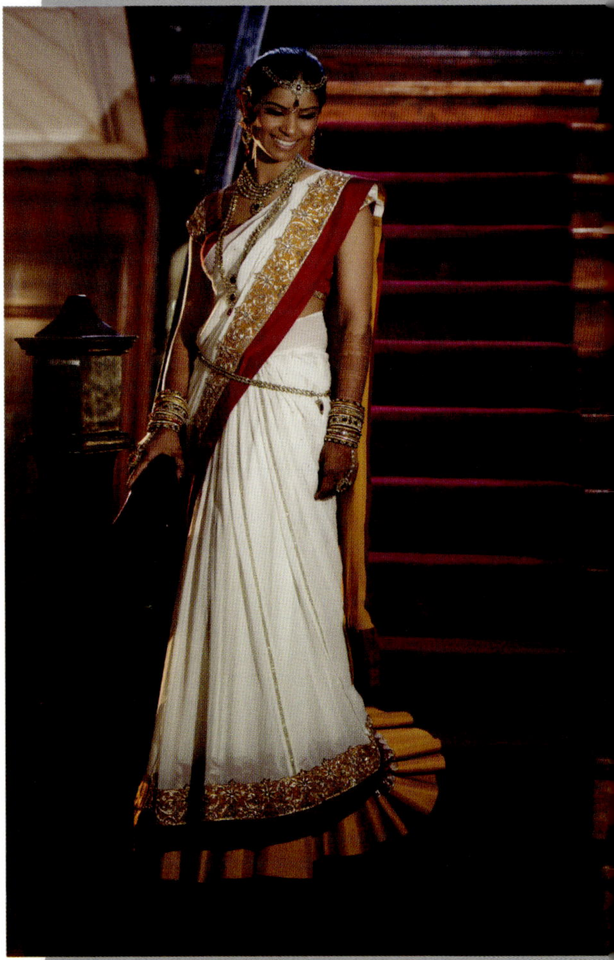

Images 4–11 and 4–12 (above and facing page). These images were made in an old building that was restored to its former glory. My assistant was behind the bride to camera left with an LED light that had a warm filter on it. This light created a warm highlight on her arm and face that helped separate her from the background. The main light source was also an LED with a warming filter placed to camera right (as you can see from the shadow her nose creates). The warmth of the filters gave me rich, royal, opulent colors that enhanced the jewelry and trim on her sari. *Tech Specs:* Nikon D3s, 4000 ISO, Lens: 70–200mm f/2.8, Aperture: f/2.8, Shutter speed: 1/160 second, Mode: A.

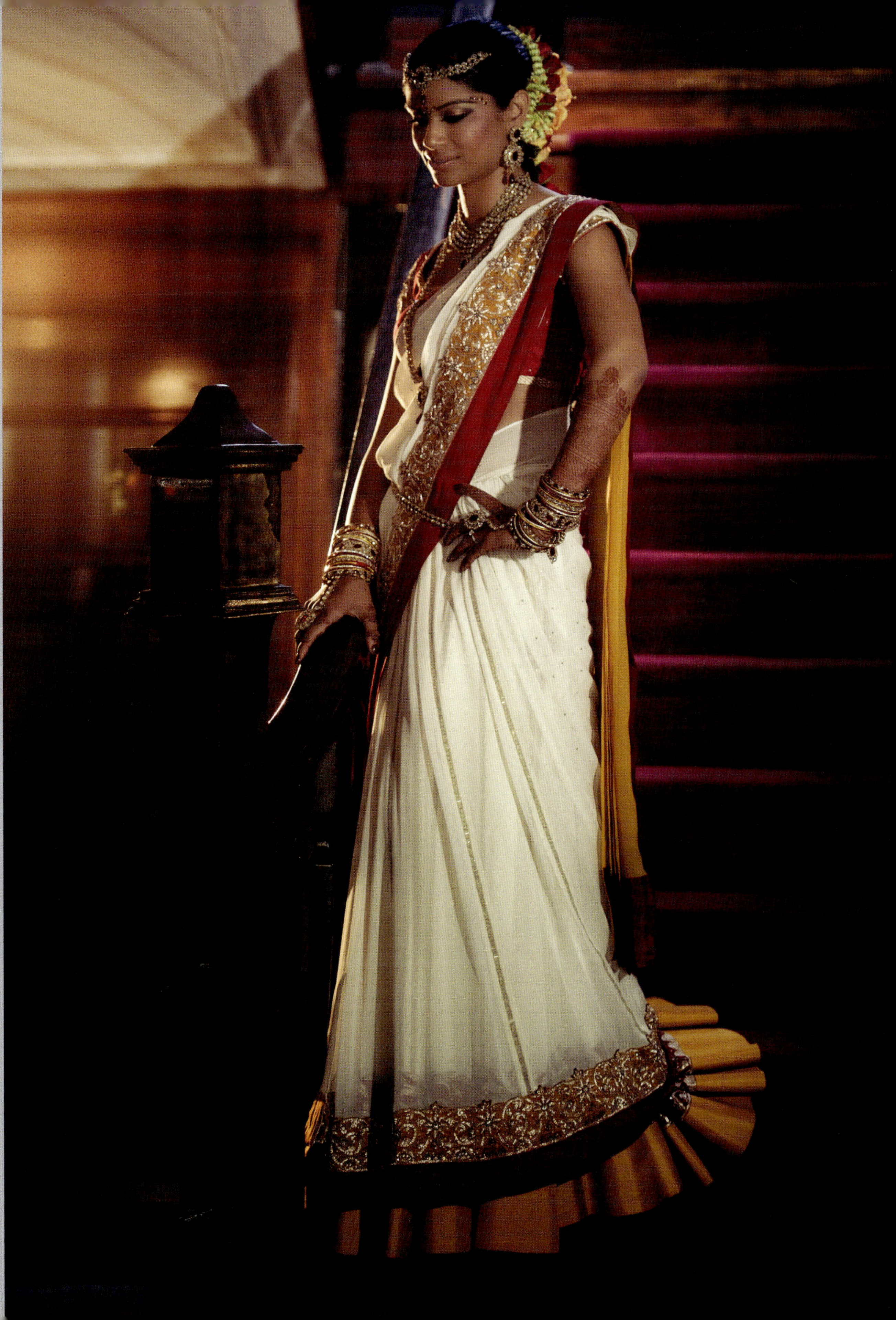

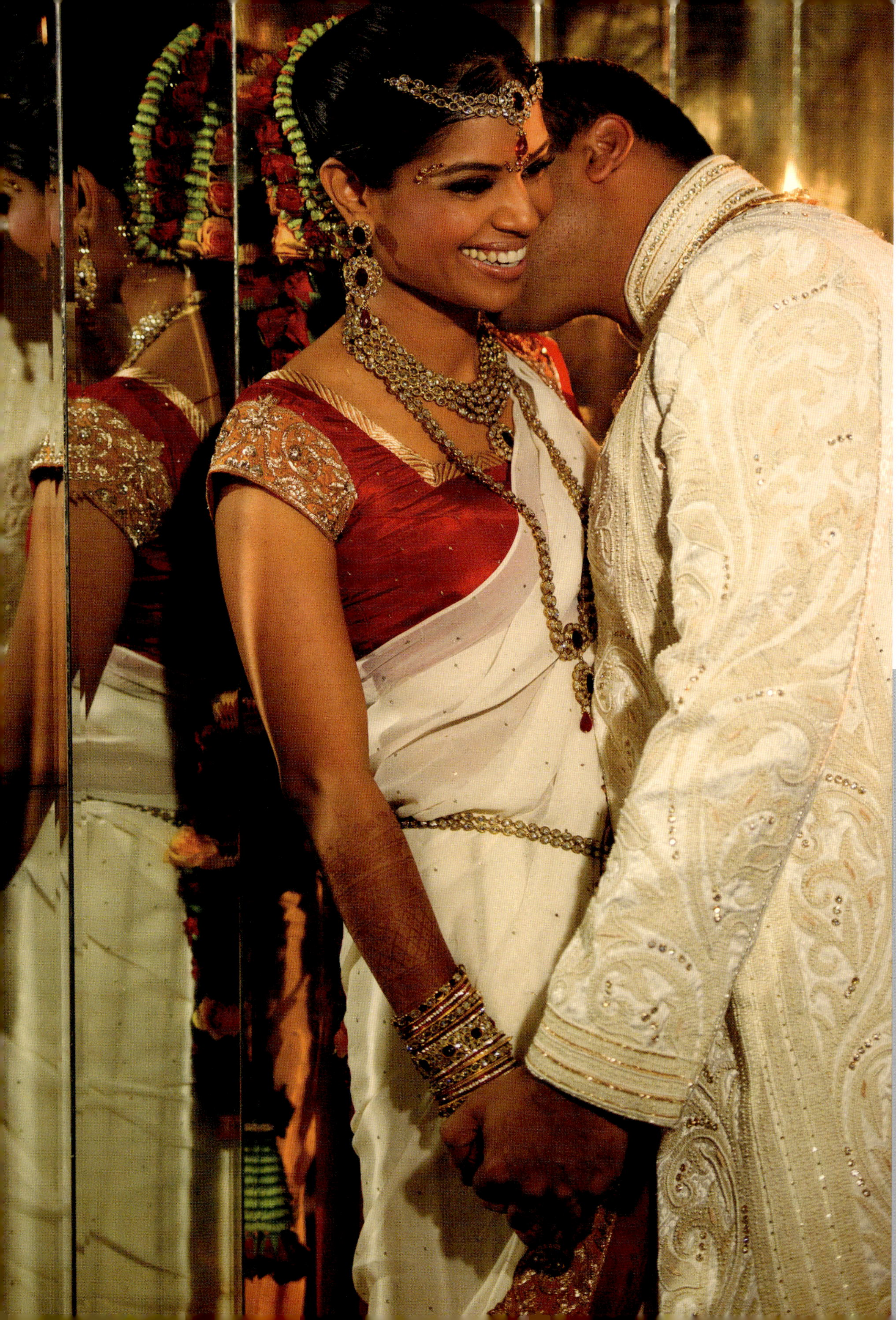

Another problematic influence on the color balance can come from what the subject is wearing. For example, if the subject is wearing a red sweater, the camera will detect that large area of warm coloration and try to neutralize it. That will result in an image that does not show the true color of the sweater—or anything else in the scene, since the same correction will be applied unilaterally to all of the colors. For this reason, I personally don't use the automatic white balance setting.

Color Temperature (K) White Balance

Another option on most cameras is the "K" white balance setting. This lets the photographer fine-tune the white balance by dialing in a specific number value for the color temperature of the lighting.

Custom White Balance

There is, lastly, the option of generating a custom white balance setting for the lighting scenario where you're shooting. This is the most accurate way to ensure a correct color rendition, but it does require a little effort—and on a shoot where time is critical, that may not be too practical.

To create a custom white balance setting, you take a reading off a test image that includes an 18 percent gray card (these can be purchased from a photographic equipment dealer). Filling the frame with a neutral color allows the camera's software to calculate a very accurate set of neutralizing corrections, resulting in an image that is true in color.

Image 4–13 (facing page). Not far from where I created images 4–11 and 4–12, I found this mirrored paneling. I like the reflection showing the detail in the bride's headdress. I kept the warm filters on the LED for consistency with the other images in this sequence. *Tech Specs:* Nikon D3s, 4000 ISO, Lens: 70–200mm f/2.8, Aperture: f/2.8, Shutter speed: 1/160 second, Mode: A.

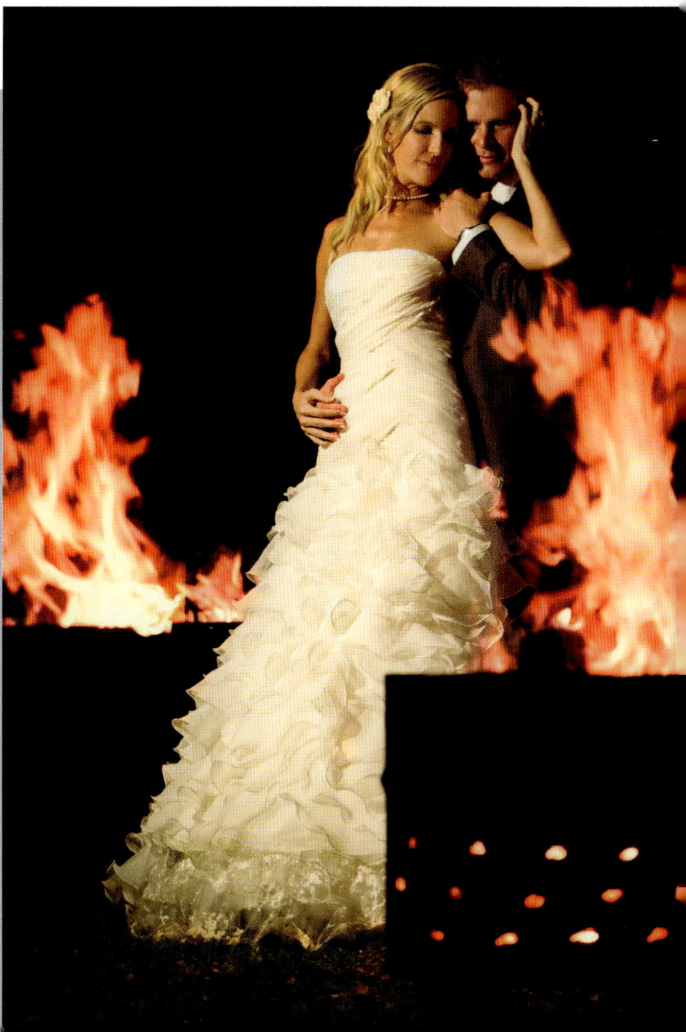

Image 4–14 (right). At this winter wedding on a farm, bonfires were provided to keep the venue and guests warm—but they also worked well for atmospheric images (likening the bonfires to the fire of their relationship). I used a Manfrotto LED with a tungsten filter to balance the color temperature of the fire and the exposure on the subjects/background. Getting that balance right took a few test shots, but then I was able to keep the fire warm and correctly exposed. *Tech Specs:* Nikon D4, 800 ISO, Lens: 70–200mm f/2.8, Aperture: f/2.8, Shutter speed: 1/100 second, Mode: M.

All the images shot after the custom white balance is created will have that same setting attached to them—until you recalibrate the custom white balance.

Because the setting is specific to one scenario, it has to be re-done for each lighting condition—which can become a little time-consuming.

Postproduction Color Correction

An alternative approach is to photograph a gray card under the lighting conditions where you will be shooting (simply have your model or assistant hold it). Then, use that sample image as a benchmark to adjust the white balance in postproduction. This works particularly well when shooting in the RAW format. (I recommend shooting everything in RAW to make full use of the latitude it offers.) If you shoot in JPG, you will still be able to use the gray card technique, but I have found the results to be a little "muddy" and inconsistent. It also reduces the bit depth of the image significantly.

To execute the color balance, open the gray-card test image in your RAW conversion software, for example Adobe Camera Raw. Then, apply any needed adjustment to the luminosity of the image. This step is very important; if you do the luminosity adjustment *after* the color balancing step, the colors have a tendency to shift. Finally, select the White Balance tool and click on the gray card in your test image. Let's look at an example.

In **images 4–15** and **4–16**, you see a gray-card test image opened in Adobe Camera Raw (along with another image shot under the same lighting). Under the histogram, it says "As Shot." In the enlarged view of the histogram, the values shown are from hovering the White Balance tool over the gray card.

Once I use the White Balance tool to click on the gray card in the test image, the program does the rest—and you'll notice that the text under the histogram changes to "custom" (**images 4–17** and **4–18**). All the color correction is done! Comparing the two sets of values, you can see that I got the white balance almost perfect in the camera. The correction neutralized only a slight red/green influence and a minor yellow cast.

You can then select any other images in that same sequence and apply the same luminosity/color changes to *all* of them at once, ensuring they are consistent with your test image. In **image 4–19**, you see a final result from our test scenario. With one click, I was able to assign it the same values as the test image, so the photograph is perfectly color-corrected and the skin tones and dress colors are true.

Creative White Balance Effects

We can use our knowledge of how the camera records and reads color to our advantage. One advantage of night and low-light photography is that it is easier to control the intensity, direction, and

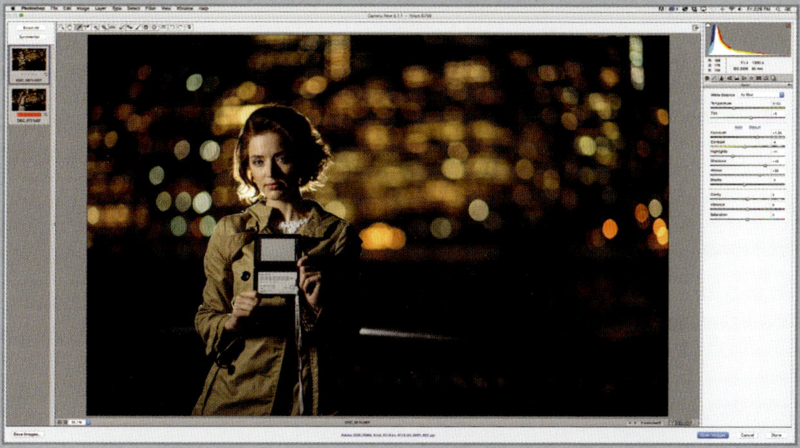

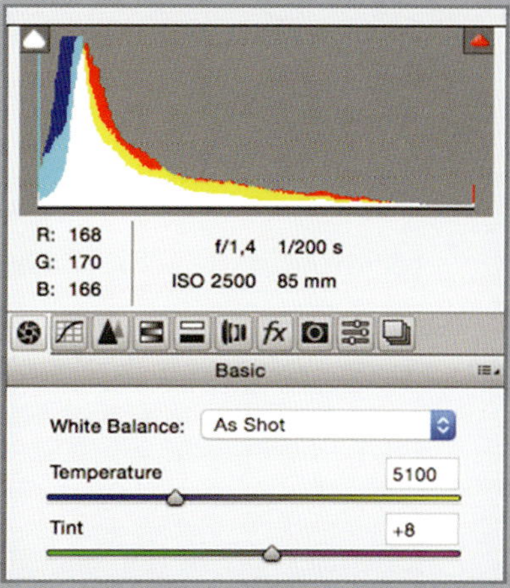

Images 4–15 and 4–16. Opening the gray-card test image in Adobe Camera Raw. A close-up of the histogram shows the color values as shot.

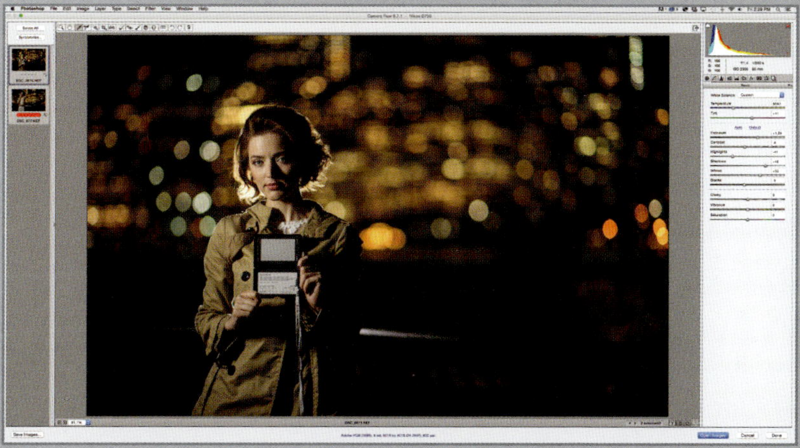

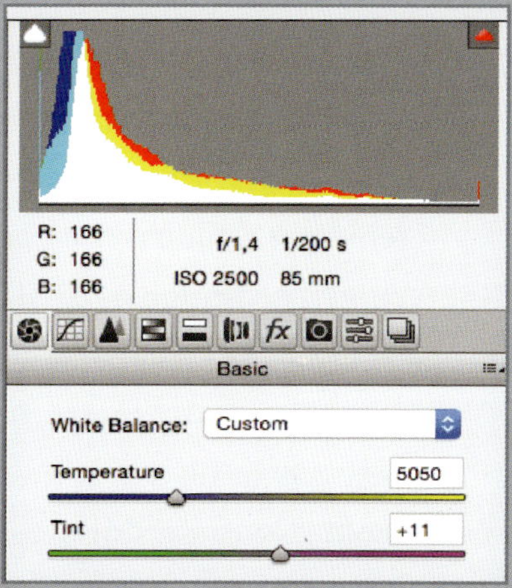

Images 4–17 and 4–18. Clicking with the White Balance tool created a custom white balance and neutralized the color. It wasn't a huge shift, but the enlarged histogram view shows how the colors were adjusted.

Image 4–19. This is the final image, color corrected using the gray card method in Camera Raw. *Tech Specs:* Nikon D750, 2500 ISO, Lens: 85mm f/1.4, Aperture: f/1.4, Shutter speed: 1/200 second, Mode: M.

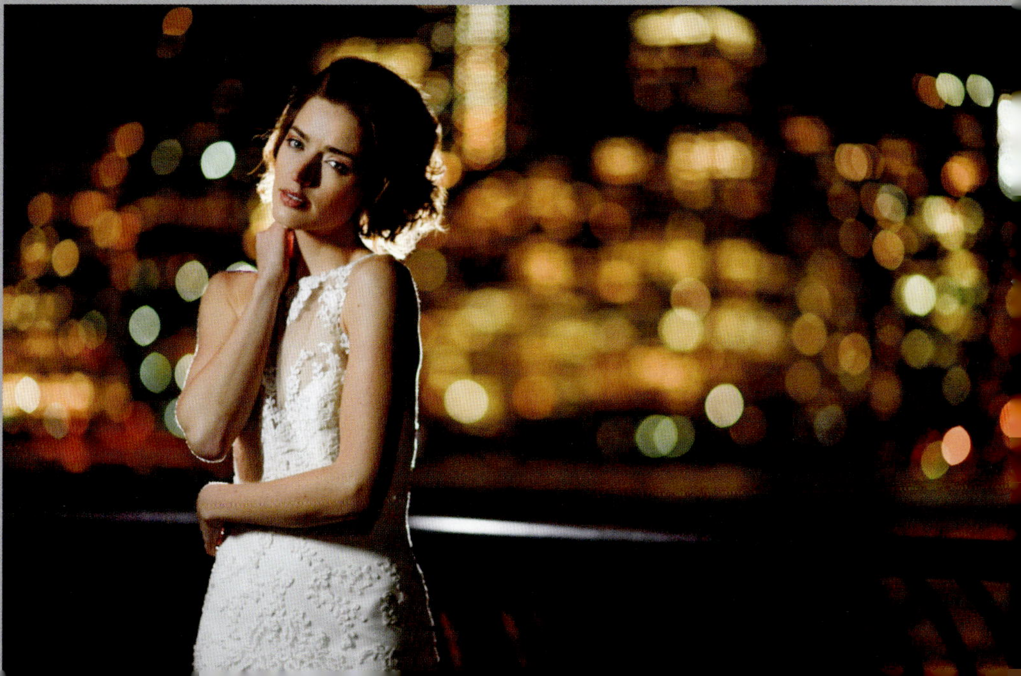

color of the light falling on your subject. So, while you could use the technique I have just described to achieve *accurate* colors, you could just as easily use the technology to achieve creative effects by "fooling" the camera. This can be achieved by manipulating the light source that illuminates your subject.

A Gelled Light on the Subject

Imagine you covered your main light with a yellow gel and then corrected the white balance, either in-camera or during postproduction, to compensate. The correction would neutralize the yellow lighting on the subject by adding blue (remember, blue is the complement of yellow; see **image 4–8**). This would provide a realistic skin tone, but adding the same blue correction to the rest of the scene (areas *not* lit by the yellow-gelled light) would also cause those tones to shift away from their real color and become more blue.

To demonstrate this technique, I covered a Manfrotto LED with a yellow Rosco gel. As you can see in **image 4–20**, I photographed a gray card to use as a color reference point—just as I did for the example in the previous section. The theory is exactly the same; it is only a little more extreme. In the image that hasn't been color-corrected (**image 4–21**), it's not surprising that the yellow gel made the model's skin and dress record as very yellow. Applying the color-balance correction setting calculated from the gray card image, however, produced a startlingly different result (**image 4–22**). The model's skin tone and dress are now more neutral—but anythings the yellow light didn't illuminate has shifted from gold/yellow to the complementary colors: purple/blue.

Image 4-20 (bottom left). With a yellow gel on the main light, I photographed the model with a gray card.

Image 4–21 (bottom right). The yellow gel on the main light resulted in the skin tones and dress being very yellow in the uncorrected image.

Image 4–22 (facing page). Neutralizing the color in the areas lit by the yellow-gelled main light produced a coordinating color shift to purple/blue in the rest of the scene. *Tech Specs:* Nikon D750, 2500 ISO, Lens: 85mm f/1.4, Aperture: f/1.4, Shutter speed: 1/80 second, Mode: M.

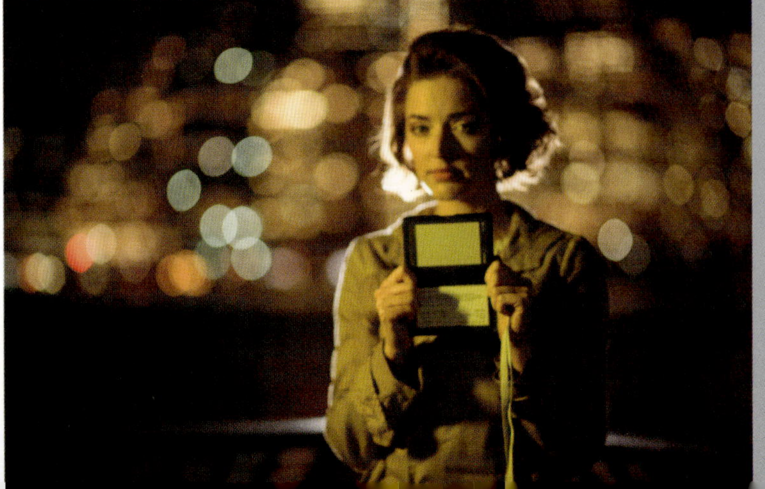

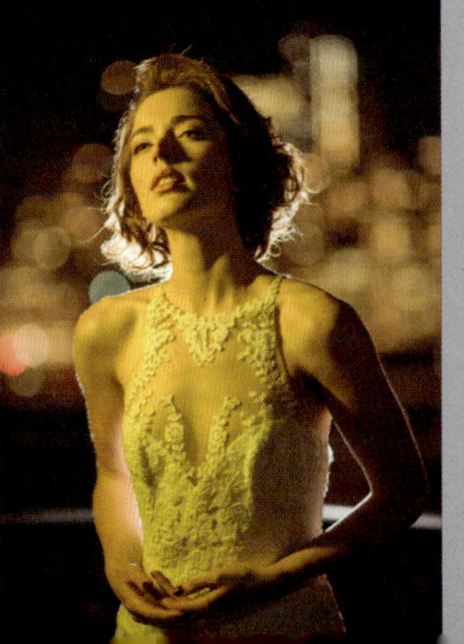

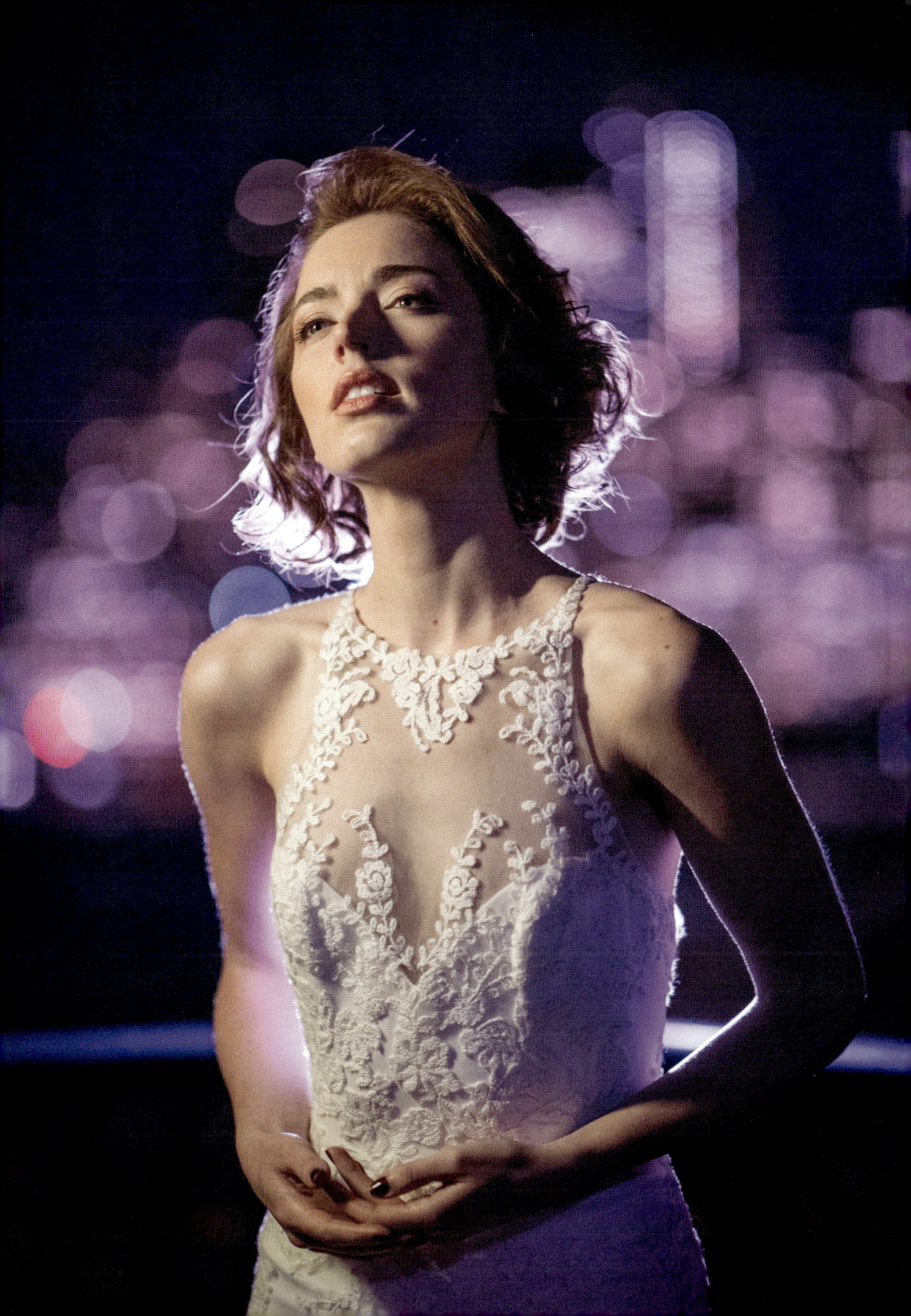

In the second image sequence demonstrating this technique (**images 4–23** through **4–25**), I used the same principle but with a cyan (blue-green) gel. I shot a test image with a gray card. Without correction, this produced very cool tones on the model and her dress. Neutralizing the blue color cast introduced red (the complement of cyan), resulting in more realistic skin tones and coloration on the dress, plus a vibrant color shift to red in the areas not lit by the cyan main light.

This technique adds even more options to your photographic repertoire. The use of a gray card in this instance may especially be of benefit, since the automatic white balance settings on even the most advanced cameras will be fooled by the multiple colors of the ambient and added light sources. That being said, if you weren't looking for realistic skin tones and liked the more surreal look, you wouldn't need to "correct" the white balance at all!

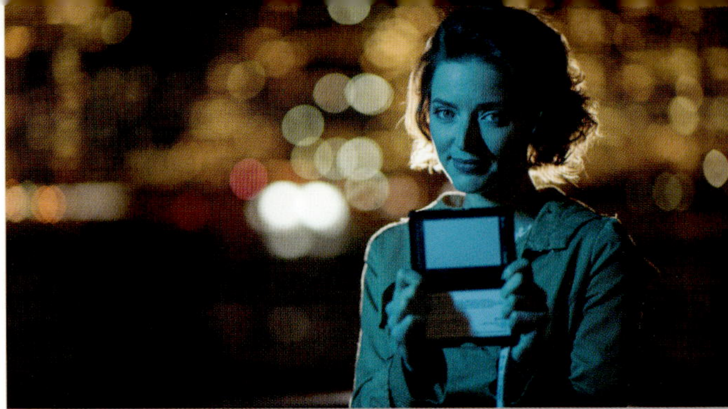

Image 4–23. With a cyan gel on the main light, I photographed the model with a gray card.

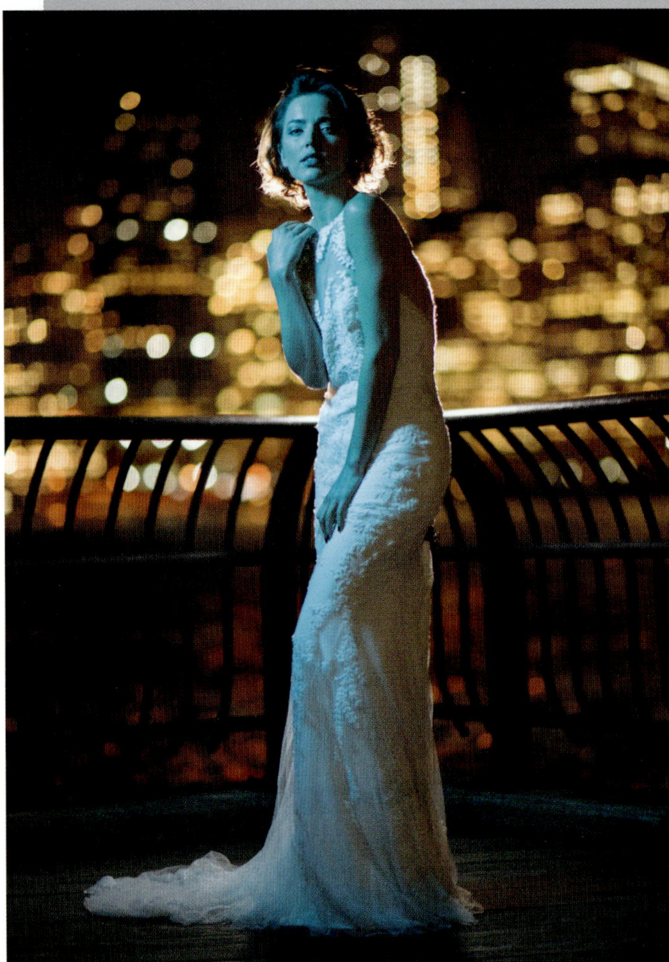

Image 4–24. The cyan gel on the main light resulted in the skin tones and dress being very cool in the uncorrected image.

Image 4–25 (facing page). Neutralizing the color in the areas lit by the cyan-gelled main light produced a coordinating color shift to red in the rest of the scene. *Tech Specs:* Nikon D750, 2500 ISO, Lens: 85mm f/1.4, Aperture: f/1.4, Shutter speed: 1/80 second, Mode: M.

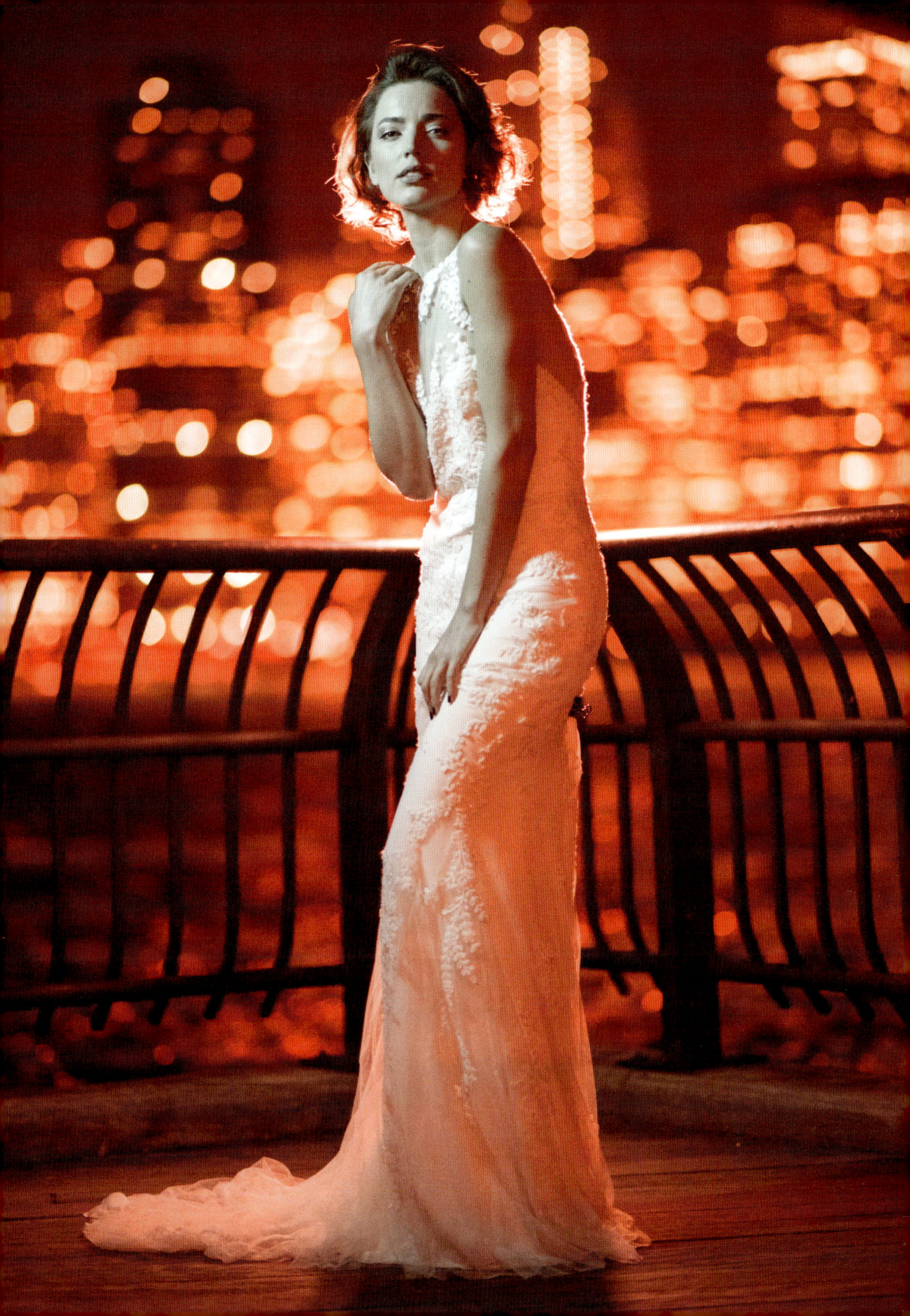

5. The Need for Speed

The most common solution for photographers looking to overcome low-light challenges is to call on the trusted speedlight. Used correctly, these very "intelligent" light sources enable photographers to shoot some incredible images. Later in the chapter, we'll also look at the use of larger (but still portable) strobe lights in low-light location photography.

Combating the Dreaded "Direct Flash" Look

Because the surface area of the speedlight is very small, its direct, unmodified light produces very harsh shadows throughout the scene and "hot spots" on the subject's skin. While you may *want* these results for a very specific look from time to time, it has to be acknowledged that—right or wrong—these tend to be regarded as characteristics of an "amateurish" lighting style. The hot spots on the subject's skin can be removed in postproduction, but we all know how time-consuming that is. With this in mind, I recommend that you either use light modifiers or bounce the flash off a reflective surface to improve the look that the speedlights produce.

Getting your speedlight off the camera is another great way to minimize the flat look that direct flash produces. There are three ways to do this. I use the SC29 TTL extension cord to allow me to fire my speedlight hand-held away from the camera. Alternately, you can use an on-camera speedlight (or the built-in "pop-up" flash) to trigger one or more additional off-camera speedlights. Gadgets such as the Nikon SU-800 Wireless Speedlight Commander can control an unlimited number of speedlights in three

Image 5–1 (facing page). Combining strobe lighting with ambient light can produce great images. Here, I used the ambient light from the venue to frame the couple. I lit the couple from the front with an Elinchrom Quadra strobe with a white umbrella. A second Elinchrom Quadra head (with a bare bulb) was placed behind the couple to create the defined shadows on the floor and the romantic rim lighting. To allow a fair amount of ambient light into the shot, I slowed the shutter down to 1/60 second. *Tech Specs:* Nikon D4, 4000 ISO, Lens: 70–200mm f/2.8, Aperture: f/3.2, Shutter speed: 1/60 second, Mode: M.

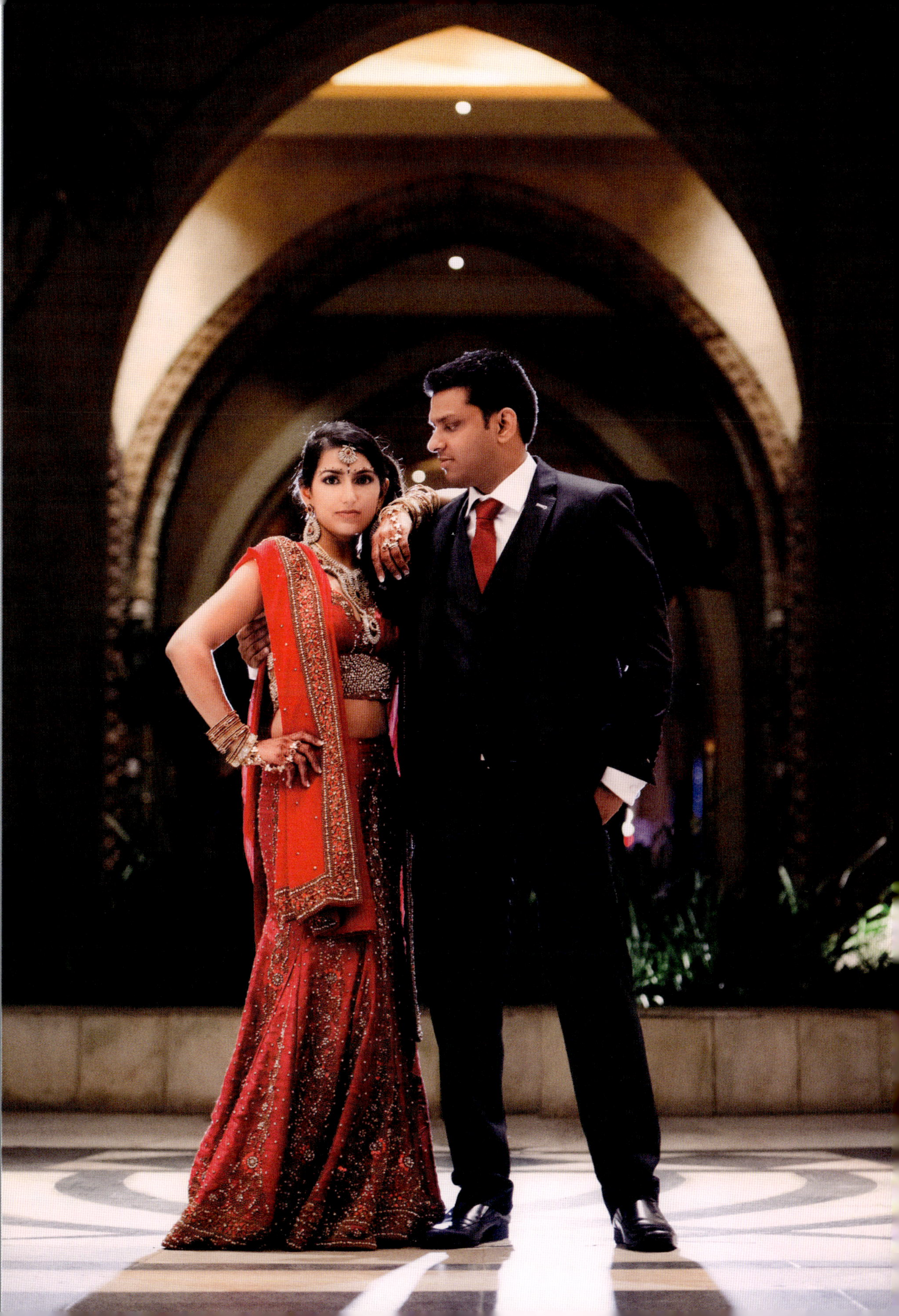

different groups. Happily, Nikon's CLS (Creative Lighting System) is surprisingly easy to understand and master.

Metering and Exposure: TTL or Manual

Today's TTL-enabled speedlights employ refined algorithms to assess the prevailing lighting conditions. Then, in conjunction with assessing the distance of the subject from the camera, the speedlight emits enough light to expose the subject correctly. From there, the user can dial in speedlight exposure compensation to fine-tune the amount of light fired.

Of course, you also have the luxury of using the speedlight on manual mode and specifying a precise amount of light to be produced each time it is fired—regardless of the camera settings or any changes in the ambient light.

For low-light photography, I use my speedlights mostly in TTL mode. I tend to shift to manual only when I need a constant output of flash power for consistency when shooting more than one frame. I may also switch to manual when the TTL system is "fooled" by the additional artificial light.

Practical Example

Let's take a look at some images created using a speedlight.

Test 1: Direct, Unmodified Speedlight, Automatic Exposure

Image 5–2 was shot with the speedlight pointed directly at Ineke. As you can see, the lighting is not very flattering. The color temperature of the light is quite cool—and, because it is coming directly from the camera, it's also flat (it doesn't reveal much shape, dimension, or form). This image was shot with the camera in program (P) mode and with the speedlight

Image 5–2. Shot in TTL mode with the on-camera speedlight pointed directly at the model, this portrait of Ineke is not very successful. *Tech Specs:* Nikon D4s, 100 ISO, Lens: 85mm f/1.4, Aperture: f/5.6, Shutter speed: 1/60 second, Mode: P.

Image 5–3. Switching to manual mode, I opened up the aperture and increased the ISO setting to allow more of the ambient light to register. *Tech Specs:* Nikon D4s, 500 ISO, Lens: 85mm f/1.4, Aperture: f/1.4, Shutter speed: 1/60 second, Mode: M.

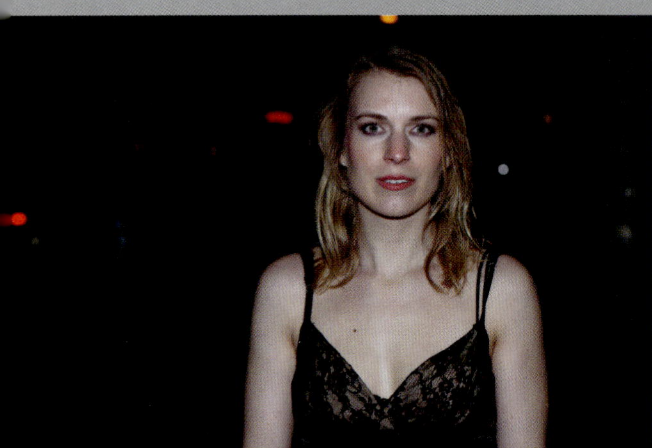

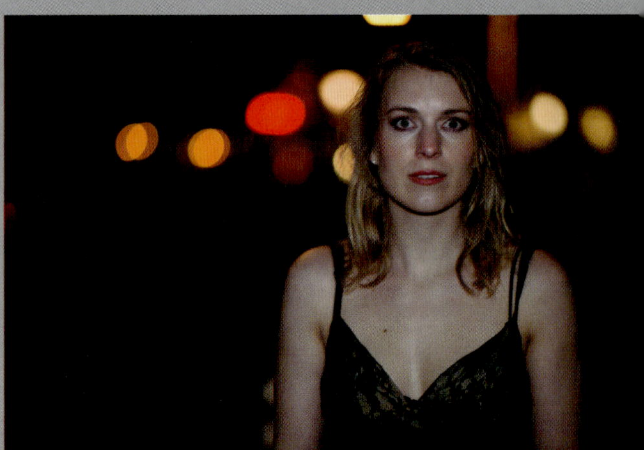

in TTL—settings that only an amateur or ignorant professional would tend to use. Notice that the background is also dark and lacks substance. This is because there was not enough ambient light to affect the sensor at the settings being used. We can definitely improve on this look.

Test 2: Direct, Unmodified Speedlight, Manual Exposure

The first things I did to improve the shot were to switch to the manual mode, open up the aperture, and increase the ISO (**image 5–3**). This made an immediate difference in the amount of ambient light captured by the sensor. The light falling on her is still cold and not flattering, but that's something we can overcome, too.

Test 3: Bounce Flash

Image 5–4 shows me taking the shot, under a bridge on a rainy night in Amsterdam. If you look closely, you will notice the next step I took to improve the image of Ineke: I twisted the speedlight. Instead of having it point directly at Ineke, I turned it to point at one of the posters on the wall. This is called bouncing the flash. The light from my small speedlight spreads out as it moves toward the wall, then continues spreading out as it bounces back onto the model. This reduces the intensity of the light on the model, but it also produces a much softer effect than the direct flash. Additionally, it allows me to create a directional lighting look without even taking my flash off the camera.

As you can see in **image 5–5**, the main light now appears to come from the side, in the direction of the poster. In this case, the bounce surface (the poster) presented one concern: it had a lot of yellow in it. Knowing that the bounced light would pick up this coloration, I took

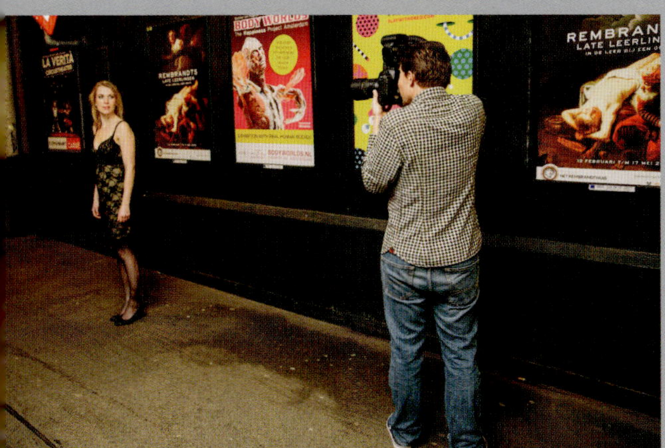

Image 5–4. Shooting with my flash turned to bounce off the yellow poster to camera right.

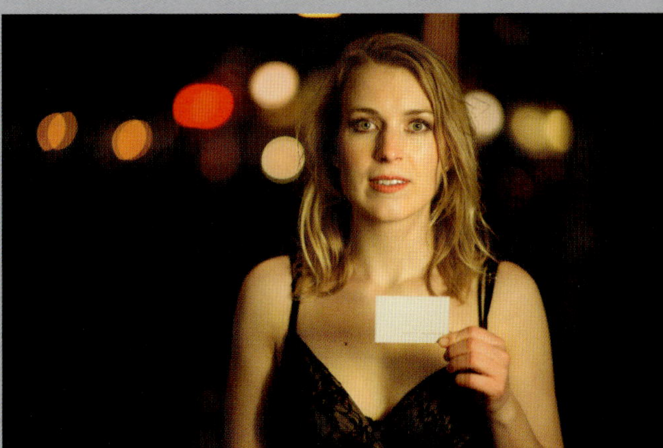

Image 5–5. Knowing that the lighting would pick up the yellow tones from the bounce surface, I shot a test frame with a gray card. This made it easy to color balance all the subsequent images from this scene.

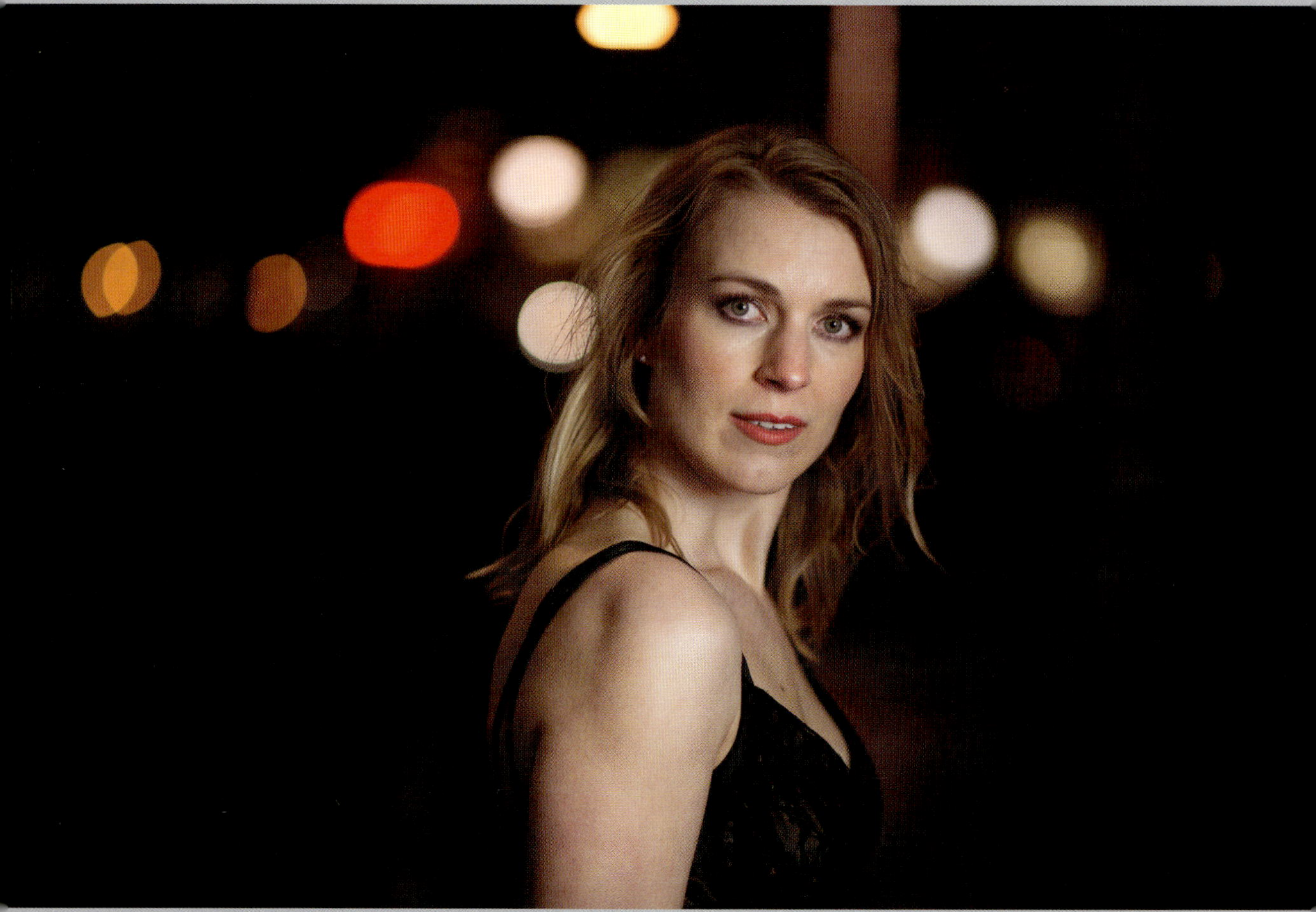

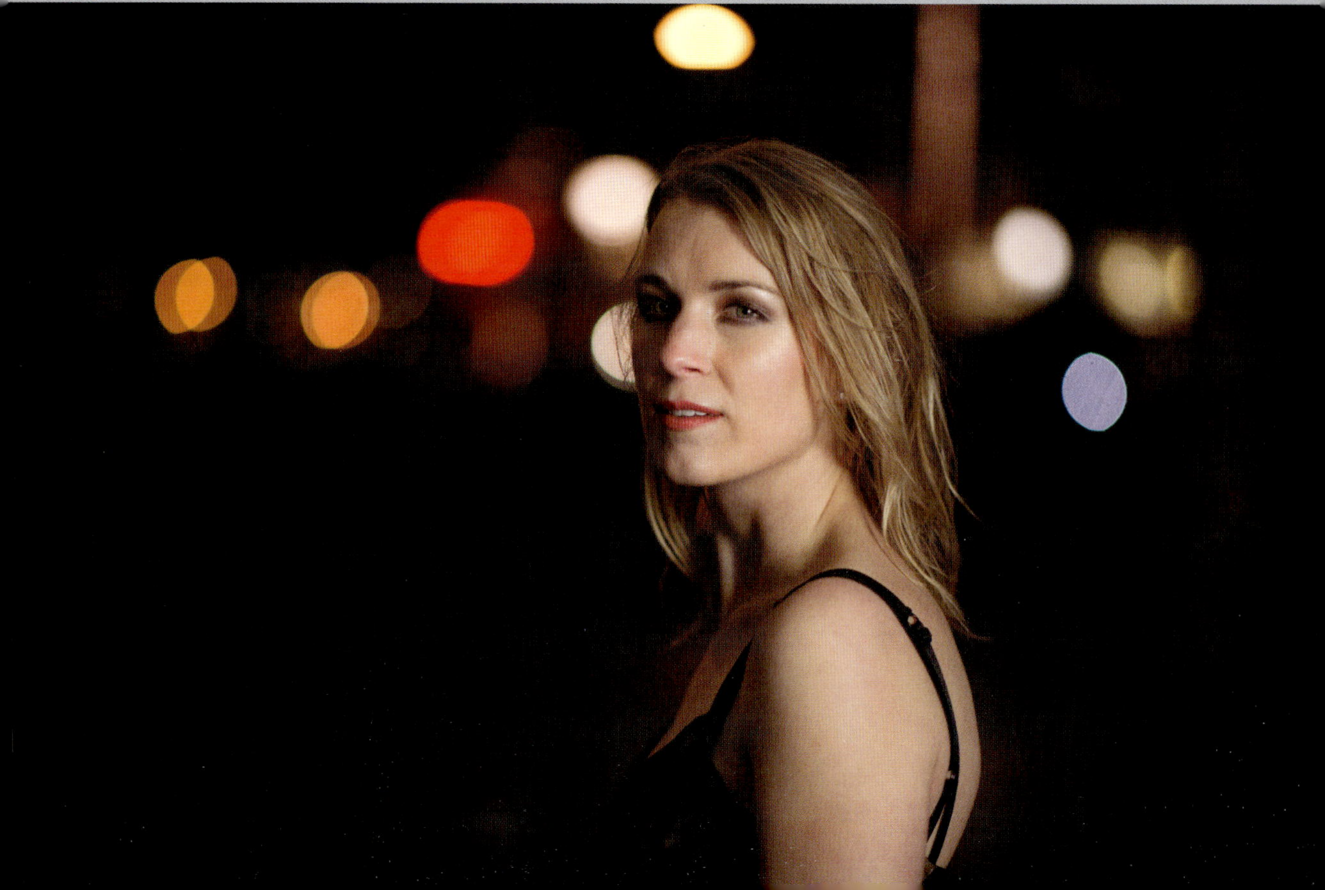

Image 5–6 (facing page, top). Short lighting with bounce flash. *Tech Specs:* Nikon D4s, 500 ISO, Lens: 85mm f/1.4, Aperture: f/1.4, Shutter speed: 1⁄60 second, Mode: M.

Image 5–7 (facing page, bottom). Broad lighting with bounce flash. *Tech Specs:* Nikon D4s, 500 ISO, Lens: 85mm f/1.4, Aperture: f/1.4, Shutter speed: 1⁄60 second, Mode: M.

a test shot of the model holding a gray card and processed the images using the postproduction color-balance technique described in chapter 4. The result was an image with nice dimension and shape—and a pleasing color balance.

Tests 4 and 5: Bounce Flash for Short/Broad Lighting

At this point, I had conquered most of the problems we identified in the direct flash image. The camera/flash settings were adjusted for a better balance between the subject and background, and bouncing the flash was a big improvement over the hard, flat lighting of the direct, on-camera flash. All that was left to do was position Ineke so the light hit her face in a flattering way.

I have often been asked which direction one would point the speedlight to create short or narrow side lighting. The rule of thumb when bouncing flash is to point it in the same direction as the subject's nose is pointing. In **image 5–6**, Ineke's nose is pointing to camera right—the same direction as the flash (and the wall it's bouncing off). In **image 5–7**, for comparison, I had Ineke turn her face in the opposite direction. Even though the speedlight is not directly pointed at her and we still have side lighting, this broad side lighting is not as flattering as the short lighting in the previous image.

Dragging the Shutter

As a wedding photographer, I photograph a lot of images of guests dancing. If I shot these using the default flash setting (1⁄60 second at f/5.6 or smaller, depending on my ISO setting), the subjects would be correctly exposed by the speedlight, but they'd be shown against a very dark, if not black, background. Shots like this lack any ambiance—and may even look a little silly, with someone caught in the middle of a dance move with little or nothing to give the pose context. Why is the background so dark? Because too little ambient light is recording in the capture.

“Shots like this lack any ambiance—and may even look a little silly, with someone caught in the middle of a dance move with little or nothing to give the pose context.”

The Basics

Dragging the shutter is a great technique for combating this problem and capturing the mood and atmosphere of the event. Using this approach, the pop of bright flash illuminates the subject (and helps freeze their action), but then the shutter stays *open* and allows the lower-intensity ambient light to continue to build up in the exposure. This helps balance the subject/background exposure levels, so you get a better overall sense of the context.

> “The flash ‘froze’ the subjects while they were dancing, and the shutter was open just long enough to allow the ambient light to have an influence in the final image.”

To implement this technique, you need to shoot in manual mode with a medium ISO—I would suggest around 1000 or 2000 ISO. Set your shutter speed to around 1/15 second and your aperture to f/4 or f/2.8. This is a good starting point. Once you have taken a test shot, you can decide whether you would like the background to be brighter or darker relative to the subject. If you want it brighter, use a slightly longer shutter speed; if you want it darker, switch to a slightly shorter shutter speed. Keep in mind that ambient lighting conditions vary widely, so this technique may take some practice.

Rear- vs. Front-Curtain Sync

I’m often asked whether to use rear-curtain sync or front-curtain sync when dragging the shutter. Basically, this refers to when the flash fires—either at the beginning or the end of the exposure. If you are shooting at 1/60 second or higher, it isn’t really going to make too much difference whether the flash fires at the beginning or end of the exposure. The camera’s default setting would be at the beginning of the exposure, which is where I like to keep it. When using a longer shutter speed, I want the flash to fire as I press the shutter. I want that pop of flash to “freeze” the action as I see it—right when I trip the shutter. If the pop of flash is set to occur at the end of my 1/8 second exposure, timing the shot feels a lot more like guesswork.

Practical Example 1: On the Dance Floor with One Light

Image 5–8 illustrates this technique. After switching to manual mode, I selected a shutter speed of 1/15 second and an aperture of f/2.8. My ISO was set to 640. I also used an SC-29 TTL extension cord to get my Nikon SB900 speedlight off the camera and avoid the flat-lighting

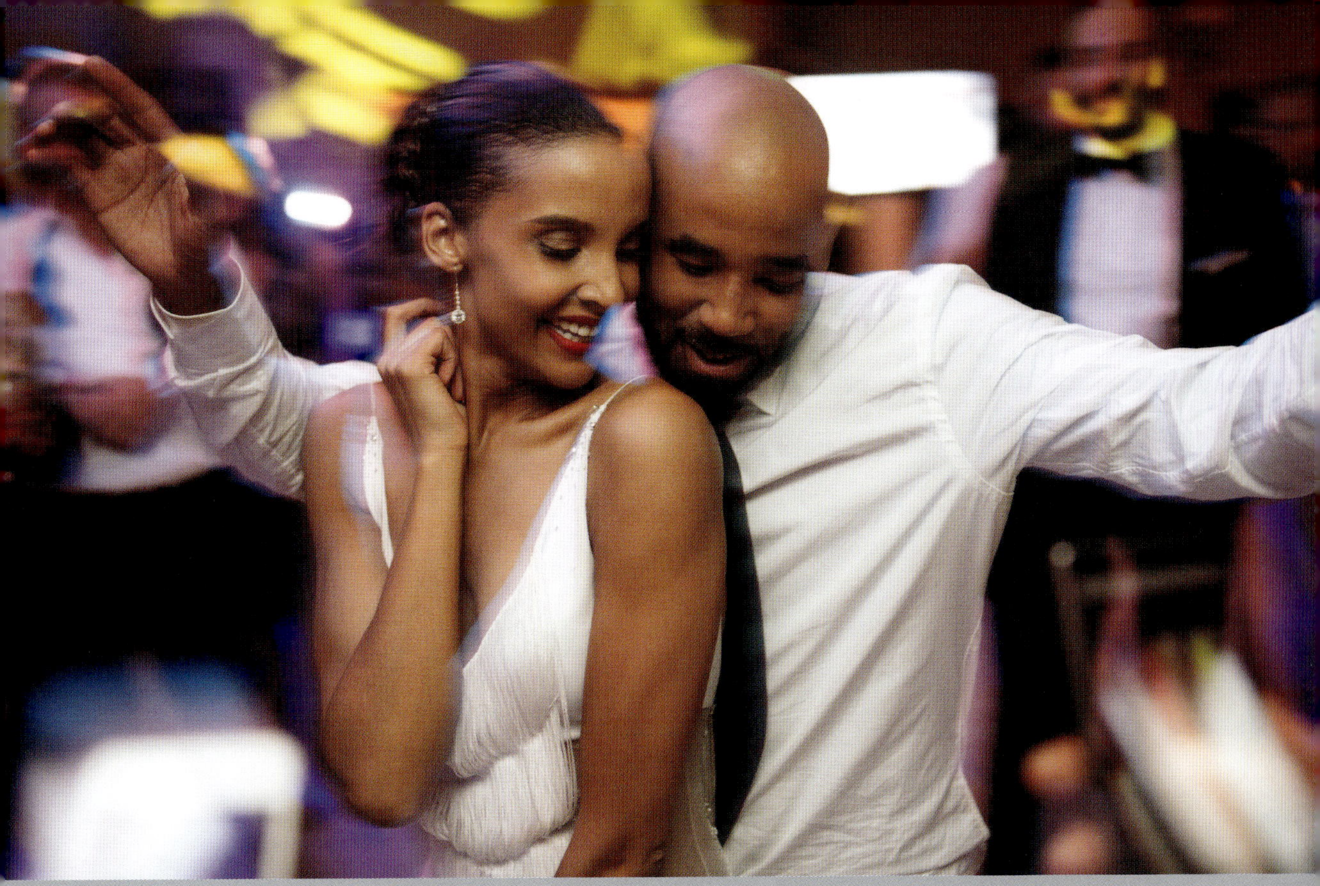

Image 5–8. A pop of flash helped freeze the subjects, while dragging the shutter allowed the ambient light to record and reveal the setting. *Tech Specs:* Nikon D750, 640 ISO, Lens: 24–70mm f/2.8, Aperture: f/2.8, Shutter speed: 1/15 second, Exposure compensation –0.3EV, Mode: M.

look. The speedlight was set to TTL and I adjusted the output to –0.3EV, as I wanted the speedlight to complement the ambient light but not dominate it. The image has depth and dimension as well as a sense of movement. The flash "froze" the subjects while they were dancing, and the shutter was open just long enough to allow the ambient light to have an influence in the final image. (*Note:* Keep in mind that your settings will vary; it really depends on the amount of ambient light that is around.)

Practical Example 2: On the Dance Floor with Two Lights

Nikon's amazing Creative Lighting System (CLS) facilitates the wireless communication between either speedlights or a commander control unit and the speedlights. This enables us to fire *and* control the output of multiple off-camera speedlights from the master unit. I utilized this system in **image 5–9** (next page), which shows bride Claire dancing at her wedding reception. The master speedlight was on the SC29 TTL

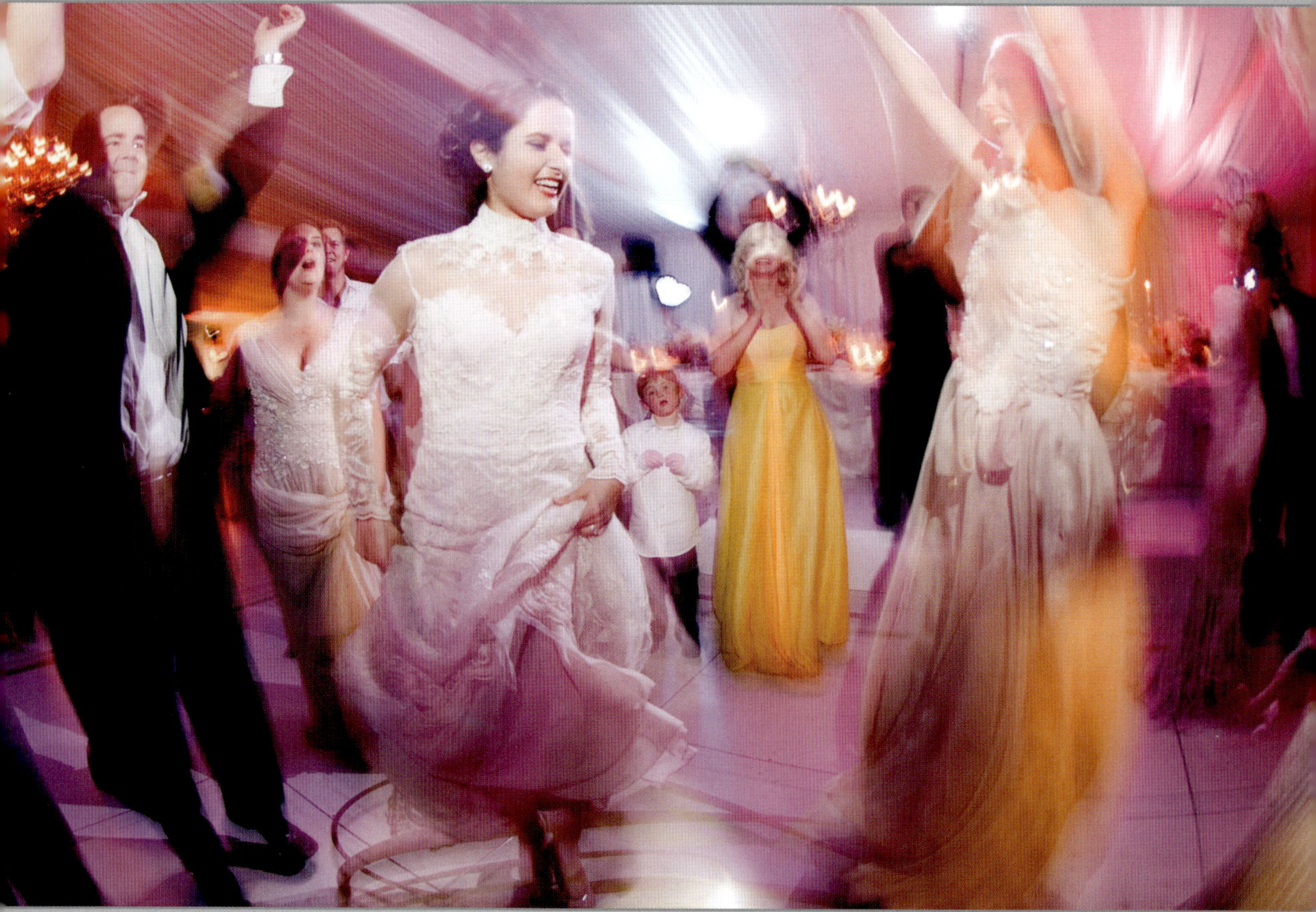

Image 5–9. The main light was a speedlight connected to the camera with a TTL extension cord. My assistant held a second blue-gelled speedlight in the background. Dragging the shutter allowed just enough of the ambient to register, giving us a better sense of the energy and ambiance. *Tech Specs:* Nikon D4, 125 ISO, Lens: 10.5mm f/2.8, Aperture: f/4, Shutter speed: 1/4 second, Mode: M.

extension cord and the second speedlight, which I had covered with a blue gel, was attached to a monopod and held by my assistant behind the bride. If you look carefully at the image, you will notice him holding the monopod with the attached speedlight in the background, to camera right. It doesn't bother me that you can see him there; most people wouldn't notice him because he blends into the background and appears to be a guest. I combined the CLS system with "dragging the shutter" to create an image with a dynamic atmosphere—one that is truly representative of the party.

Exploring the capabilities and limitations of your speedlights is a never-ending journey of learning and growing. You really ought to read the manual to appreciate just how intelligent they are! If you want to work more extensively with speedlights, I recommend picking up a book by my good friend Neil van Niekerk. His popular books *On-Camera Flash* and *Off-Camera Flash* (both from Amherst Media) are comprehensive guides to using speedlights for weddings and portraits.

For More Power: Compact, Portable Strobes

Although speedlights work very well, especially under difficult lighting conditions, I personally enjoy shooting with off-camera portable strobes, such as the Elinchrom Quadra—a portable battery and flash kit that is ideal for location photography. While speedlights provide around 50 watt-seconds of light, the Elinchrom Quadra has a maximum flash output of 400 watt-seconds. If I am only using one flash head on this system, I tend to use the "B" output socket on the power supply. The system is asymmetrical and the "B" socket has a lower output than "A," which allows me to shoot with a great light source onto which I can add many different modifiers. With the use of TTL remote triggers, this system allows you to keep the "automatic" function of the TTL system while benefiting from a better light source and a more consistent, reliable triggering system.

Modifiers and Positioning

One of my favorite modifiers for this system is the small Elinchrom Octa Softbox. You can use it as intended to produce a wonderful flattering, soft light on the subject. For more of a fashion look,

Image 5–10. From this hotel's rooftop, I wanted to capture the city lights in the background. I started off by setting my exposure so that the city lights were as bright as I wanted them to be. The primary light source landing on the bride was from an Elinchrom RangerRX with an Octa Softbox light modifier attached. I set the power so the light on her matched my settings for the city lights. Two Manfroto LEDs were placed on either side of the bride to create depth and contour the subject. They also created a highlight that prevented her dark hair from blending into the dark background. *Tech Specs:* Nikon D4, 200 ISO, Lens: 70–200mm f/2.8, Aperture: f/2.8, Shutter speed: 1/100 second, Mode: M.

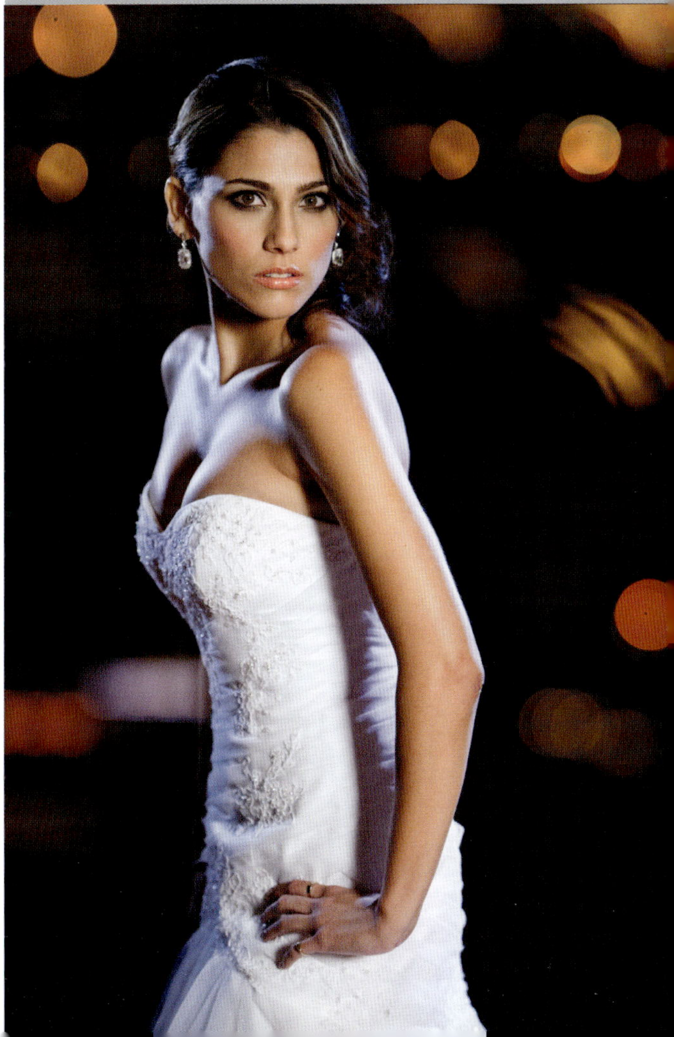

you can remove the front diffuser from the softbox and have it function more like a silver beauty dish. Attaching a small spigot (a special metal adapter) allows me to mount the flash head onto my monopod—turning the monopod into a boom. This allows my assistant to maneuver the unit easily for on-the-go lighting.

Test 1: Default Setting

Let's look at a sequence of images demonstrating how these things all come together. As with the test that we did with the speedlight in a previous section, I started off with what would be the default factory setting that the camera would use in the program mode. This would be at 100 ISO with the aperture at f/5.6 and the shutter speed at 1/60 second. As you can see in **image 5–11**, the quality of light falling onto Bahareh is very good, but there is very little ambient light in the background. This image was shot in the beautiful city of Amsterdam and there was amazing light from the bridges over the canal, as well as a traffic light. Those elements just aren't present in this image.

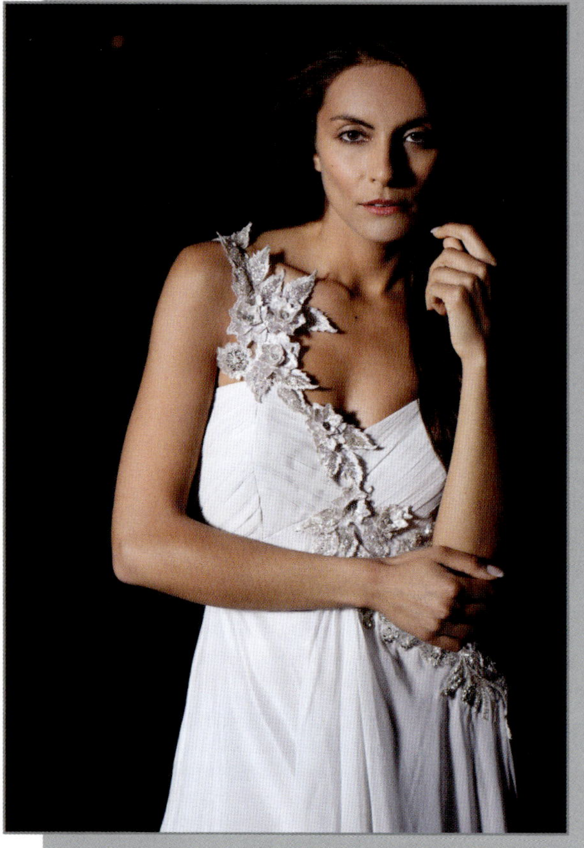

Image 5–11. Using the default settings of a camera in program mode produced nice lighting on the subject, but the background reveals almost nothing of the setting. *Tech Specs:* Nikon D4s, 100 ISO, Lens: 85mm f/1.4, Aperture: f/5.6, Shutter speed: 1/60 second, Mode: M.

"The aperture controls the subject exposure; the shutter speed controls the background exposure."

Test 2: Dragging the Shutter

For this image, I used the same setup as the previous image, however this time I left the shutter open for a little longer than the default 1/60 second. I opened it for 1/15 second to allow more time for the ambient light to fall onto the sensor. You can see that the exposure on Bahareh's skin and dress is exactly the same; this is because the light being emitted from the strobe

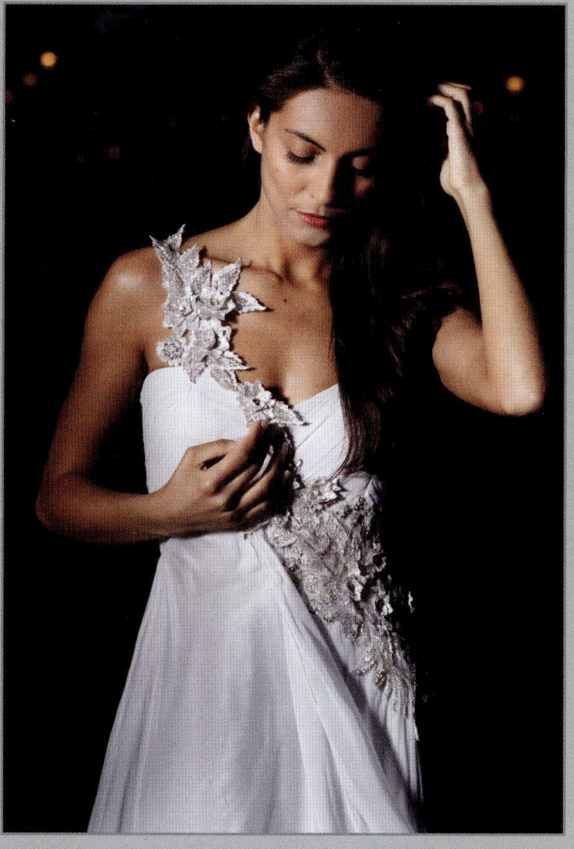

Image 5–12. Dragging the shutter at 1/15 second helped bring in some background detail—but not quite enough. *Tech Specs:* Nikon D4s, 100 ISO, Lens: 85mm f/1.4, Aperture: f/5.6, Shutter speed: 1/15 second, Mode: M.

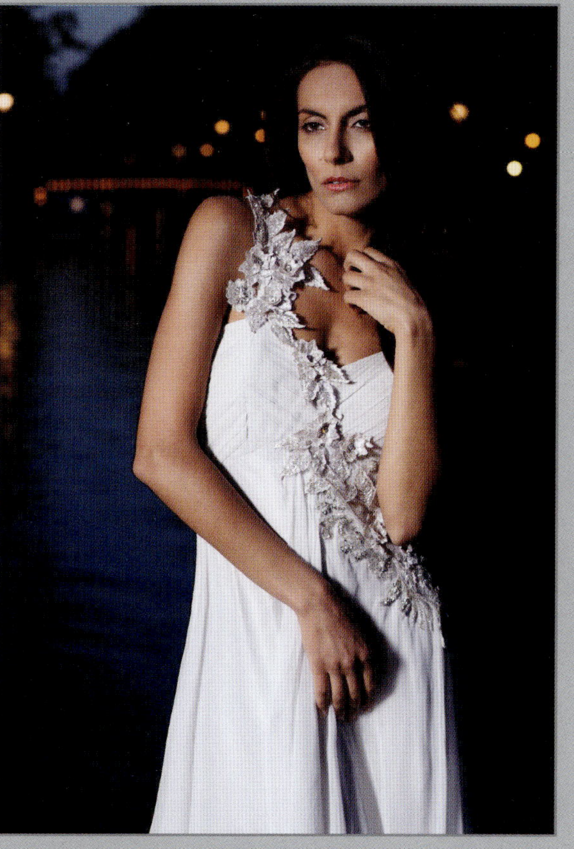

Image 5–13. Dragging the shutter at 1/4 finally brought the Amsterdam evening into view. *Tech Specs:* Nikon D4s, 100 ISO, Lens: 85mm f/1.4, Aperture: f/5.6, Shutter speed: 1/4 second, Mode: M.

is the same strength or output. Its level is not impacted by the change in shutter speed. This is where the familiar adage for strobe photography comes into play: "The aperture controls the subject exposure; the shutter speed controls the background exposure." Although **image 5–12** is better than the previous image, the lights of Amsterdam deserve a little more respect than even this.

Test 3: Dragging the Shutter Even More

For **image 5–13**, I opened the shutter even longer—1/4 second. The ambient light is now a lot more prevalent than in the first image. When getting to slower shutter speeds like we have in this image, you need to be careful of ghosting. This could occur when the camera is not held as steady as it could be or when the subject moves during the exposure.

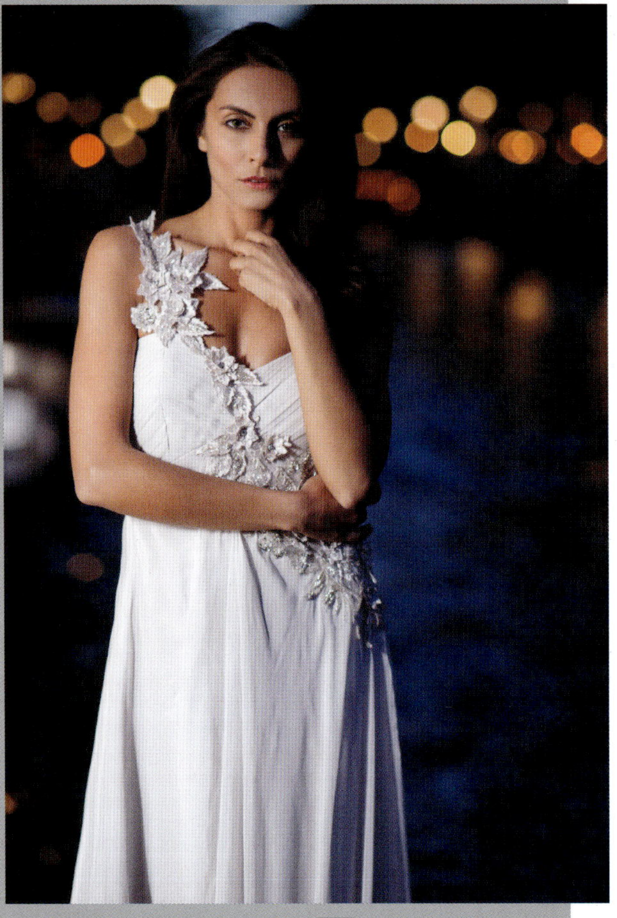

Image 5–14. Opening the aperture and boosting the ISO let me capture the light on the background—and introduce some nice bokeh. *Tech Specs:* Nikon D4s, 800 ISO, Lens: 85mm f/1.4, Aperture: f/2, Shutter speed: 1/60 second, Mode: M.

Test 4: Wider Aperture, Better Bokeh

Now we need to look at other options for allowing more ambient light onto the sensor. There are three components to exposure: shutter speed, aperture, and ISO. In the previous image, we used a longer shutter speed to control the level of the ambient light. In **image 5–14**, I took my shutter speed back to my starting point for this sequence (1/60 second) but opened the aperture to f/2 and increased the ISO to 800. Effectively, this allowed 5 stops more ambient light onto the sensor than we had in **image 5–11**. We get 2 stops by opening the aperture from f/5.6 to f/2 and 3 stops by increasing the ISO from 100 to 800. I had to reduce the strobe output to compensate for opening the aperture to f/2. You will now notice how much more aesthetically pleasing the bokeh in the background is; this is because wider apertures produce better bokeh as the depth of field reduces. (*Note:* In the next chapter, we'll spend some more time looking at how to create and refine this effect.)

Test 5: Motion Blur

For a final experiment with the same lighting setup and exposure settings, I purposely moved the camera during the longer exposure. There was very little ambient light falling onto Bahareh, which resulted in her being "frozen" by the nearly instantaneous burst of light from the flash. Moving the camera during the exposure resulted in the streetlights being portrayed as light trails. Depending on how you move your camera during the exposure, you can create interesting shapes with the ambient light. In **images 5–15** through **5–18**, I tried a few variations.

Images 5-15, 5-16, 5-17, and 5-18. Shooting at the same settings as the previous image, I moved the camera during the exposure to blur the ambient light. *Tech Specs:* Nikon D4s, 800 ISO, Lens: 85mm f/1.4, Aperture: f/2, Shutter speed: 1/60 second, Mode: M.

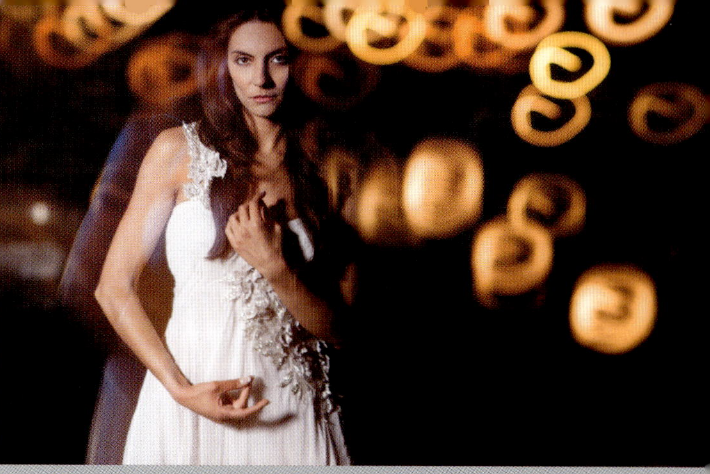

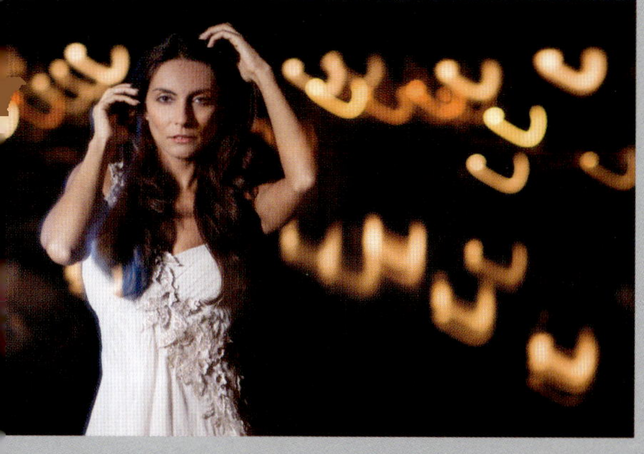

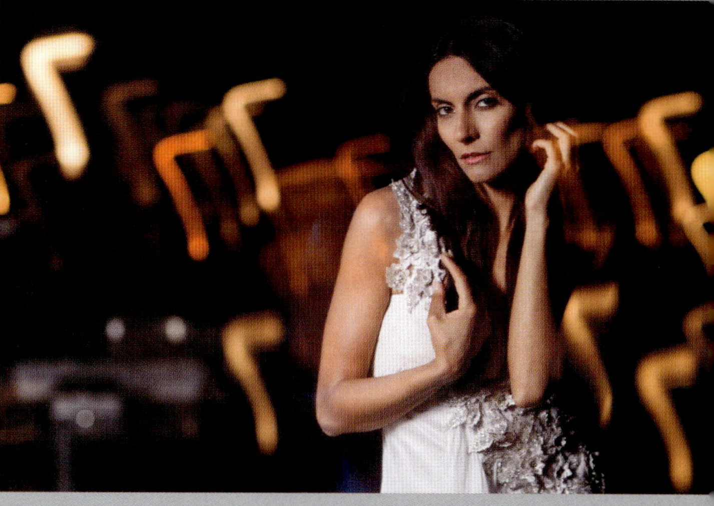

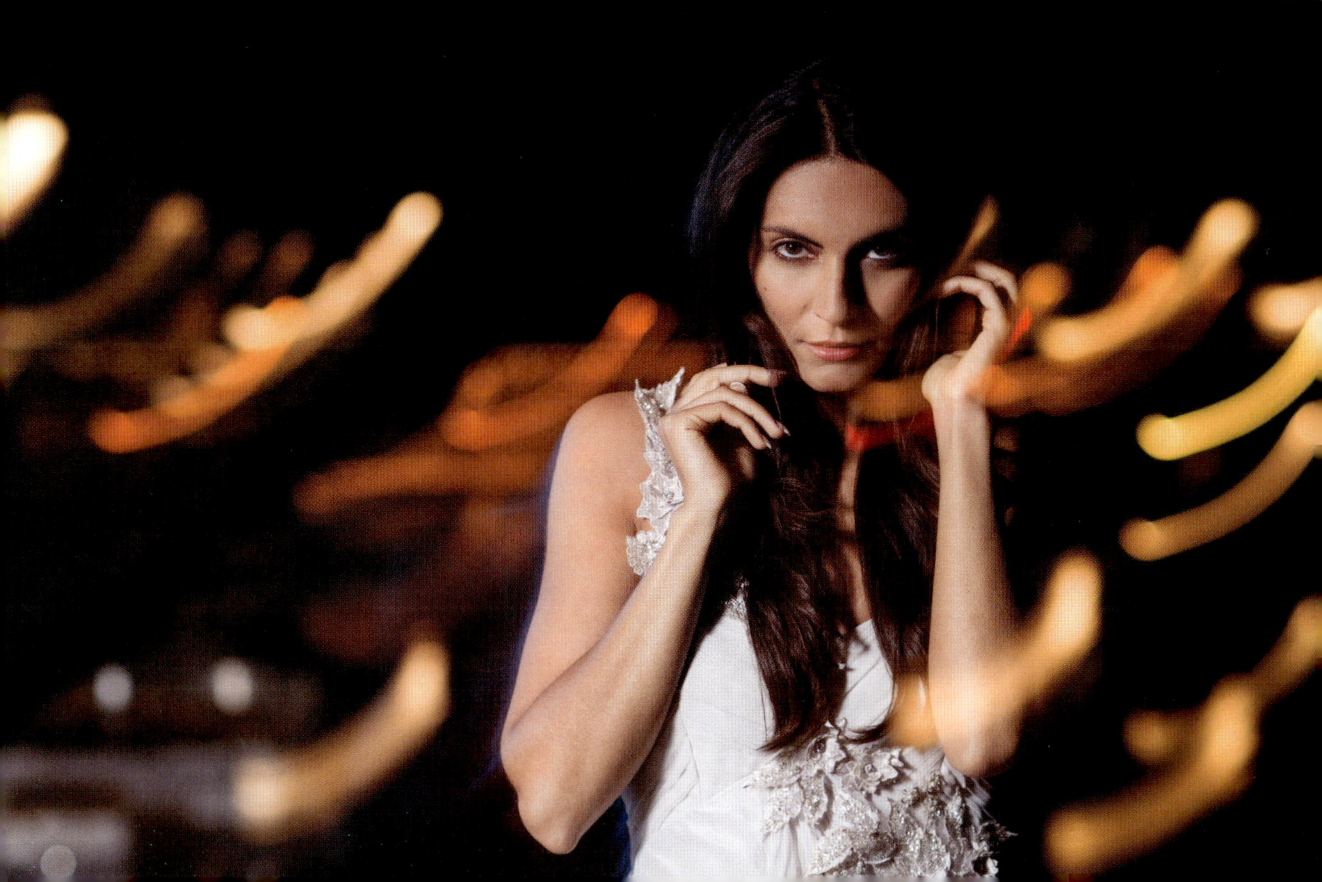

6. Special Effects and Subjects

The Beauty of Bokeh

Low-light photography has opened our eyes to many wonderful options. One of its best assets is how attractive the ambient light in the background of the images appears. And you should be able to achieve great bokeh on that pretty background, since the low light means you'll usually be shooting at large apertures—often f/2.8 or bigger.

Image 6–1. This image was created near the Brooklyn Bridge in New York City. I was lucky enough to be asked by Nikon to test their new D750, which has fantastic low-light capabilities. The round, soft, out-of-focus highlights in this image perfectly demonstrate the appeal of bokeh in your low-light images. *Tech Specs:* Nikon D750, 2500 ISO, Lens: 85mm f/1.4, Aperture: f/1.4, Shutter speed: 1/80 second, Mode: M.

The Look of the Bokeh

While bokeh is a feature of an image, it is actually the lens that determines the size and shape of the bokeh that we see. Usually visible more in the highlights than any other tonal range, bokeh is affected by the shape of the diaphragm blades (the aperture) of the lens. A lens with more round-shaped blades will have rounder, softer spheres of out-of-focus highlights. A lens with more hexagonal-shaped blades will echo that particular shape in the blurred highlights.

Lens, Aperture, and Subject/Background Distance

For great bokeh in your images, first and foremost you'll need to use a fast lens. In

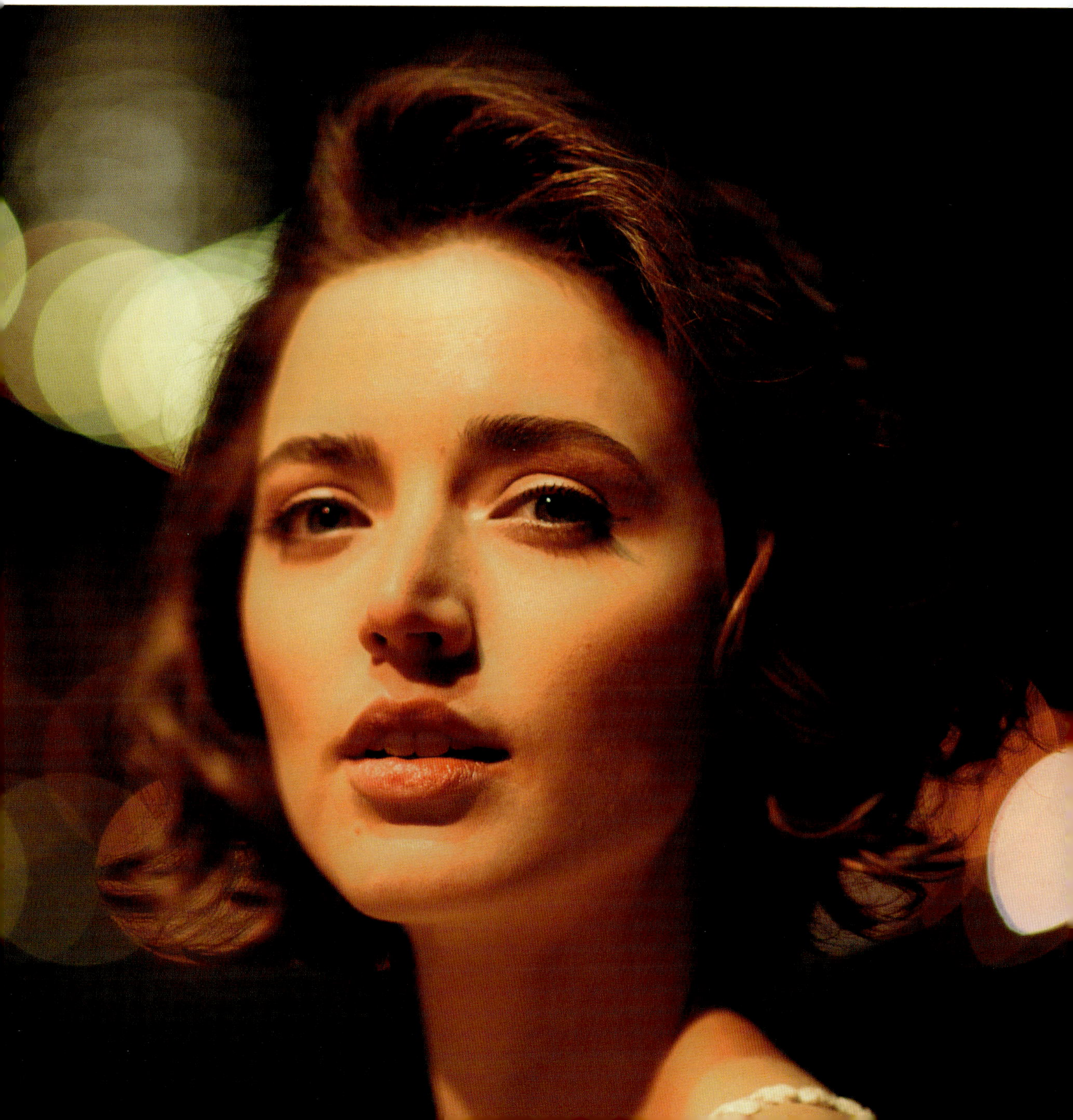

fact, the faster the lens, the better. Opt for a lens with a maximum f/2.8 aperture—or, preferably, an even faster lens with a maximum aperture of f/2, f/1.8, or f/1.4.

Next, shoot with the lens wide open by choosing the aperture priority, flexible program, or manual modes. In the aperture priority mode, you'll set the f/stop while the camera chooses the best shutter speed for the exposure. In the flexible program mode, you'll choose the widest possible aperture and shutter speed combination. In the manual mode, you'll dial in both your aperture and your shutter speed.

Finally, in order to boost the chances of visible bokeh in your images, you'll need to increase the distance between your subject and the background. With the focus on your subject, this helps ensure that the background will fall beyond the depth-of-field range and be farther out of focus. Selecting a background with nice highlights will further enhance the visible bokeh and really add to the creativity of the image.

Foreground Bokeh

You can also create interesting bokeh in the foreground of an image by shooting through/past various objects—such as a prism, clear bottle, crystal, drinking glass,

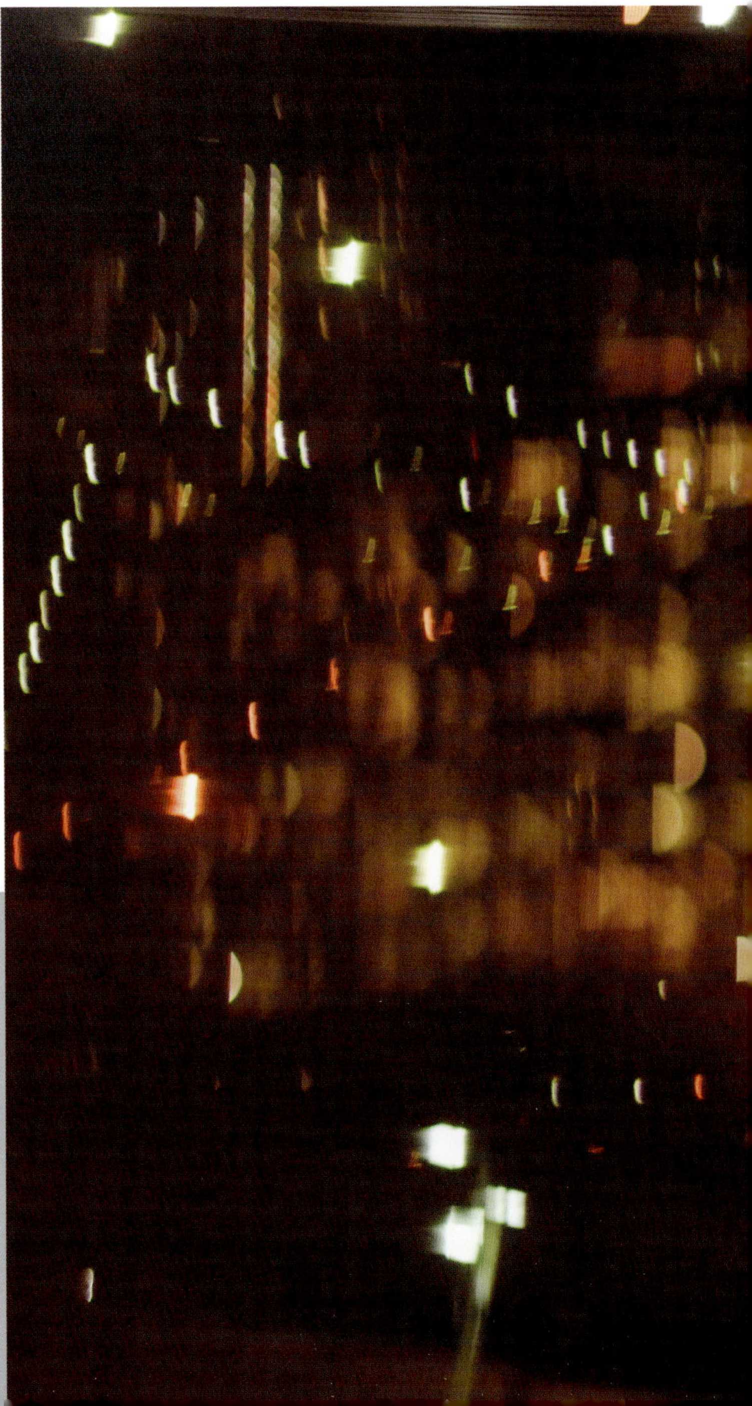

Image 6–2. A prism in front of the lens was used to create foreground bokeh. *Tech Specs:* Nikon D750, 2500 ISO, Lens: 85mm f/1.4, Aperture: f/1.4, Shutter speed: 1/200 second, Mode: M.

or even a CD or mirror. These techniques offer so many unusual, varied, and unpredictable results. Shooting through a string of fairy lights also creates some very appealing foreground bokeh.

Image 6-2 is from the series of tests I did with the Nikon D750. Annelise was lit from camera right with an Ice Light covered with a Rosco blue gel. I like the play on warm and cool created by the contrast of the Ice Light and the warm street light. I held a glass prism in front of the lens to reflect the lights of the Brooklyn Bridge and create the foreground bokeh. This technique takes some getting used to, but I am really enjoying the unpredictable results—adding depth and dimension to my photography.

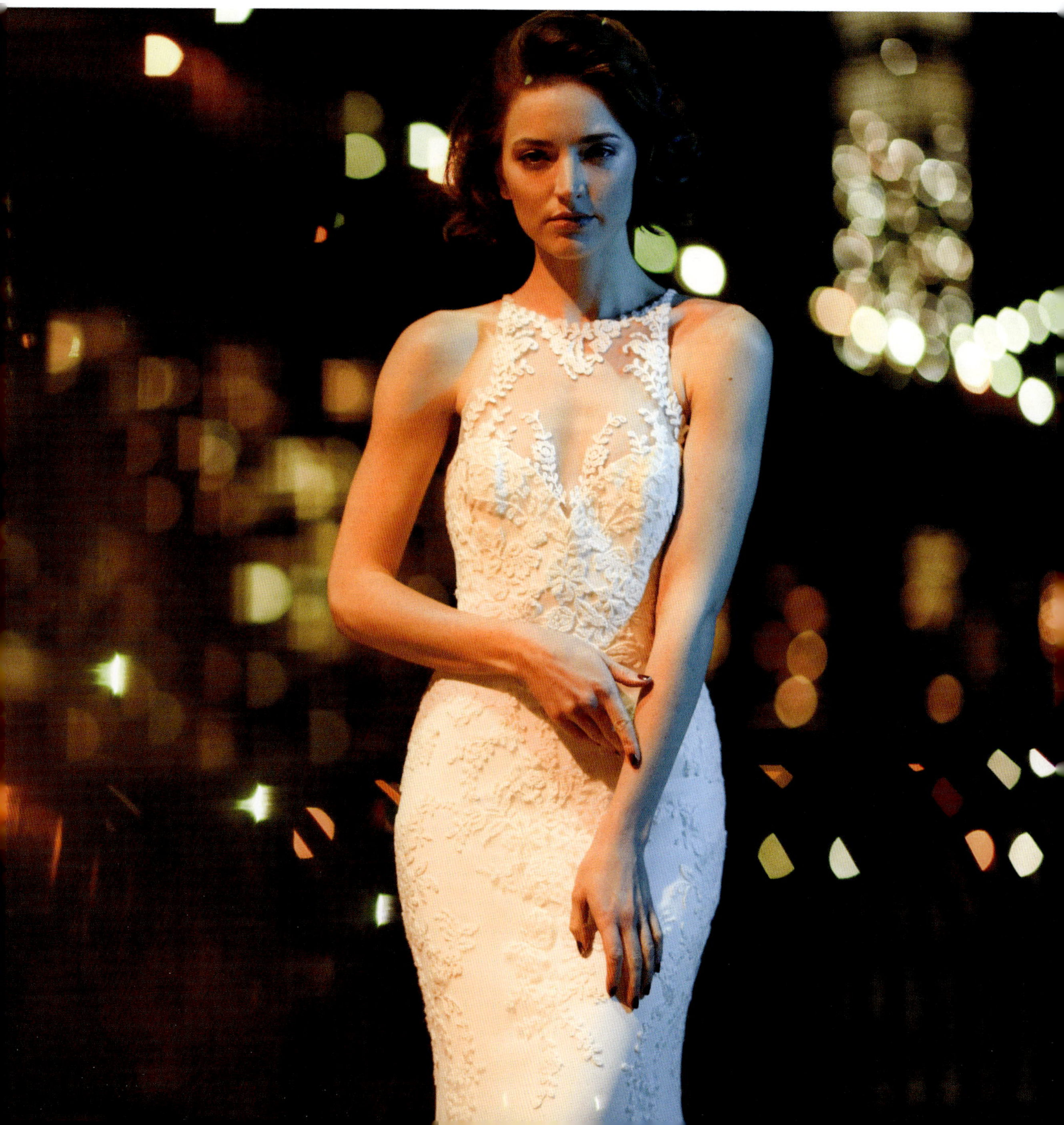

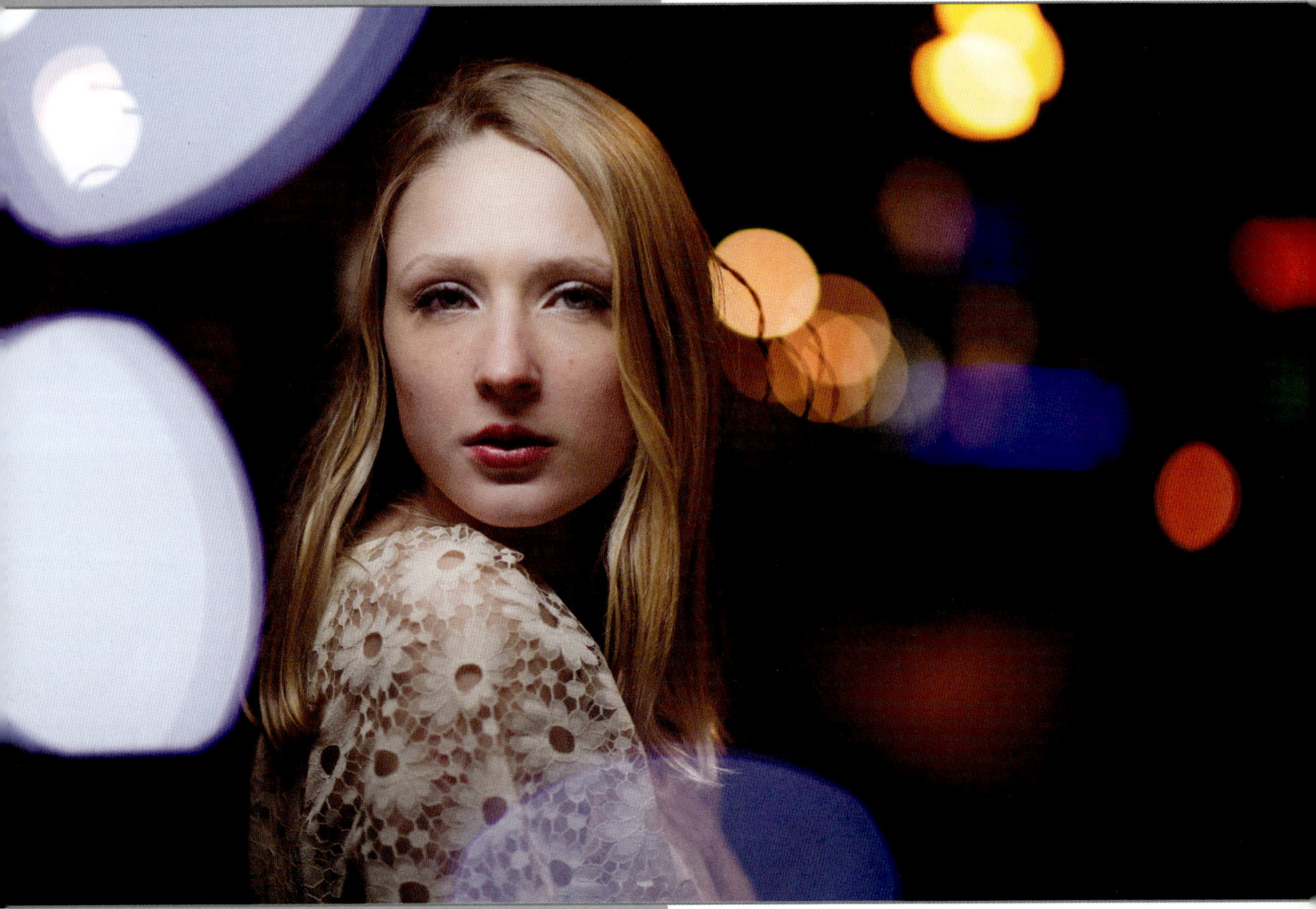

Image 6–3. A string of fairy lights was used to create foreground bokeh. *Tech Specs:* Nikon D4s, 4000 ISO, Lens: 85mm f/1.4, Aperture: f/1.4, Shutter speed: 1/2000 second, Mode: A.

This image of Loes (**image 6–3**) was created during a low-light workshop. I had a delegate hold up a string of battery-powered fairy lights in front of the lens to create the foreground bokeh. I always keep a string of these lights in my camera bag, just in case the opportunity arises. When background scene isn't particularly exciting, I can easily transform it into something more interesting using this technique. As in the previous image, the model was lit with the Ice Light; its great window light properties resulted in the soft, flattering light. I see that I shot the image at 4000 ISO—maybe a little too much, considering I didn't need the

"When background scene isn't particularly exciting, I can easily be transform it into something more interesting using this technique."

1/2000 second shutter speed. I should have dropped the ISO by 3 stops to 1000 and set the shutter speed to around 1/250 second. Fortunately, I got away with it because of the high ISO capabilities of the great camera.

I combined two techniques to create **image 6–4**. I lit Bahareh from camera left with an Ice Light that was covered with a blue gel. I then corrected the white balance in postproduction, resulting in a very warm background. I used a prism to create the foreground bokeh and was pleasantly surprised to see that it caught a reflection of the model—how nice to get this right in the camera! The lights reflecting off the water of the canal in Amsterdam can still be seen, as can the streetlights. Overall, it's an interesting image.

The Illusion of Fog

I have had a lot of fun creating the illusion of smoke or fog in my low-light images. When I'm near a power source, I use a smoke machine to produce a steady stream of mythical-looking mist. Where a power source is not available, I have my assistant

Image 6–4. To create this image, I combined the foreground bokeh technique described in this chapter with the gelled main light technique from the end of chapter 4. *Tech Specs:* Nikon D4s, 2000 ISO, Lens: 85mm f/1.4, Aperture: f/1.4, Shutter speed: 1/80 second, Mode: M.

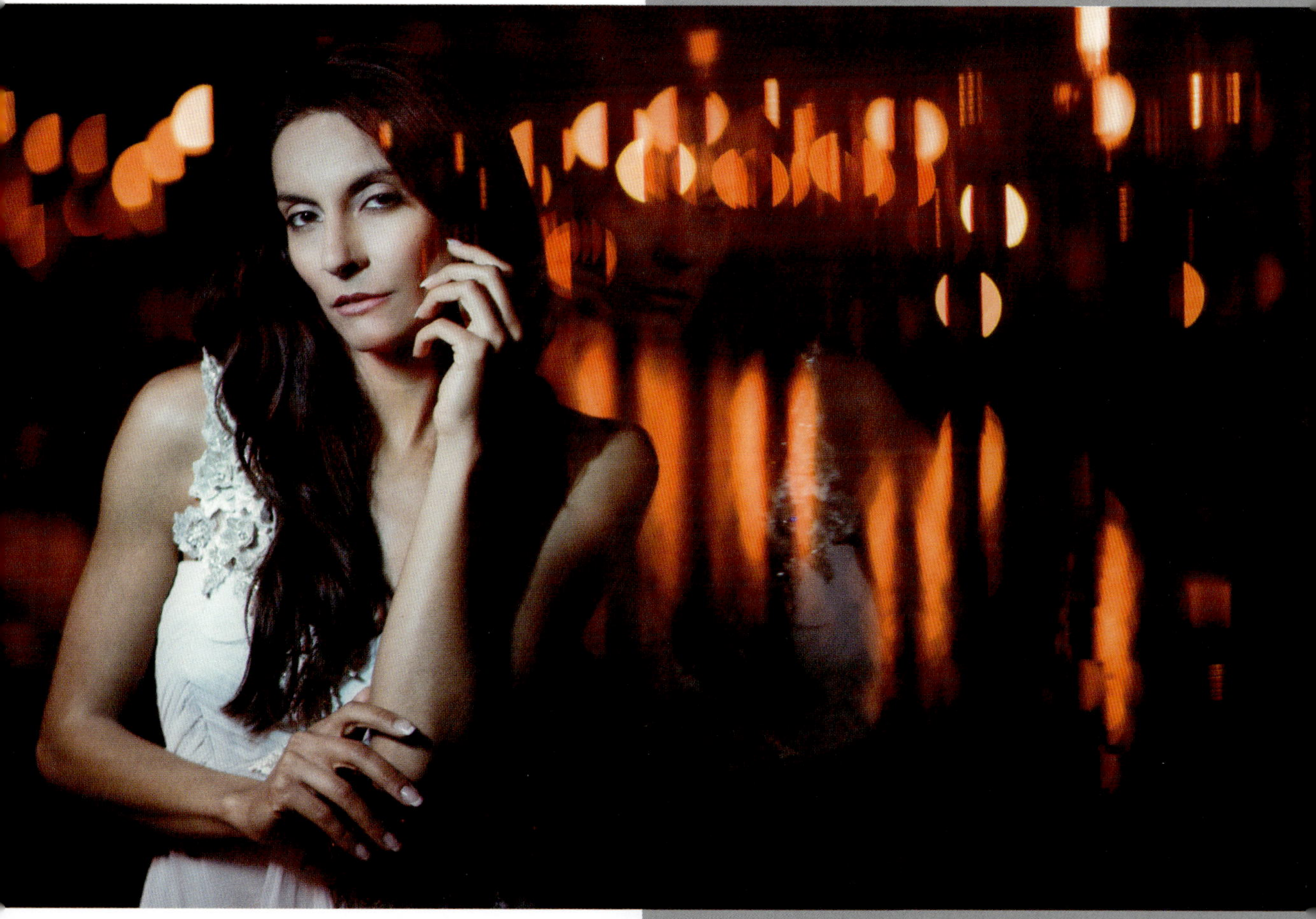

Images 6–5, 6–6, and 6–7 (this page and facing page). As they were leaving the reception, I used a Manfrotto LED to light the bride and groom from the front and had a guest hold the Lenser T7 flashlight behind them. My assistant threw some talcum power into the air behind them for steamy effect that added dimension. I love the bokeh created by the traffic and nearby building lights. An image like this takes just minutes to shoot—ensuring the couple can leave quickly after a long day of celebration. *Tech Specs:* Nikon D4, 10000 ISO, Lens: 70–200mm f/2.8, Aperture: f/2.8, Shutter speed: 1/160 second, Mode: M.

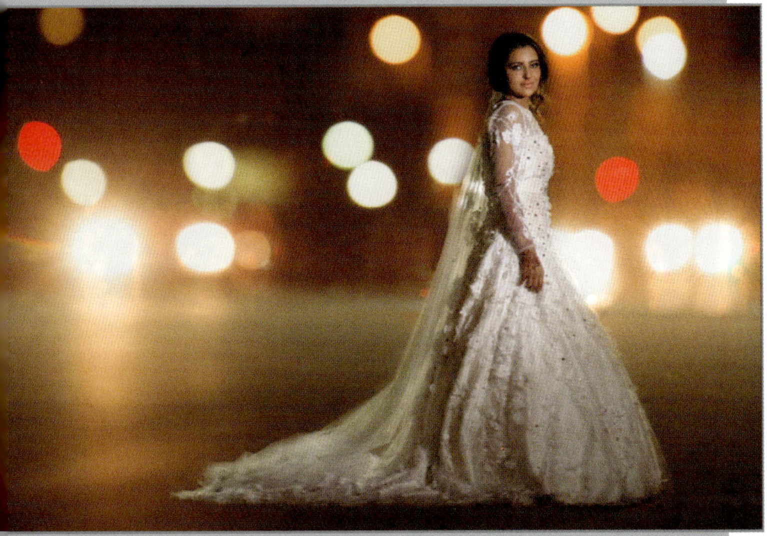

blow some talcum powder or even cooking flour into the air, generally behind the subject. Colored smoke bombs are very effective; however, you need to keep an eye on the laws and health/safety regulations of the area where you are shooting.

Lighting and Shooting

For best results, the "smoke" needs to be illuminated from behind. I also suggest shooting a few images in sequence. As the smoke or powder settles or gets blown by the wind, the shapes and intensity will change. You'll want to have a few options when choosing your images—and you could even use multiple images to create your final image with the best "mist" effect.

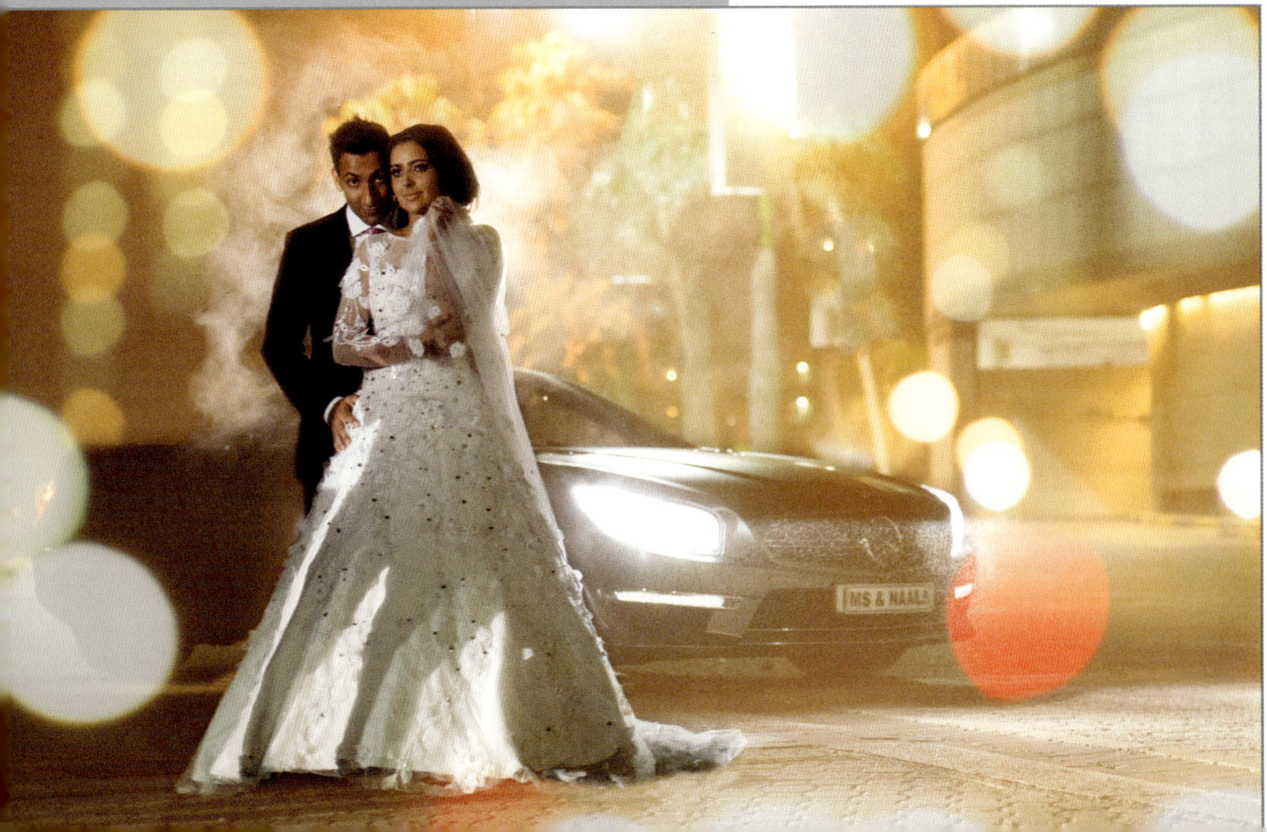

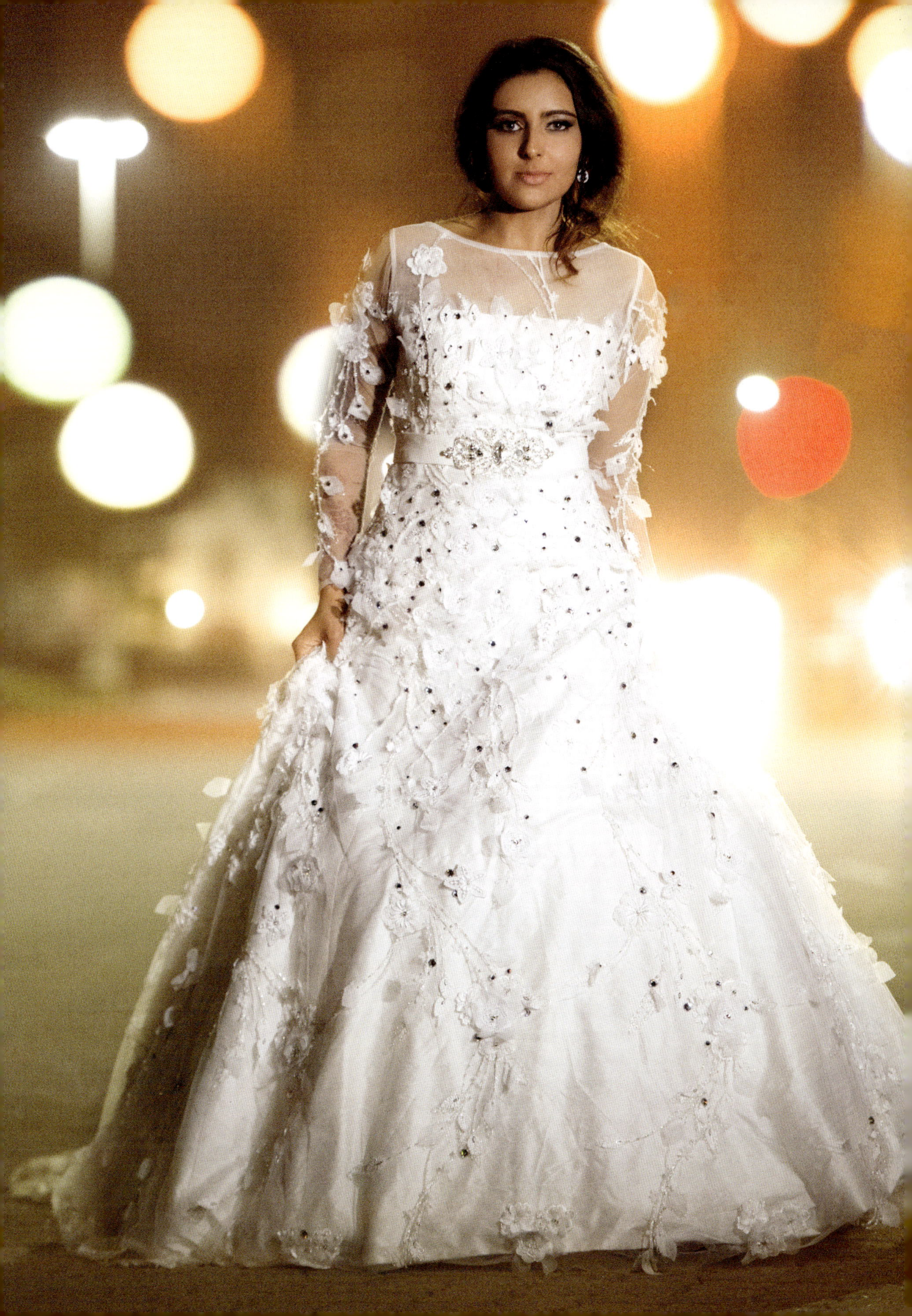

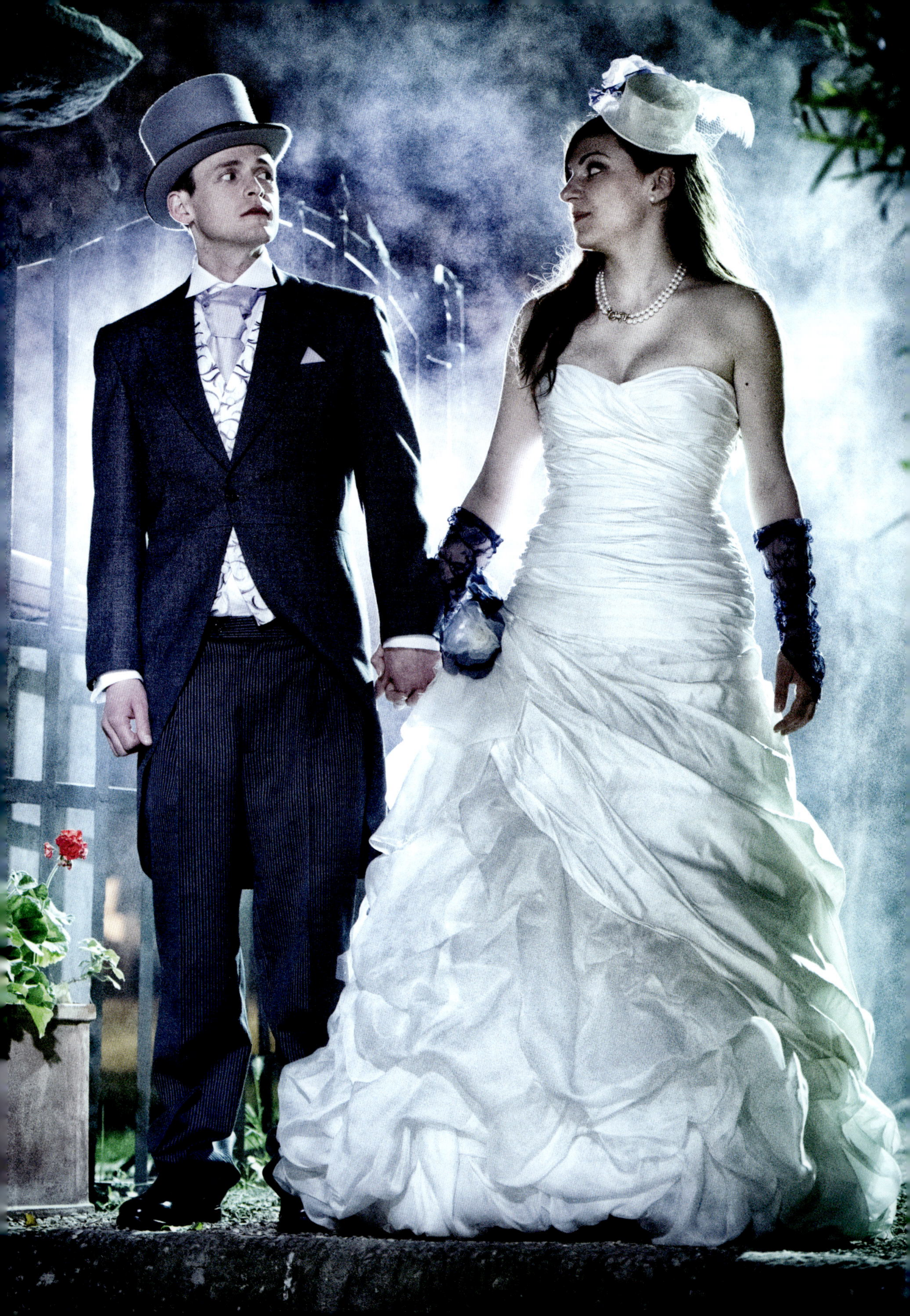

Practical Examples

Images 6–8 through **6–11** were created in Florence, Italy, at the wedding of Sarah and James—a very quirky couple who were both up for anything. I had my assistant blow some talcum powder behind the couple and lit it with the Manfrotto LED. The lighting from the front (on the couple) was floodlighting that was already present in this beautiful garden. Drawing inspiration from Tim Burton's movie *Corpse Bride*, I transformed the pretty garden gates into something more like the entrance to a cemetery—and the wind blew the powder in a way that made it work perfectly. Unbeknown to me and other guests, Sarah and James had a *Corpse Bride*–themed cake! We all had a good laugh, realizing that we were so in sync with each other. They absolutely loved the images and the shots got a lot of action on social media. I really liked the red flower at the bottom left-hand corner of the image (facing page). I only noticed it afterward—but it was a fortuitous element that made the image work even better.

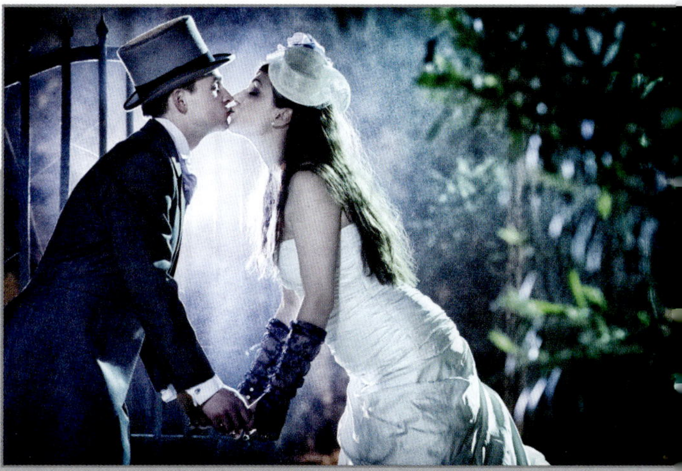

Images 6–8, 6–9, 6–10, and 6–11. Backlighting some talcum powder blown into the scene behind my subjects gave this low-light image a cinematic look. *Tech Specs:* Nikon D4, 8000 ISO, Lens: 70–200mm f/2.8, Aperture: f/3.2, Shutter speed: 1/80 second, Mode: M.

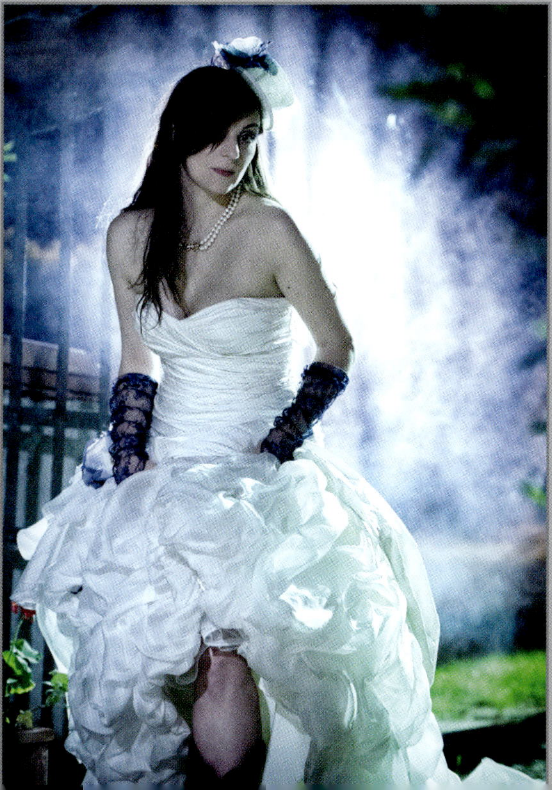

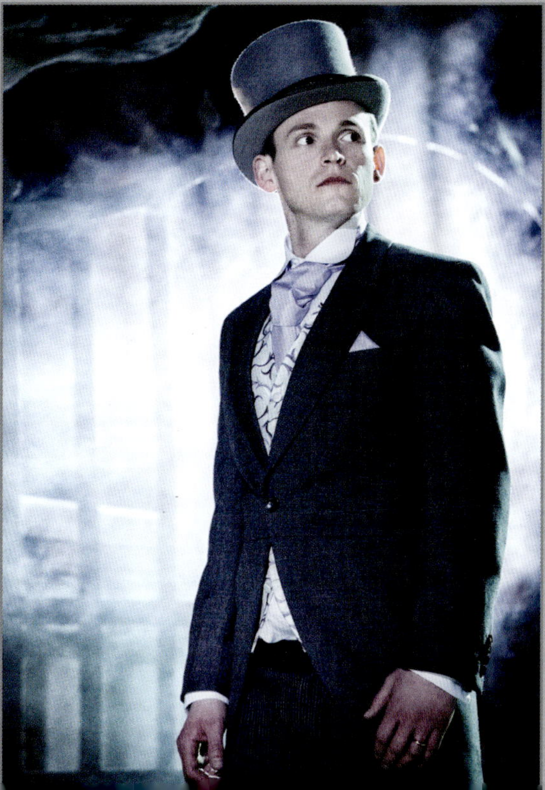

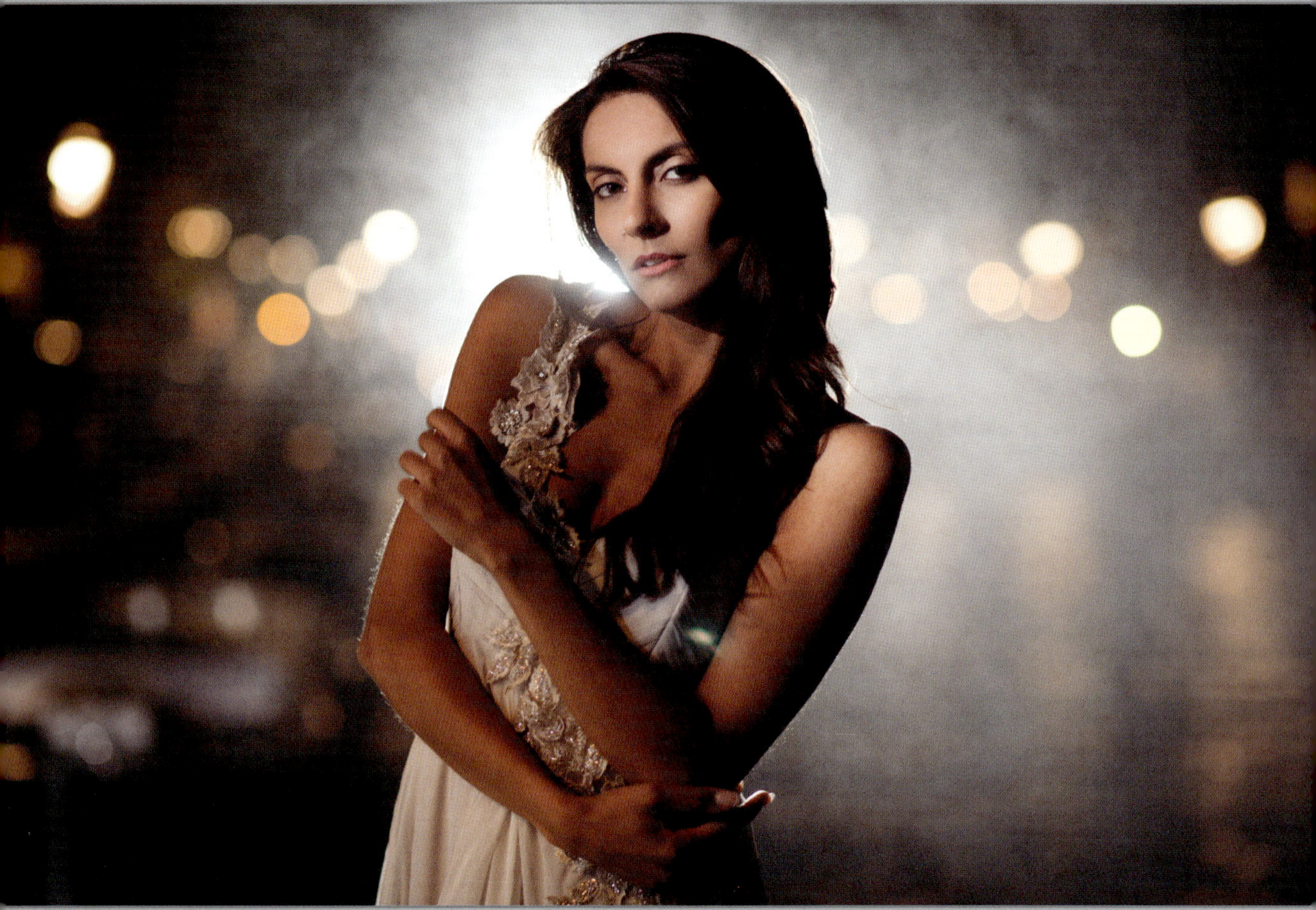

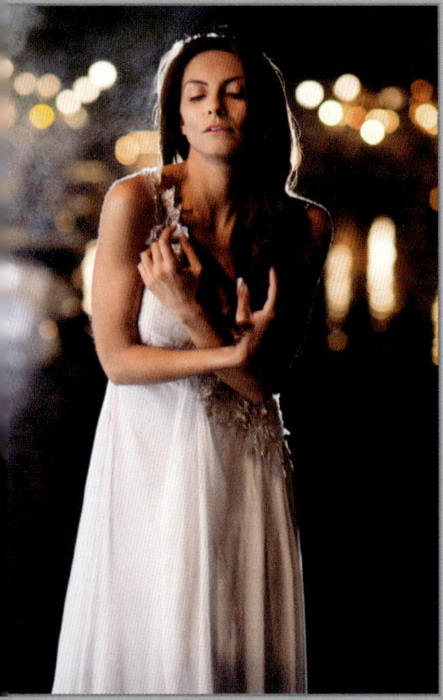

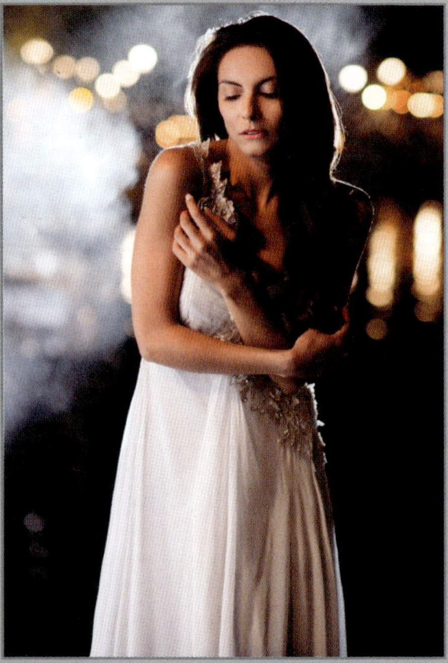

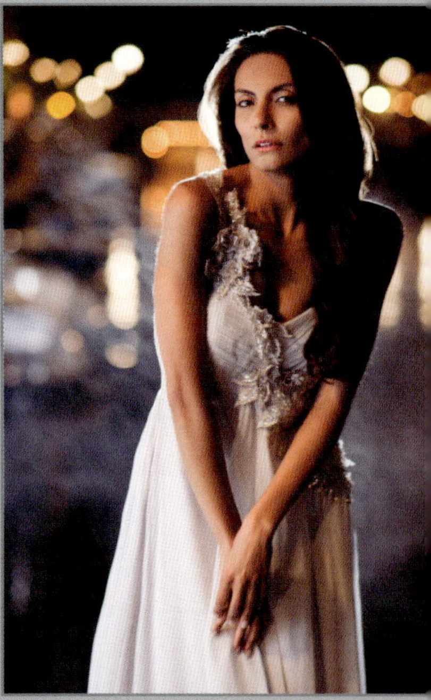

Images 6–12, 6–13, 6–14, and 6–15. The "fog" can shift quickly, so shoot a sequence of images to ensure you catch the best effect. *Tech Specs:* Nikon D4, 8000 ISO, Lens: 70–200mm f/2.8, Aperture: f/3.2, Shutter speed: 1/80 second, Mode: M.

Images 6–12 through **6–15** show another shoot where I used talcum powder to add mood and mystery to the images. I lit the model with the Elinchrom Quadra portable strobe from camera left and placed an Ice Light behind her on a light stand to illuminate the powder. In this sequence of captures, you can see how quickly the "fog" changes shape and intensity—so keep shooting to achieve the desired result. I would also suggest shooting in the manual mode for this type of image as the shifting thickness and position of the "fog" may interfere with the camera's light metering ability.

Cityscapes: Urban Night Photography with Michiel Buijse

As I've noted, part of the joy of shooting portraits at night and in low-light situations is how the lighting transforms our backgrounds. This is especially true when shooting in urban environments. I invited accomplished low-light photographer Michiel Buijse (www.behindthelenscap.nl) to share his advice for capturing the beauty of cities at night. These are concepts that can clearly translate to portrait and wedding photography—genres in which the beauty of places and spaces is often very important to telling our stories and depicting the subjects within them.

The Basics

In addition to needing a camera that is capable of taking photos in a manual mode, Michiel suggests some additional requirements. "You don't want to shoot handheld with exposure times of 30

Image 6–16. Photograph by Michiel Buijse.

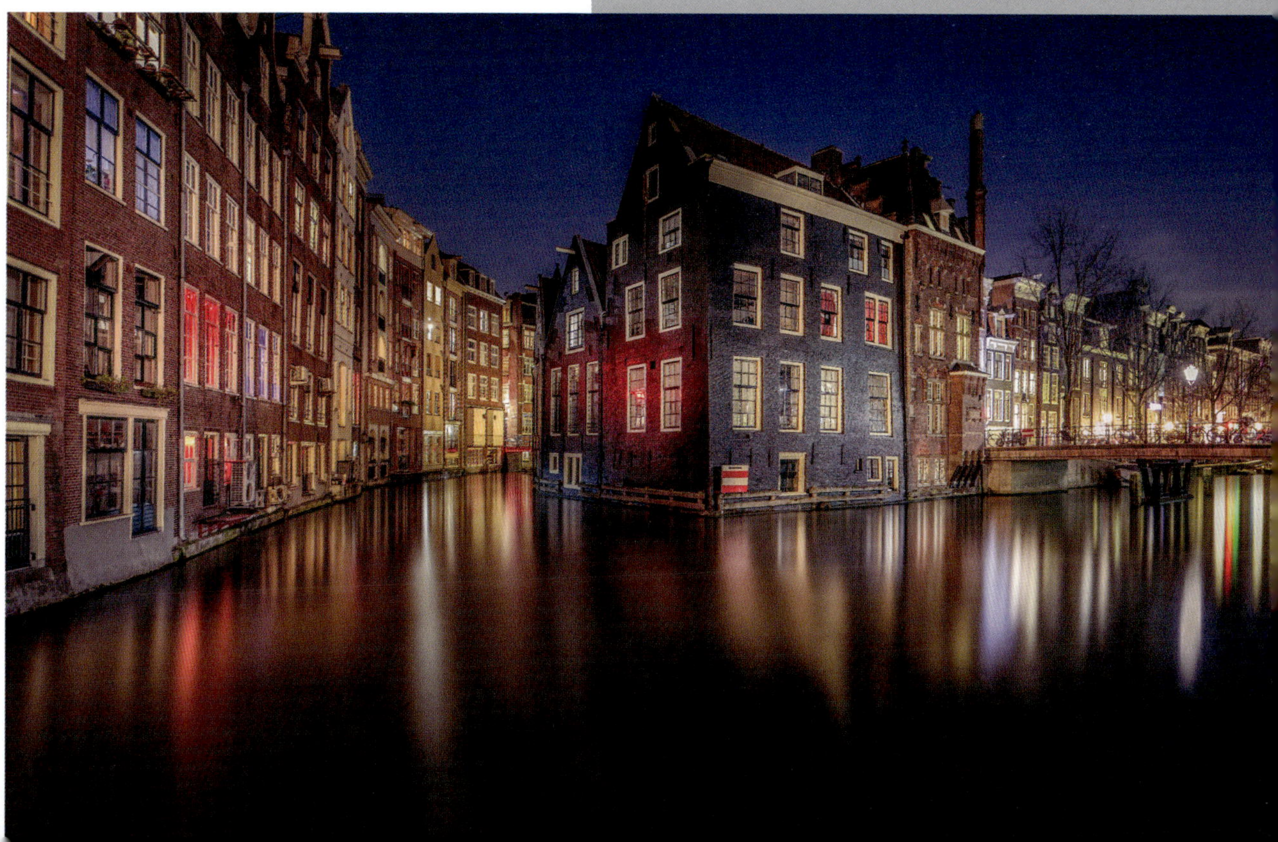

seconds and more—because, inevitably, you will get camera shake. That brings me to one of the most important pieces of equipment for shooting in low light: the tripod. This is really necessary for great night photos. Secondly, you need a remote trigger. This can be a cheap one with a cable or a little more expensive wireless one. Any of them will do just fine. The key is that you don't have to touch your camera for pressing the shutter button and, therefore, you can avoid camera shake when taking the shot."

He also turns off any vibration reduction or image stabilization feature. "Since we are using a tripod, we don't need the lens vibration reduction or image stabilization. In fact, this feature can work against us when using a tripod and result in images that are not sharp," says Michiel.

However, he does suggest using a lens hood. "Most people use a lens hood only during the day to prevent lens flare from the sun. At night, they just remove it. But what if I tell you that there are a thousand more light sources that can produce lens flare when you shoot at night, especially when you are capturing cityscapes? I'm

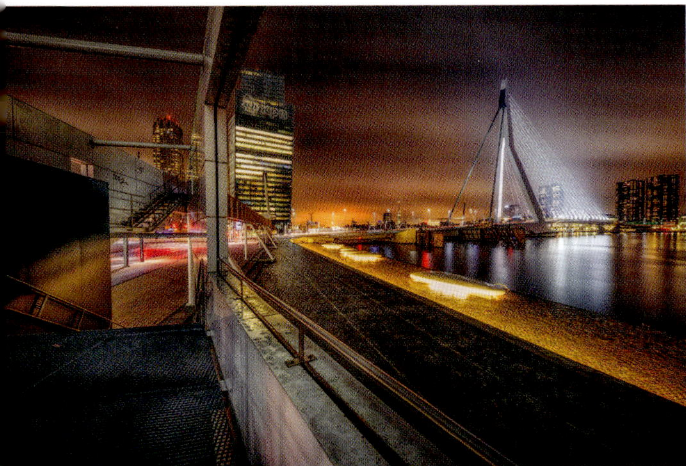

Images 6–17 and 6–18. Photographs by Michiel Buijse.

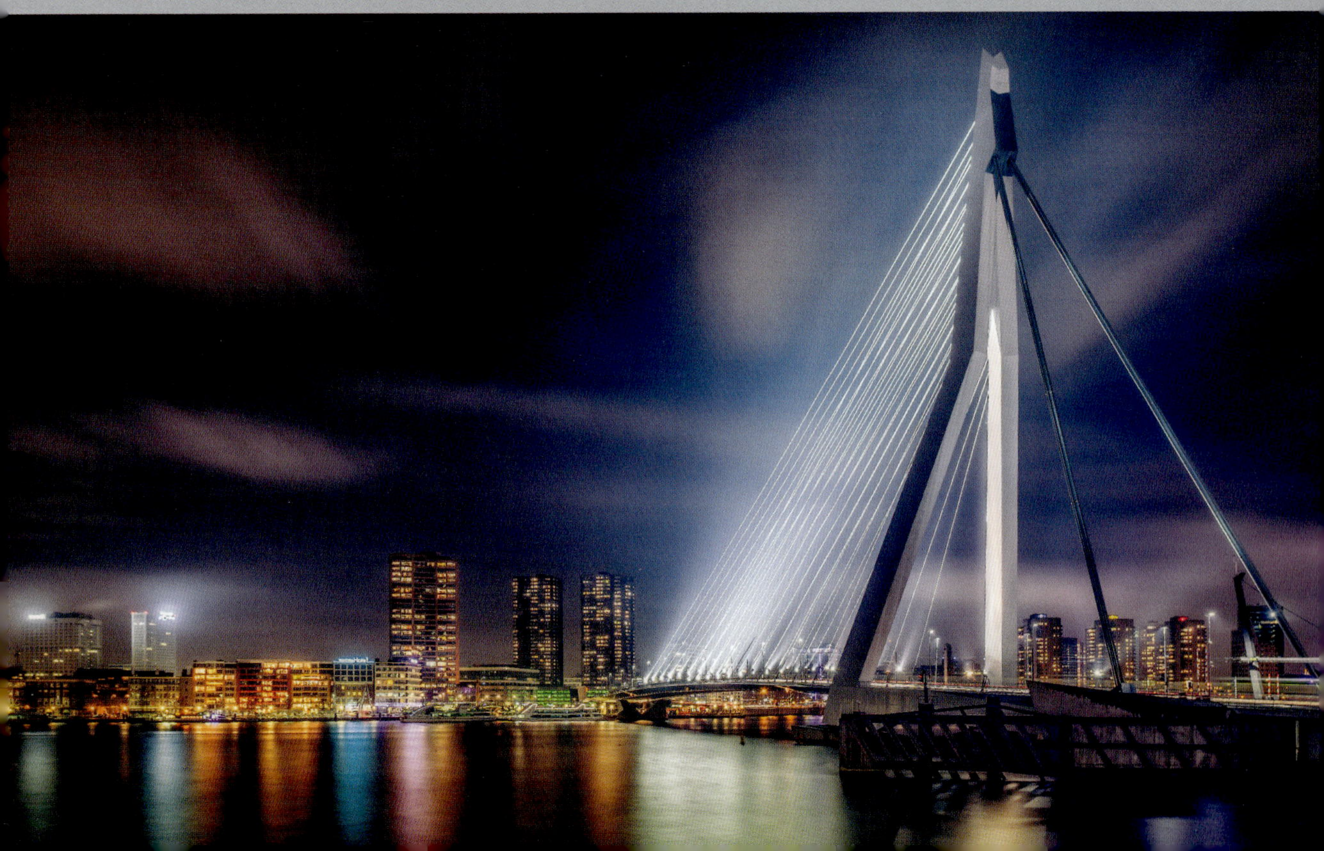

talking about all the streetlights, passing traffic, lights in trees or on bridges—all those tiny light sources can produce lens flare."

Filters are another potential problem. "When you use UV or polarizing filters during night photography, they will most likely produce some kind of lens flare. Many photographers have a polarizing filter screwed on their lens. This works perfectly during daytime when the main light source is coming from a certain direction. At night in a city, however, the light sources are coming from all different directions. Also, this filter reduces 2 or 3 stops of light and your exposure time will be even longer. For example an exposure of 30 seconds without a polarizing filter will become 2 minutes with this filter screwed on."

ISO, File Format, and White Balance

There are some in-camera settings that Michiel also recommends adjusting for night shooting.

"When we photograph people in low light," says Michiel, "it's a known fact that we should crank up the ISO to a level where the shutter speed is fast enough to avoid movement of our subject. However, when it comes to shooting cityscapes, there are no moving subjects in our shot, so we can set the ISO to 100. With longer exposure times, we'll be able to capture more light than even the naked eye can see."

For the file format, he suggests shooting RAW. "Photos shot in low light do need some care in post-processing and RAW will give you the best results," he notes. Michiel also prefers to do any noise reduction during postproduction, so he turns off the in-camera noise reduction. "By choosing in-camera noise reduction, you can lose some fine details in the shot," he says. "When you do this during postproduction, you can selectively choose where you want the noise reduction to take place and retain some fine details where they're needed.

> "What if I tell you that there are a thousand more light sources that can produce lens flare when you shoot at night, especially when you are capturing cityscapes?"

"Shooting in RAW also means you can change the white balance to suit your needs during post-processing," Michiel adds. "Nevertheless, when I'm previewing my shots, the picture on the camera display is a JPEG image with the white balance that's set in the camera. This gives me the opportunity to see if the colors are right. I'm always looking for contrasting colors, like warm and cool tones. Looking at the preview image, I can visualize what to do with it during post."

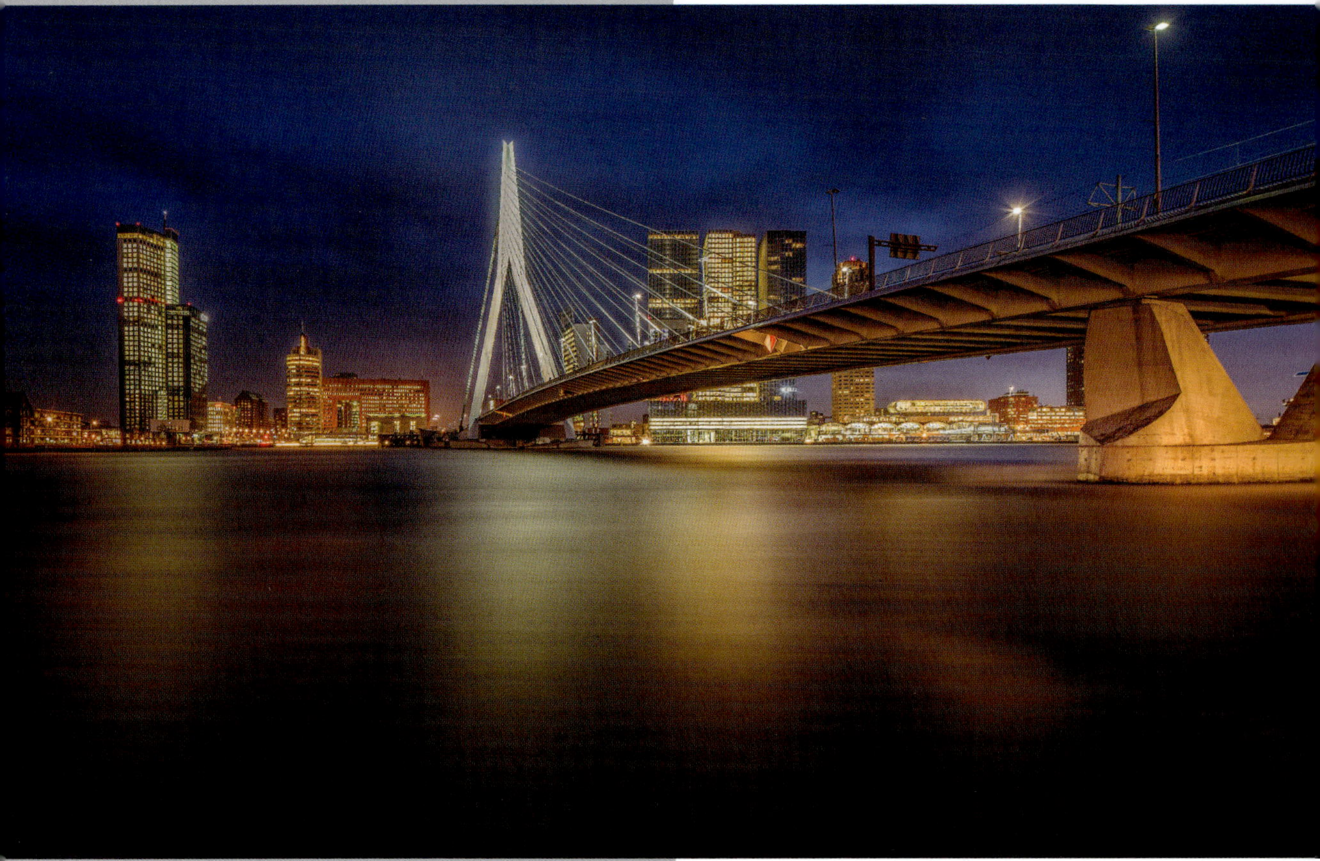

Image 6–19. Photograph by Michiel Buijse.

"For night shots, most of the light will come from artificial light sources, so a tungsten white balance will give you the best results," Michiel points out "When you shoot during twilight, a white balance for daylight or cloudy will do the trick. When twilight is over, you can switch to tungsten white balance or dial in your preferred temperature in Kelvin."

Focusing

Michiel also opts for manual focus. "When shooting in low light with autofocus," says Michiel, "you might have noticed that the camera will struggle to focus correctly. Due to the lack of contrast points, it's very hard for the camera to find a good focus point. This is why we have to focus manually. To get pin-sharp images, set your lens or camera to manual focus. By using the live view on the camera, we can focus very precisely on the subject we want to have in focus."

To do this, Michiel gets the tripod firmly set up and the remote connected to the camera so he can make his composition. "Choose the best aperture for your lens, which will give you the sharpest image," he advises. "Normally, I start at f/8. This is the sweet spot for most lenses and will give the best quality."

"With the lens or camera on manual focus, we can now use the live view to focus precisely on the subject we want in focus," he says. "Switch on live view and set the aperture and shutter speed so the light meter reads zero. This will give you an average exposure. Then, zoom in on the preview using the magnifying buttons next to your display. Do not zoom in using the lens. Find your subject on the display and use the focus ring on your lens to get a pin-sharp image. If your subject is too dark to focus on, try to lighten it with a flashlight and focus again."

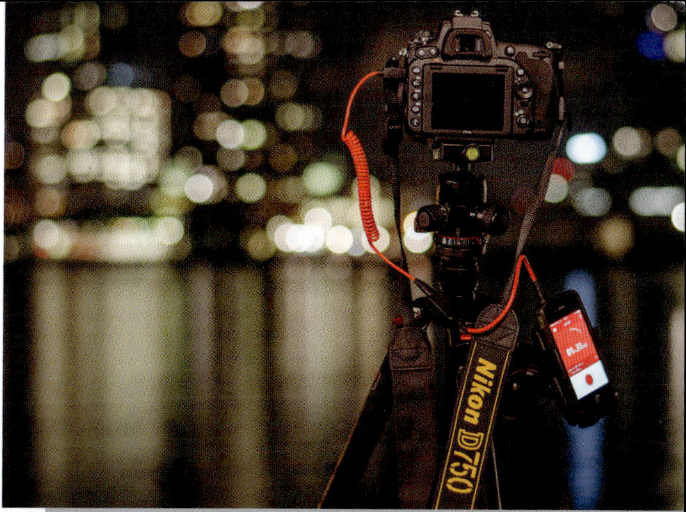

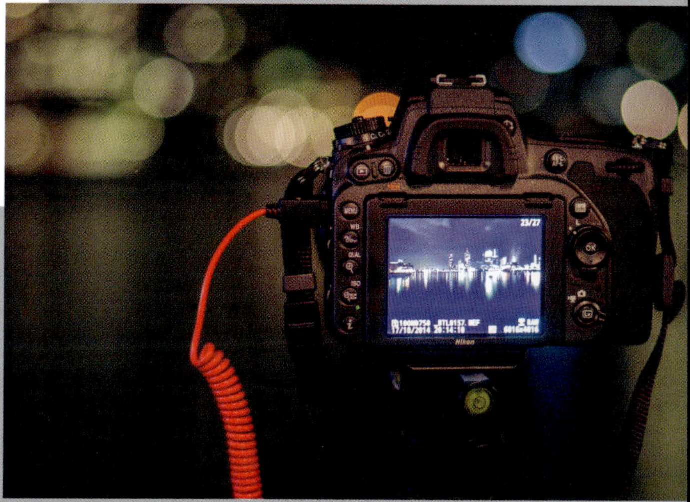

Images 6–20 and 6–21 (right, top and bottom). Michiel's gear set up for a night shot and focused using Live View. Photographs by Michiel Buijse.

Image 6–22 (below). Photograph by Michiel Buijse.

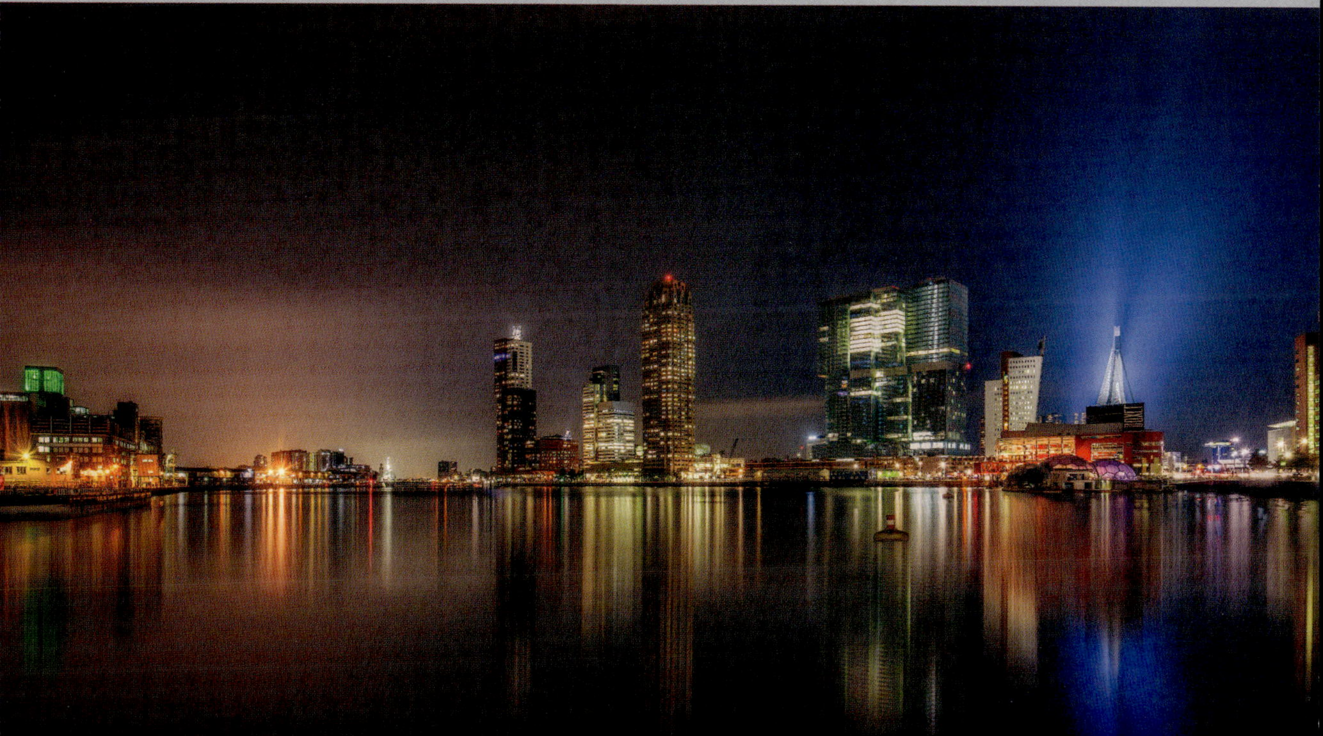

Image 6–23. Photograph by Michiel Buijse.

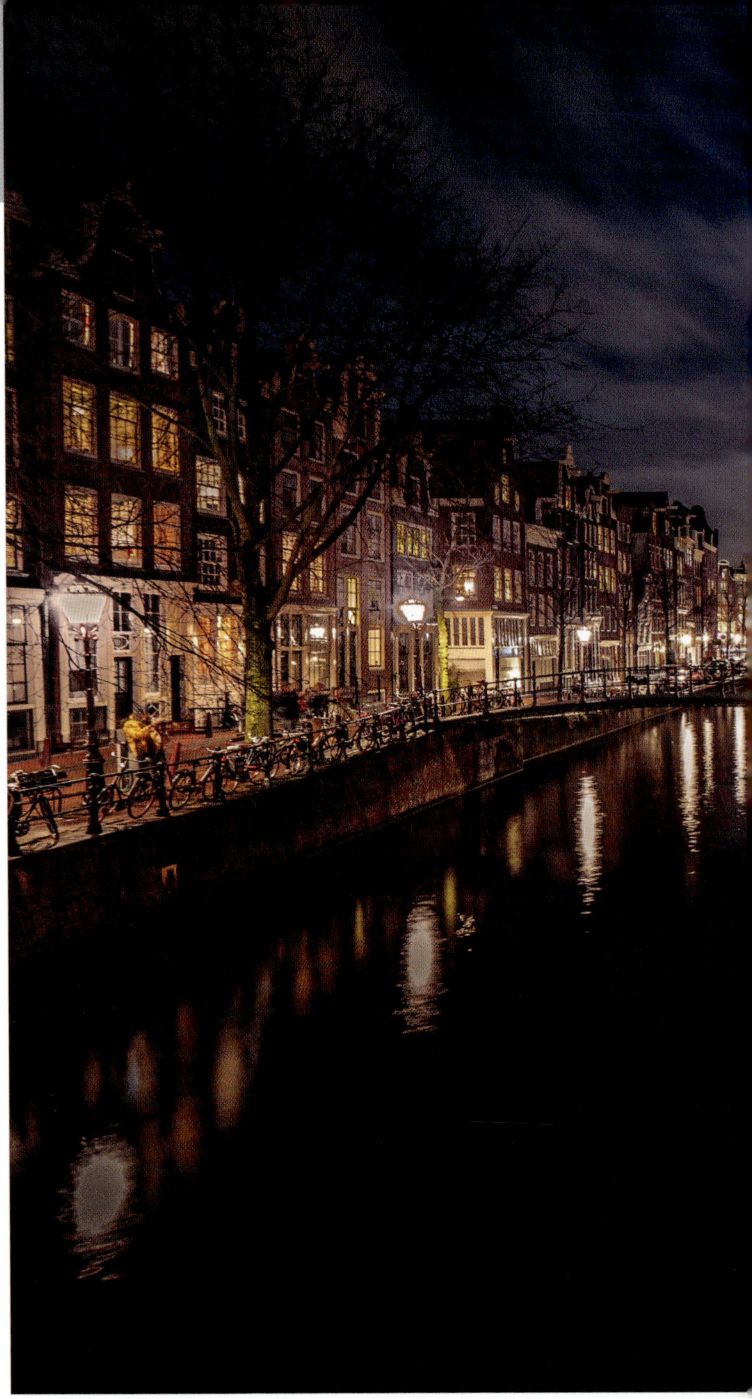

Metering and Shutter Speed

"For night shots, you will get the best results when you use matrix metering," says Michiel. "The camera will meter the light from all the small light sources. This will normally result in an underexposed image, because those light sources are too small. To make sure we get a good exposure, we will need to overexpose the shot to capture the shadow details, too. We achieve this by overexposing about ⅔ stop."

"When your shutter speed exceeds 30 seconds, you have two options: you can raise your ISO to get the correct exposure reading or switch to bulb mode and calculate the desired shutter speed. Let's say a shutter speed of 25 seconds will give you a photo that is ⅓ stop underexposed. We will need to increase the exposure by 1 stop, to get a ⅔ overexposed photo. For every stop brighter, you will have to multiply your shutter speed by two. In this example, the shutter speed will become 50 seconds—2 x 25 = 50."

Taking the Shot

"With all these steps completed, we are almost ready to take the shot," says Michiel. "There are just a few more things to keep in mind before you press the shutter button. For example, you

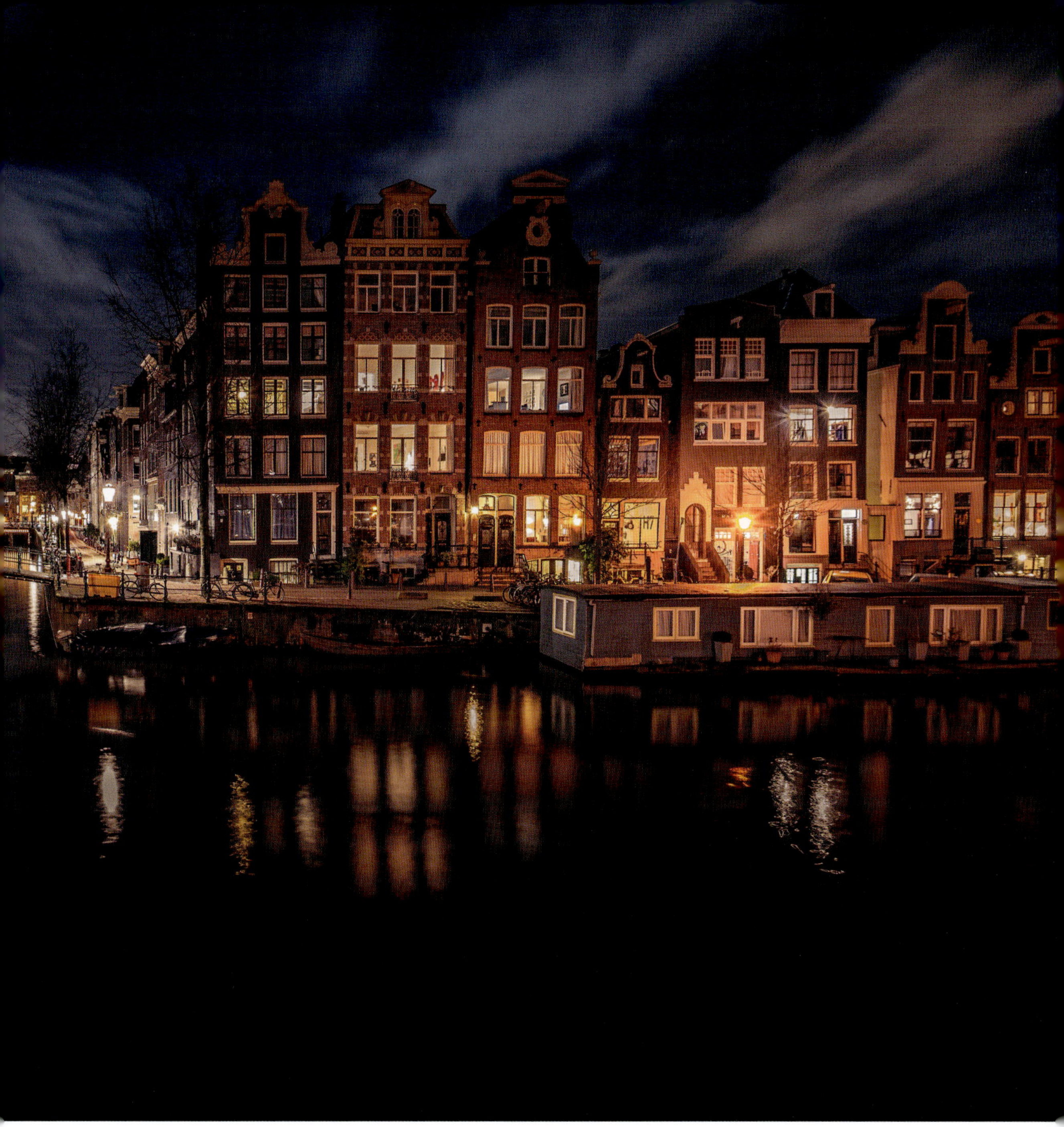

may want to close the viewfinder when there's light coming from behind you. This will prevent any light leak during the long exposure. When shooting in a city, wait for the traffic to be out of view—or in view, if you want to capture the light trails. Cars driving by can produce some vibrations, which may result in an image that is not sharp. And if you have a camera strap attached, secure it to the tripod so the wind doesn't catch it. That will also produce vibrations in the camera."

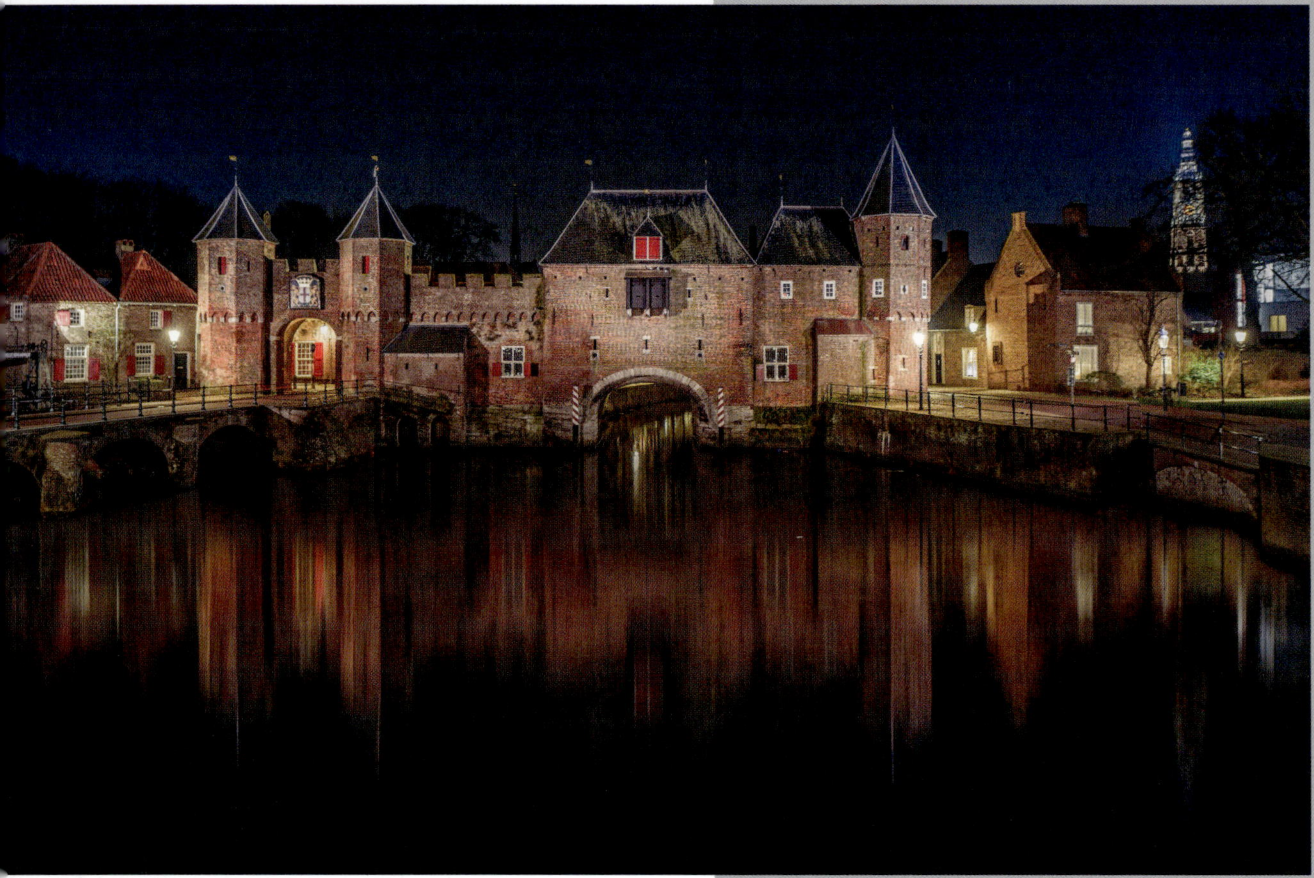

Images 6–24, 6–25, and 6–26 (above and facing page). Photographs by Michiel Buijse.

Additional Tips and Tricks

"When shooting in a city at night, keep in mind that light can come from all directions," says Michiel. "Place yourself in a way that your own (or your camera's) shadow is not visible in the shot—unless this is the thing you are after. The best practice is to place yourself just in front of a streetlight with your back against the pole. This way, your shadow will be as small as possible."

Michiel also suggests making sure your tripod is as stable as possible. "Extend the legs by starting with the thickest parts first. Make sure you place the legs on a firm surface so they can't slip away during the shot. Last, but not least important, keep the center column as low as possible. You want to keep the weight of your camera as low as possible to get the best stabilization of your camera."

"Also," Michiel adds, "keep in mind that night shots in a city have high contrast between the highlights and shadows. Sometimes the contrast is so high that you might consider taking exposure brackets and using HDR—high dynamic range—post-processing for your photos."

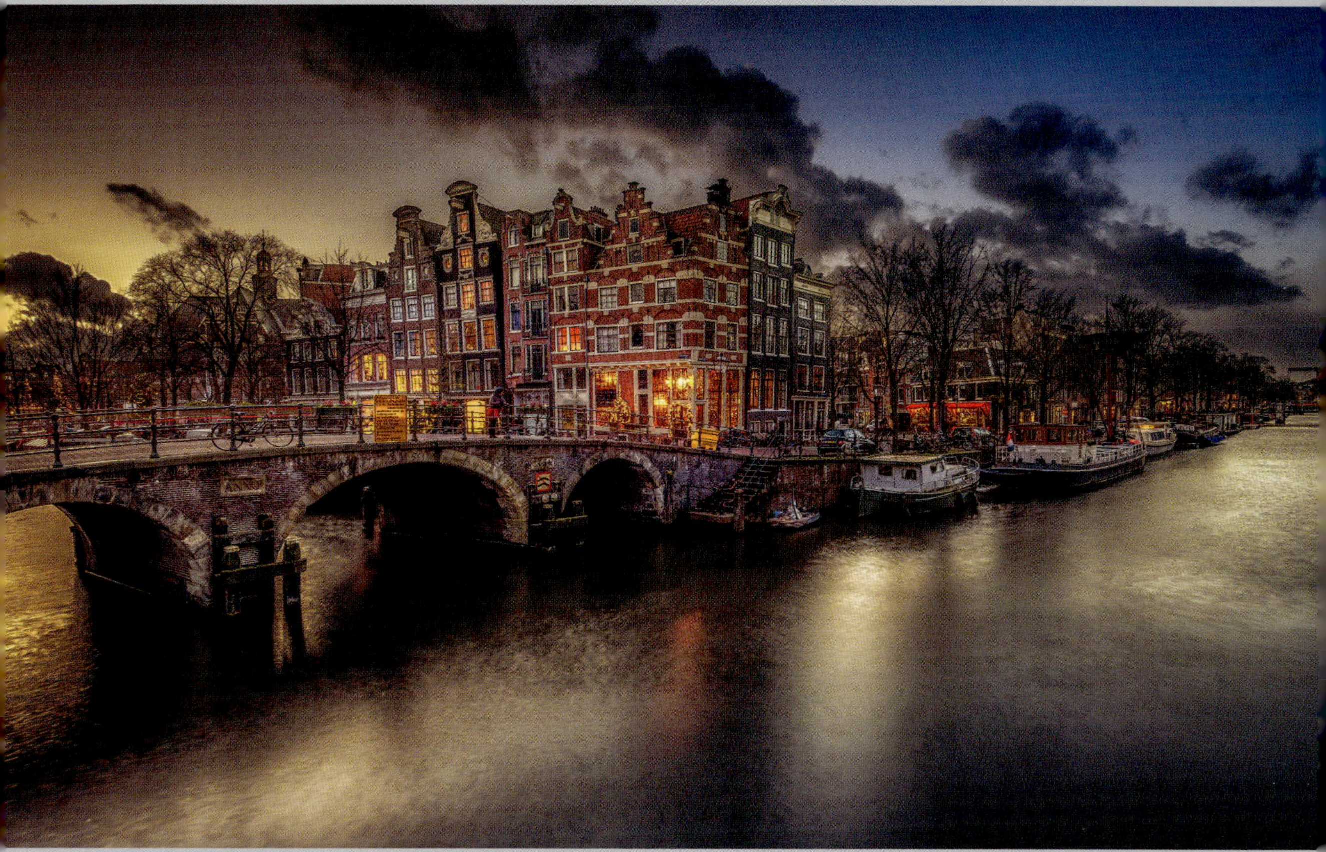

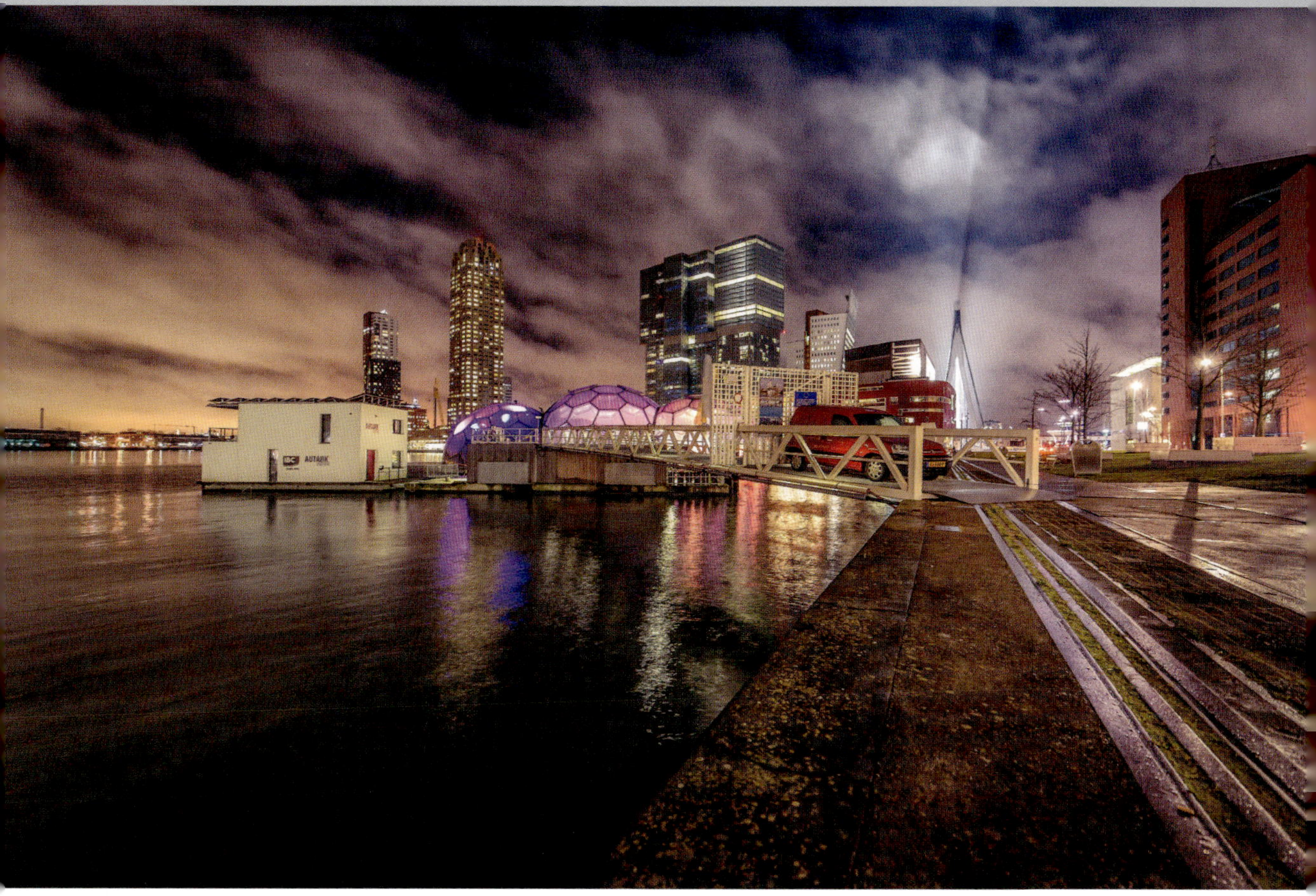

7. Bringing It All Together

To close out the book, I want to share with you a few of my favorite night and low-light images. I'll also explain how they were created, bringing together many of the lighting and shooting skills we've explored in the previous chapters. I hope these will inspire you to push your low-light photography in new directions!

In the Beginning

Image 7–2 was shot just as I had started to embrace the "low light" revolution. It was a very exciting time for me—as it was, I'm guessing, for many other photographers worldwide. Nikon had introduced the Nikon D3s, which won many awards for its low-light ability. The image was created on one of my wedding workshops in London in 2010 and the photographers attending were amazed at what could be created with a very simple, small LED flashlight. In the behind-the-scenes shot (**image 7–1**), you can see how the image was created by having one of the photographers directing the flashlight onto our gorgeous model. The backlight you can see is from the Elinchrom Ranger RX, set to its lowest output.

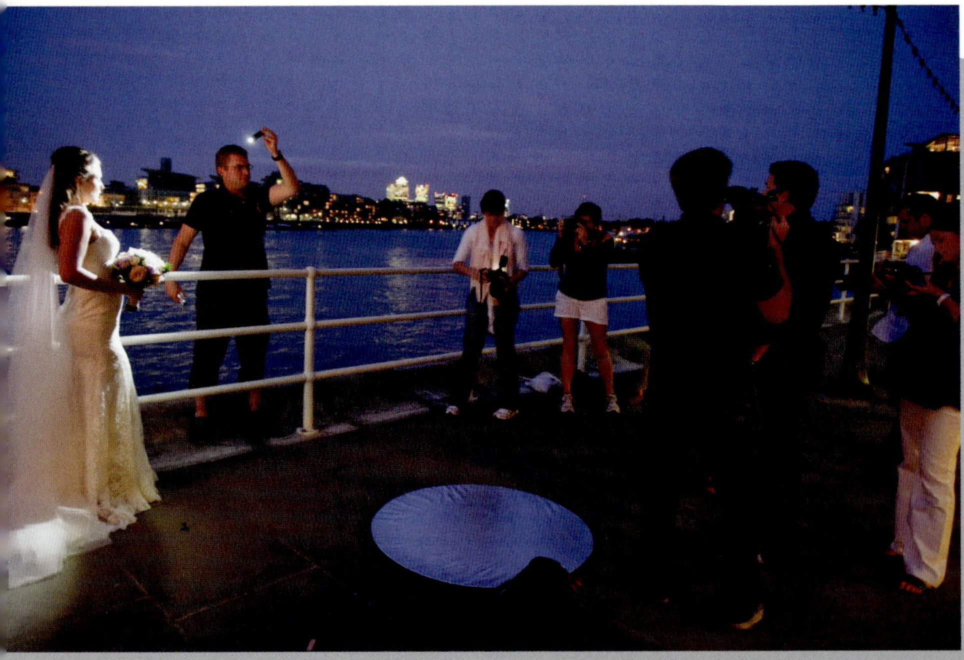

Images 7–1 (left) and 7–2 (facing page). At a wedding workshop, I photographed this model with an LED flashlight. *Tech Specs:* Nikon D3s, 4000 ISO, Lens: 70–200mm f/2.8, Aperture: f/2.8, Shutter speed: 1/100 second, Mode: M.

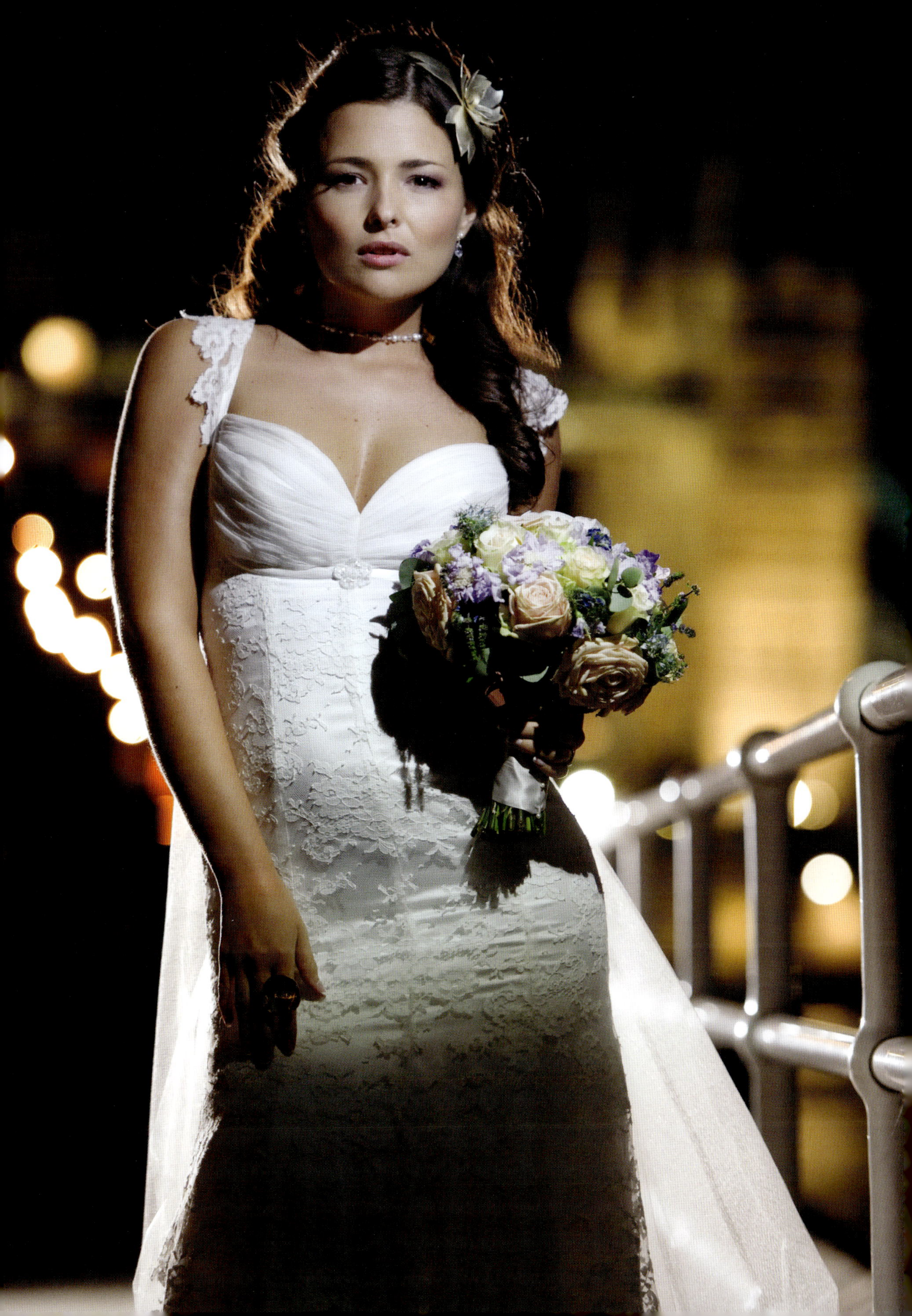

The Streets of Seattle

Image 7–3, created on the streets of Seattle, was shot very close to steel grating that offered an interesting texture. There was enough ambient light to illuminate the subject from the front; however, I felt the image needed more drama. The introduction of a Manfrotto LED from behind took care of that, resulting in an image that evokes a sultry, underworld feeling.

Three Balanced Light Sources

I loved working with Sadie (**image 7–4**), because she has such natural poise and presence. On this particular image, a lot of energy and effort went into the styling and lighting. It was styled by a good friend of mine, Christine Wright, who is a floral genius. There are three different light sources in play. You have tungsten light coming from the bare bulbs in the white metal letters behind Sadie. There are also the candles in the foreground. Fortunately, these two light sources were of a similar luminosity and I only had to control the output power of the third source, the Ice Light, in order to balance the brightness of the tungsten and candlelight. I decided to gel the Ice Light with a blue gel, as I had recently seen similar lighting in a fashion magazine that resonated with me. I am very pleased with results.

Image 7–3 (below). Backlight added drama to the ambient light through the grate. *Tech Specs:* Nikon D4, 4000 ISO, Lens: 70–200mm f/2.8, Aperture: f/2.8, Shutter speed: 1/320 second, Mode: A.

Image 7–4 (facing page). Tungsten light, -light, the light from a blue-gelled Ice Light were all balanced in this image. *Tech Specs:* Nikon D4s, 800 ISO, Lens: 85mm f/1.4, Aperture: f/1.4, Shutter speed: 1/160 second, Mode: M.

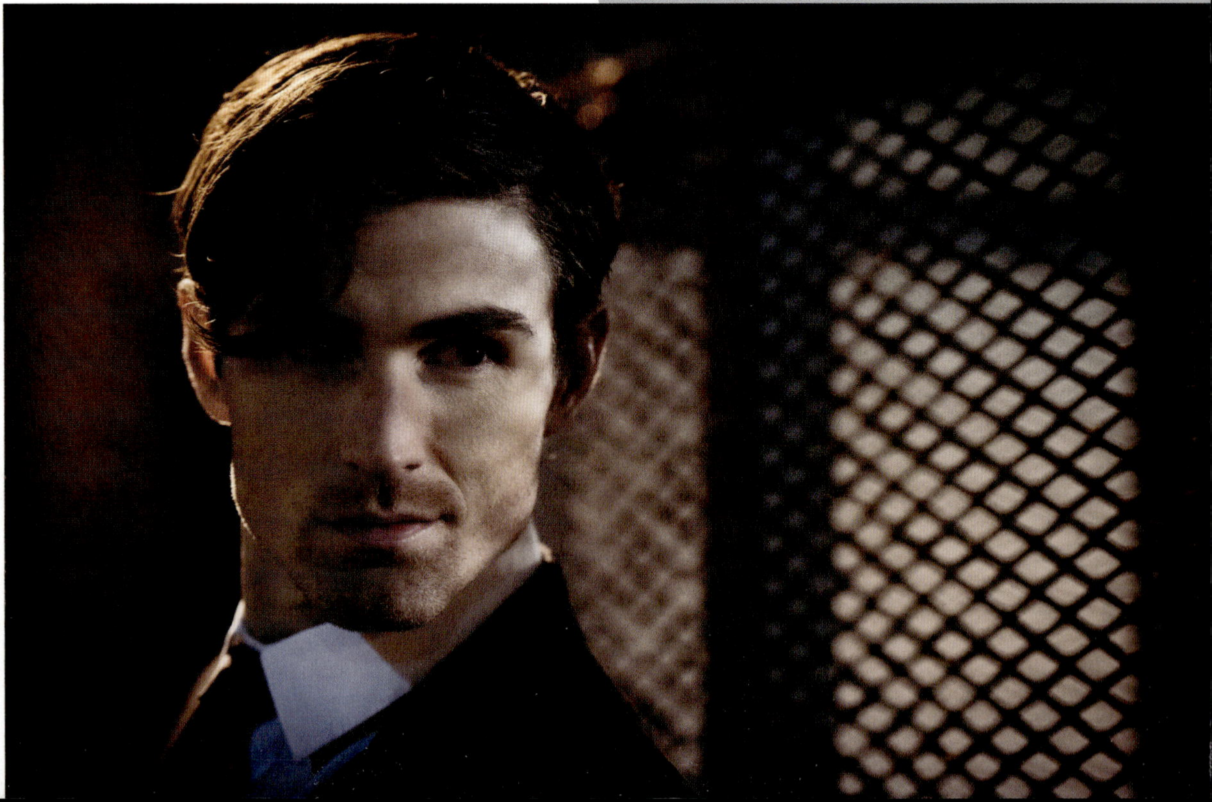

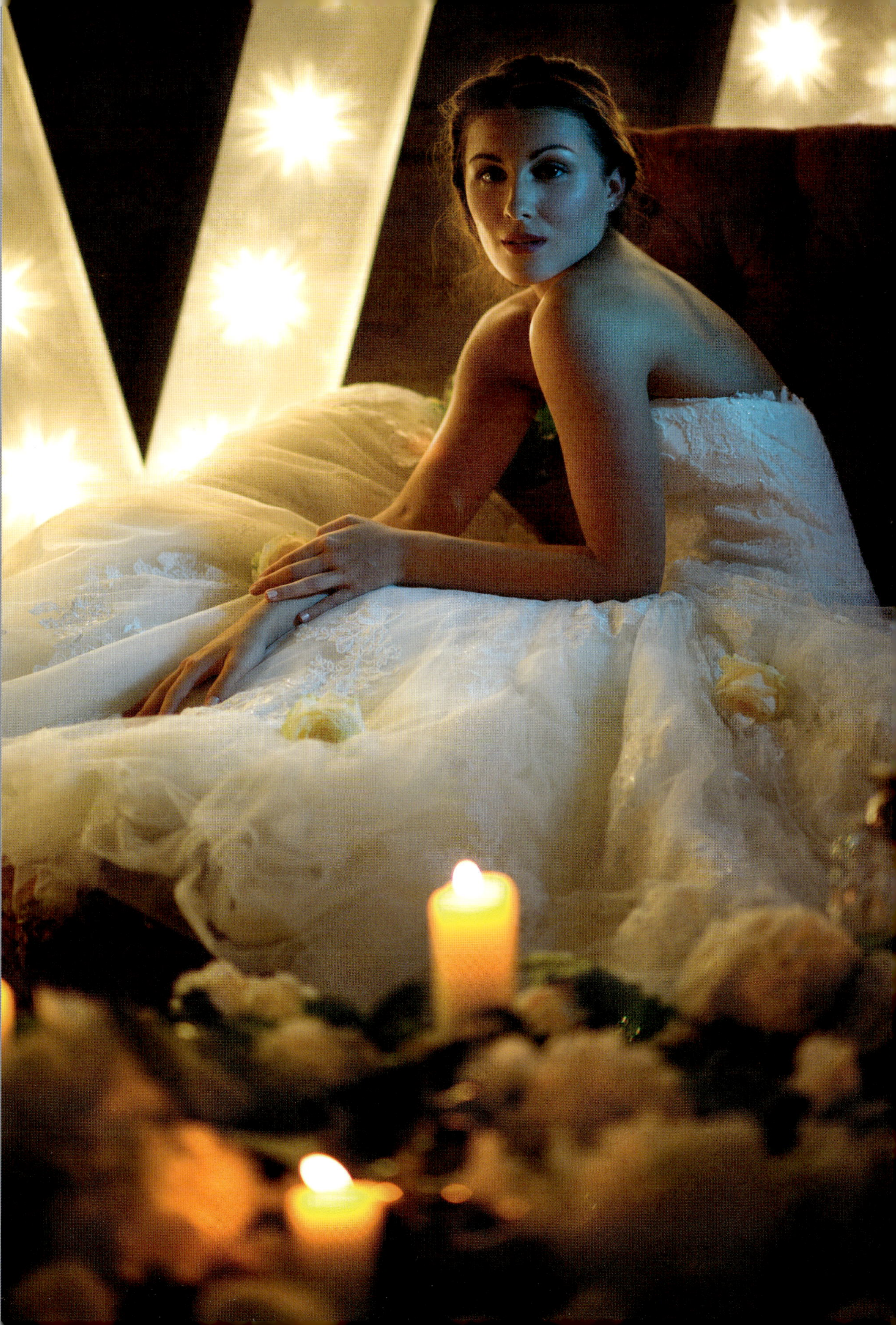

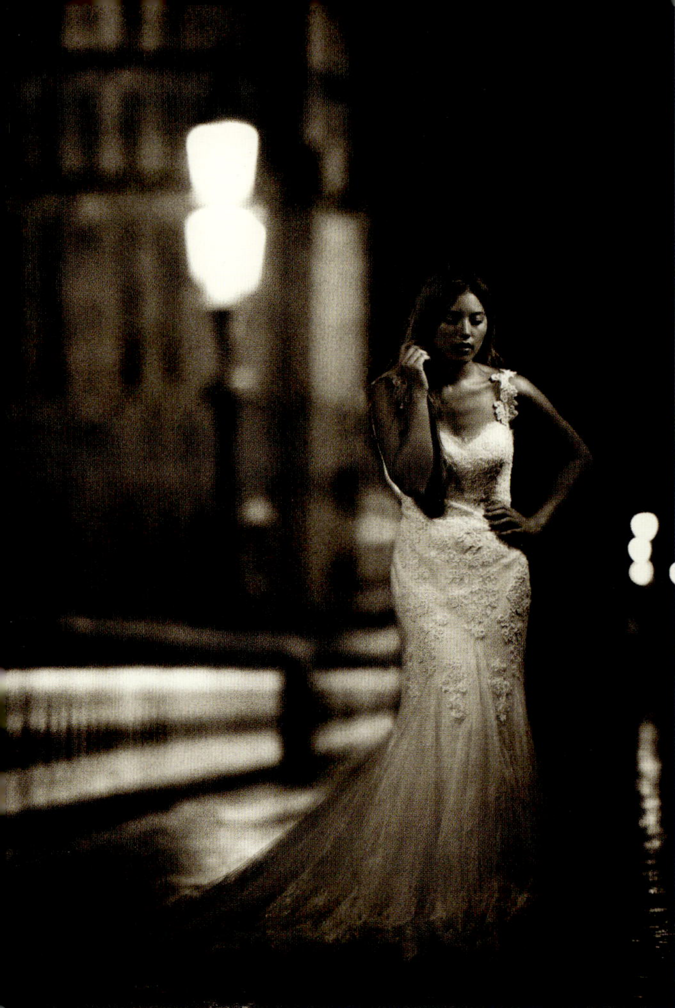

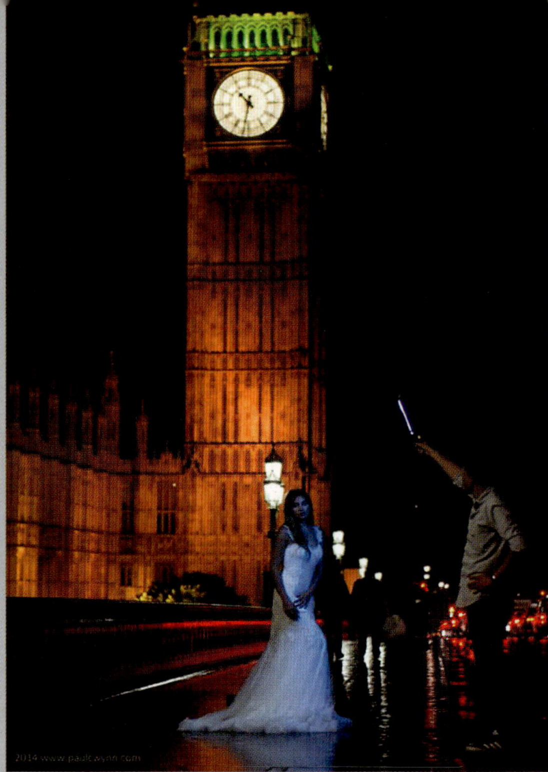

Images 7–5, 7–6, and 7–7. In color or monochrome, this low light image really works. *Tech Specs:* Nikon D4s, 10000 ISO, Lens: 70–200mm f/2.8, Aperture: f/2.8, Shutter speed: 1/200 second, Mode: A.

On the Bridge

Image 7–5 was shot on a bridge near Big Ben and the Houses of Parliament in London. I really like the combination of colors that are coming through. The light from the front landing on Chi was from an Ice Light that had a blue gel over it, as you can see from the behind-the-scenes shot (**image 7–6**). I love all the color combinations, from the warmth of Big Ben, to the car tail lights reflecting off the wet surface of the road. That being said, and in seeming contradiction, I also love the monotone image that has been processed in Nik Software's Silver Efex Pro (**image 7–7**). That version of the image is so nostalgic and evocative that I wouldn't hesitate to use either the color or the monochromatic image.

"I love all the color combinations, from the warmth of Big Ben, to the car tail lights reflecting off the wet surface of the road."

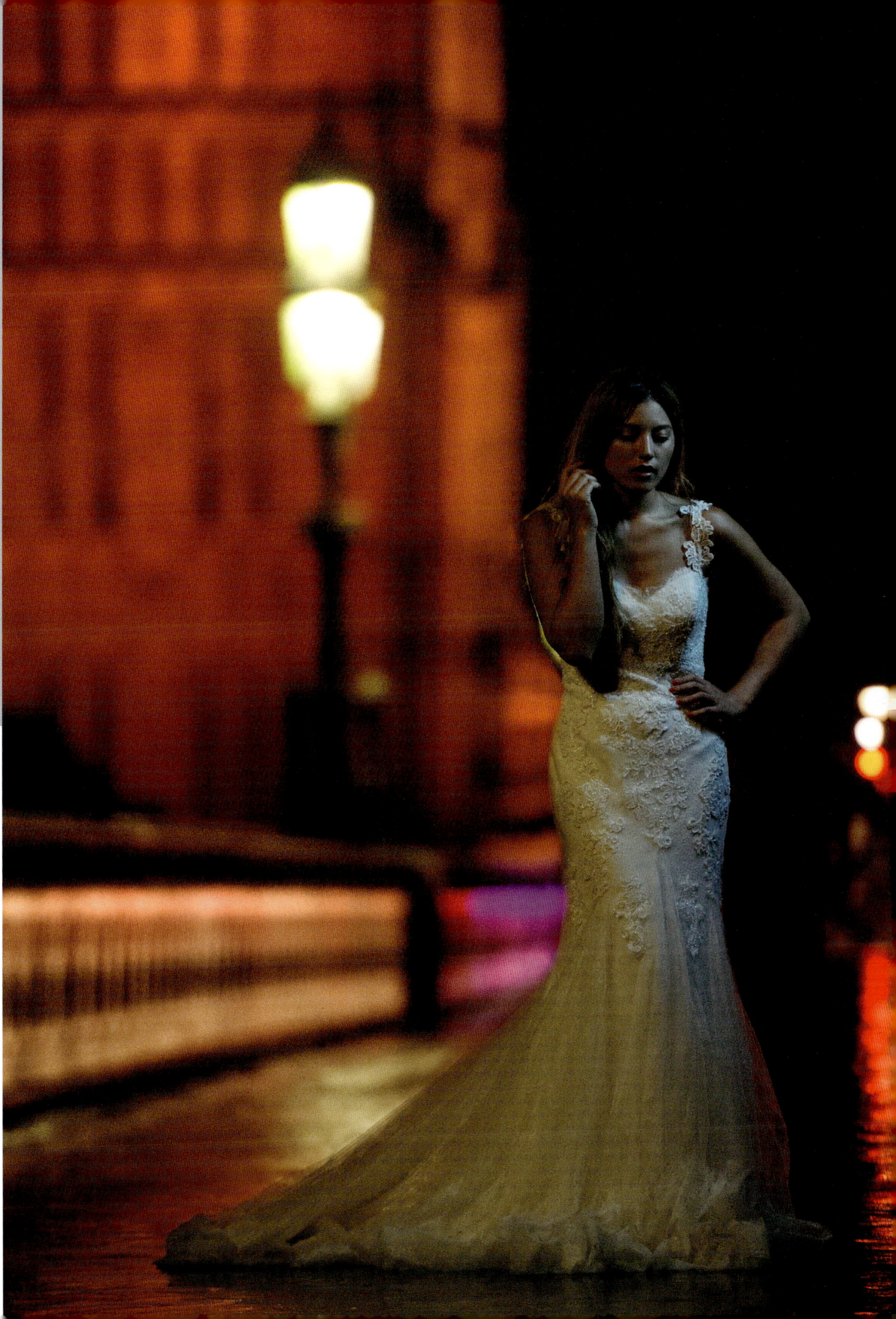

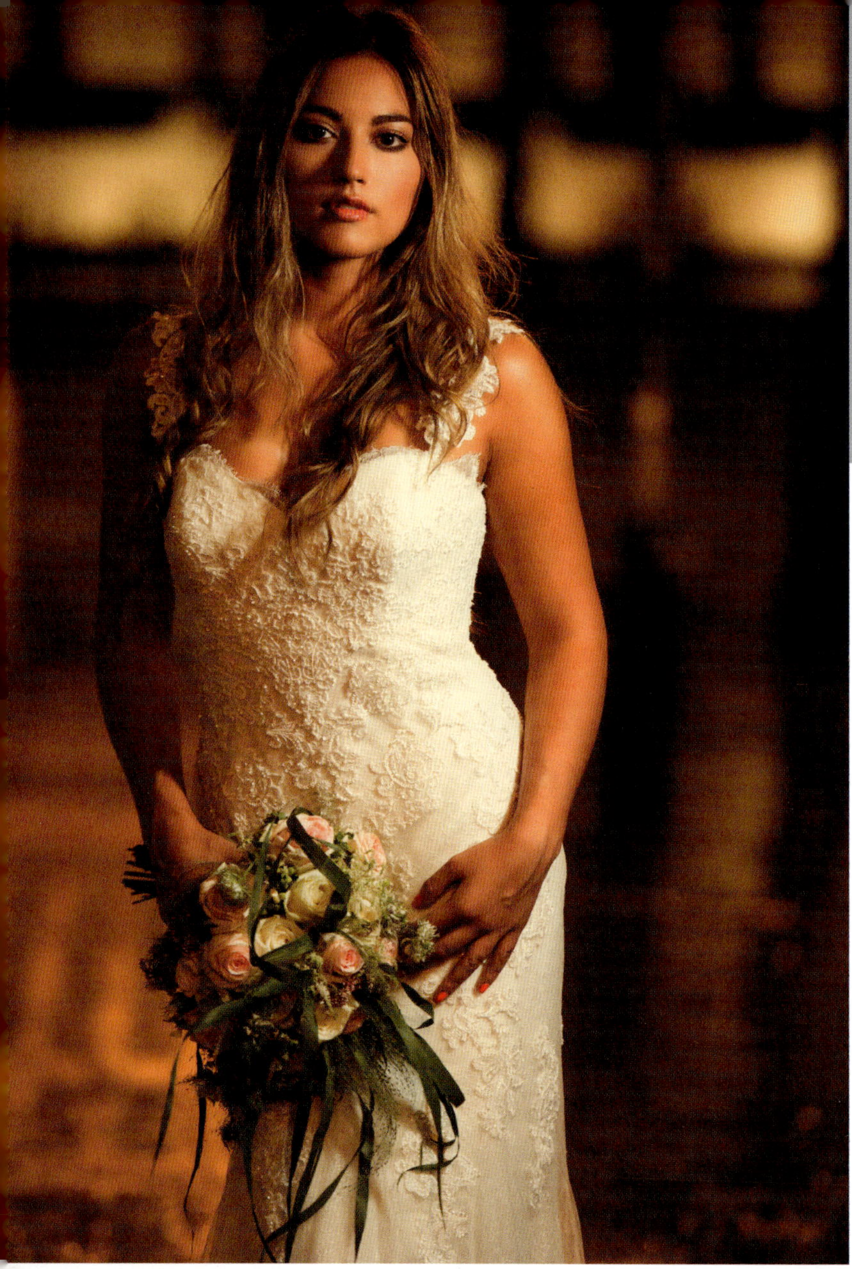

Images 7–8 and 7–9 (left and facing page). Balancing the exposures of the subject and background was critical to the success of these images. *Tech Specs:* Nikon D4s, 4000 ISO, Lens: 70–200mm f/2.8, Aperture: f/2.8, Shutter speed: 1/160 second, Mode: A.

“The key to the success of this image was getting the balance right between the two light sources, putting the subject and background exposures at the right relative levels.”

Street Light Plus an Ice Light

Images 7–8 and **7–9** demonstrate how I balanced the ambient street/city light with the light that I had at my disposal. I placed the Ice Light to camera right, illuminating Chi's left-hand side. Again, let me draw your attention to the wonderful “window light” quality of the Ice Light. The key to the success of this image was getting the balance right between the two light sources, putting the subject and background exposures at the right relative levels. One of the great advantages of low light photography is being able to control the brightness of your background—it's a useful tool that will help you create images that really resonate with you.

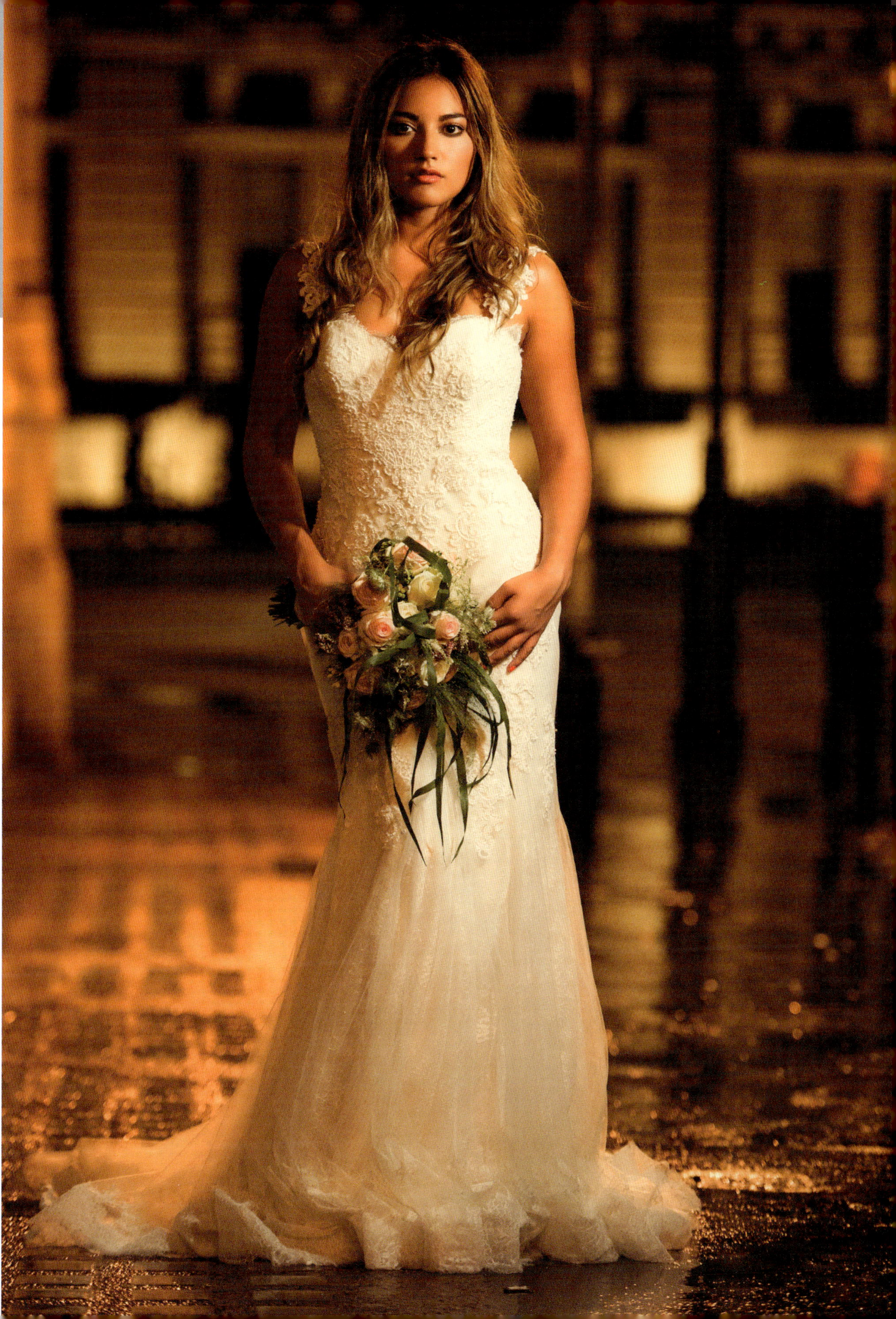

Christmas in South Africa

At Christmas in Durban, South Africa (in the southern hemisphere—hence, warm), the local council wraps an avenue of trees in beautiful fairy lights. Perfect! Armed with my Manfrotto LED, I headed toward the office park to create **images 7–10** and **7–11**. I shot right up close to the lights, creating images with amazing bokeh. The passing cars would also fortuitously illuminate the scene and provide great backlighting. Again, the key was to get the balance right between the light falling on my subject and the ambient light from the fairy lights.

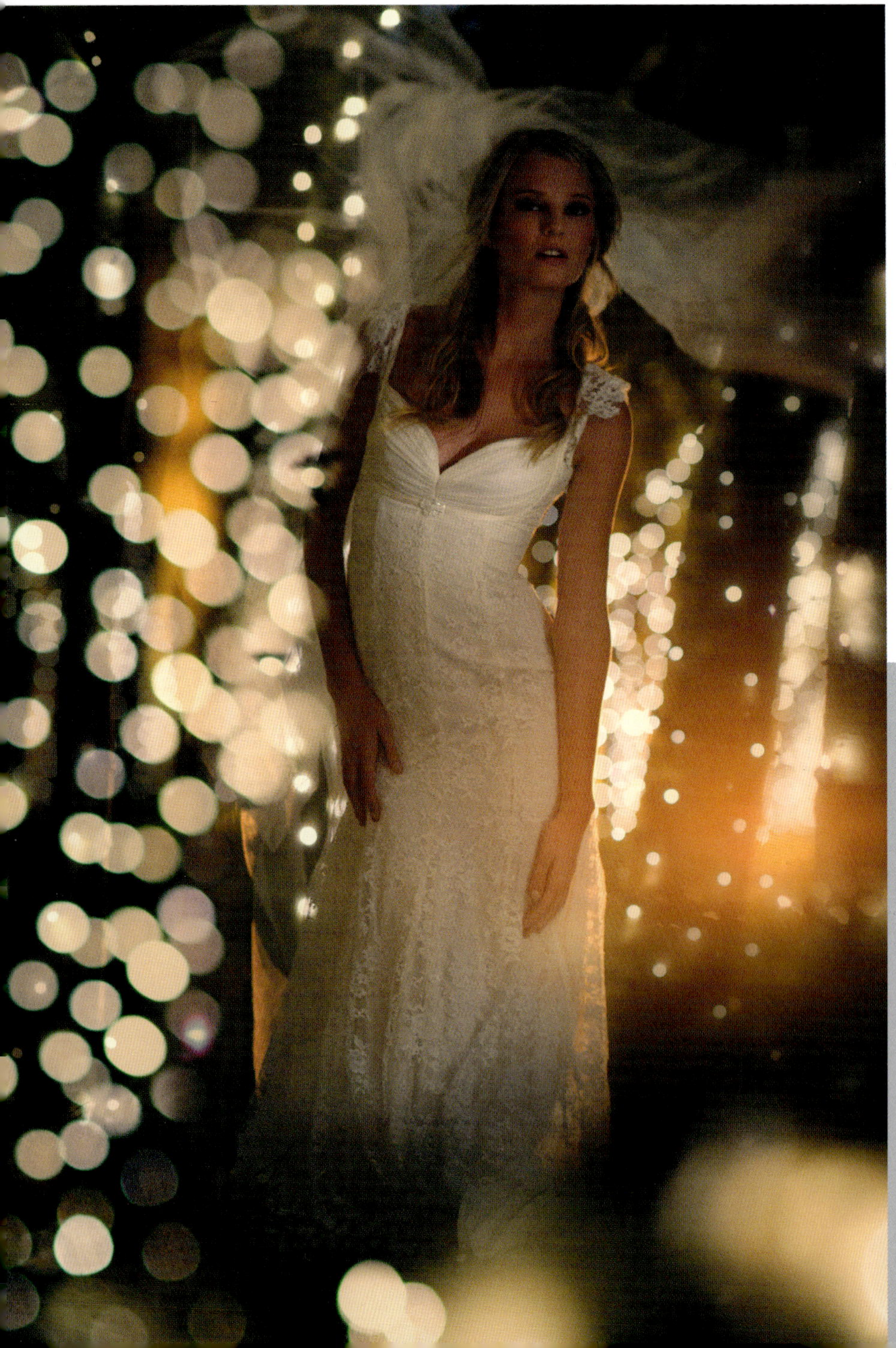

"The passing cars would also fortuitously illuminate the scene and provide great backlighting."

Images 7–10 and 7–11 (left and facing page). As we worked up close to the trees wrapped in fairy lights, passing cars occasionally provided fortuitous backlighting. *Tech Specs:* Nikon D3s, 4000 ISO, Lens: 85mm f/1.4, Aperture: f/2, Shutter speed: 1/80 second, Mode: M.

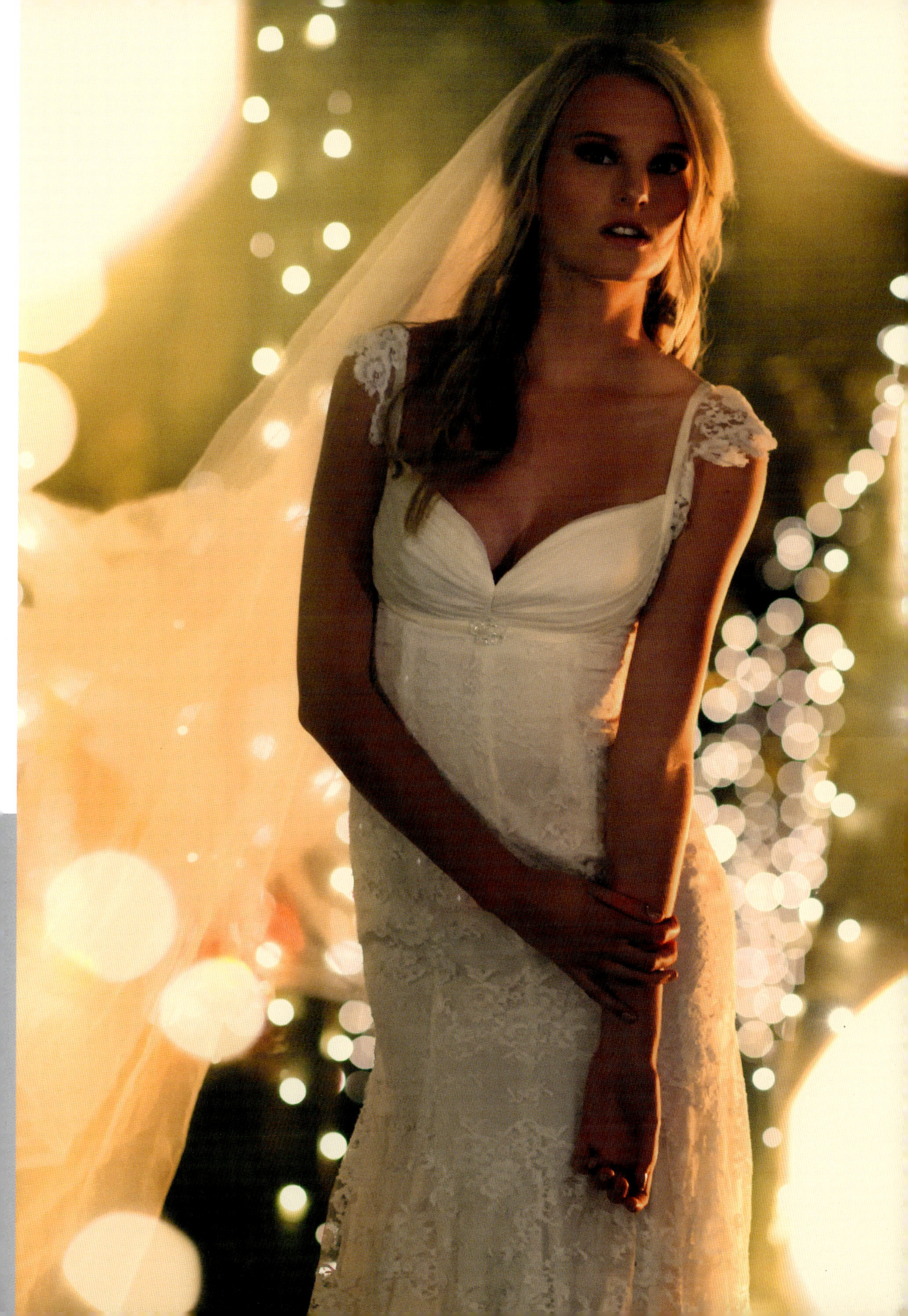

An Editorial Shoot

These images were created during an editorial shoot for a fashion label. We shot at The Oysterbox, a wonderful five-star hotel on the east coast of South Africa. We had been shooting for about three or four hours and I needed a comfort break. Having discovered that the restrooms were gorgeous, I suggested that we shoot the next scene in the men's room. After verifying the potential, the art director agreed it was a goof idea and we then shot there. The model was illuminated with a manfrotto LED, which provided great shape-forming light. The mirrors and ambient light facilitated great bokeh and reflections. For the second shot, I used the prism to create the foreground bokeh, which added a refreshing twist to the image.

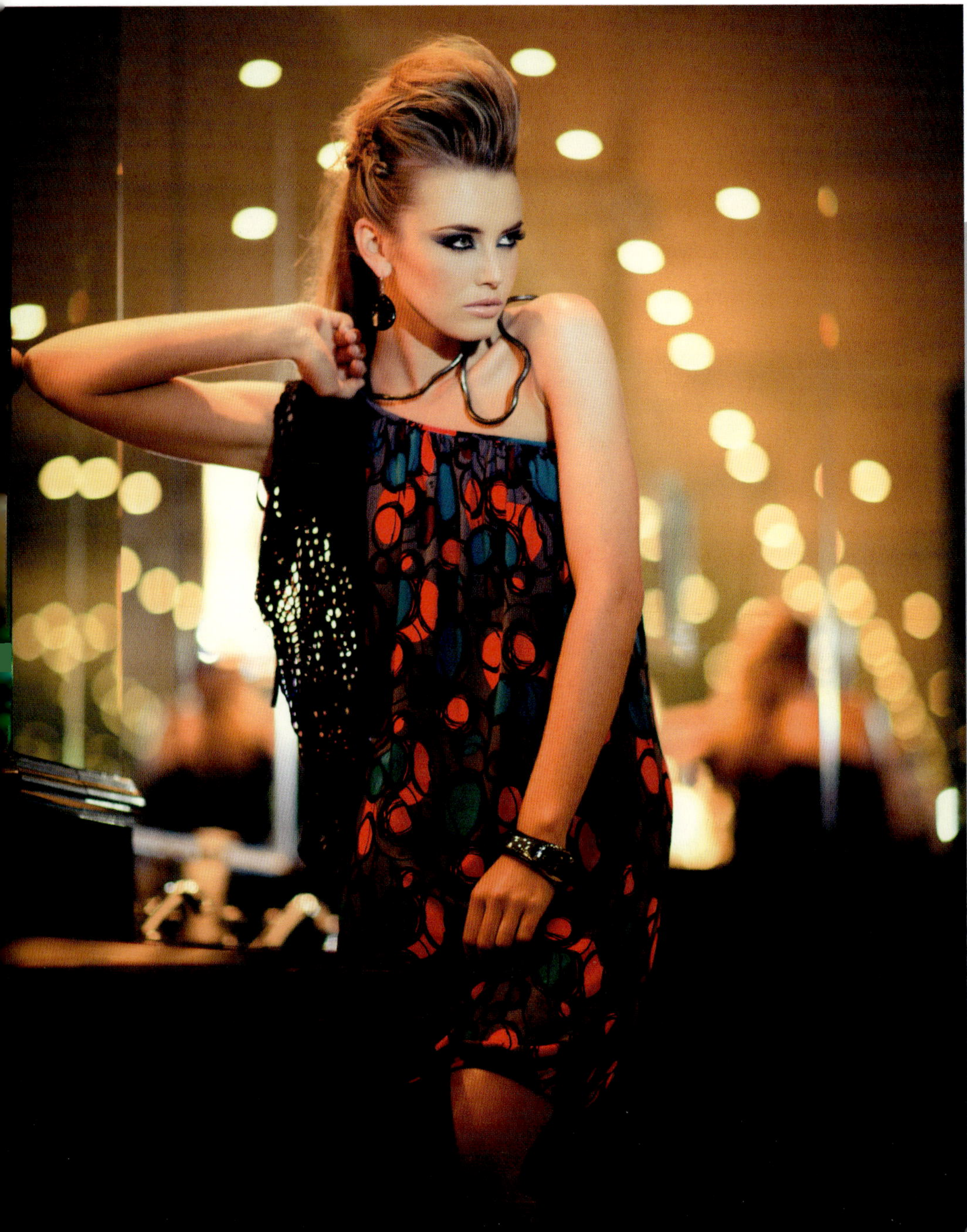

Images 7–12 and 7–13 (left and facing page). A restroom might not be the obvious choice for a fashion photo shoot—but here it worked out perfectly. *Tech Specs:* Nikon D4, 1600 ISO, Lens: 85mm f/1.4, Aperture: f/2, Shutter speed: 1/100 second, Mode: M.

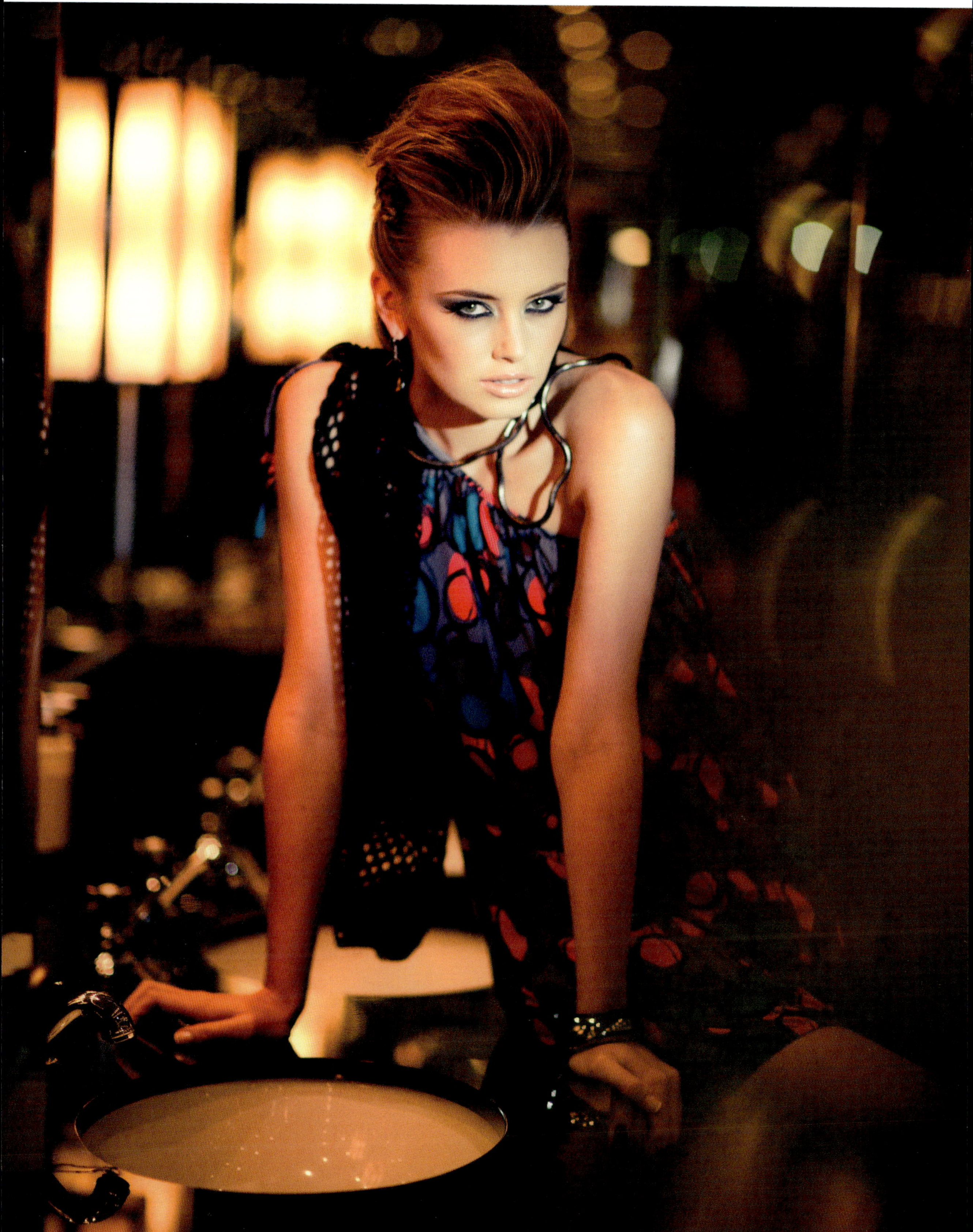

Amsterdam in the Background

This image of Ineke (**image 7–14**) was taken on a bridge over one of the many picturesque canals in Amsterdam. The cityscape was a great background. I used the Lowel GL1 to light her from the front. I had my assistant attach this light to a Manfrotto boom and elevate it to emulate street lighting. We also placed an Ice Light on a light stand behind her, for the rim lighting you see. Placing the fairy lights on the ground to the side of her added a

Image 7–14. I elevated a Lowel GL1 to emulate the look of a streetlight. This was paired with backlight from an Ice Light and fairy lights on the ground. *Tech Specs:* Nikon D4s, 2000 ISO, Lens: 85mm f/1.4, Aperture: f/1.4, Shutter speed: 1/200 second, Mode: M.

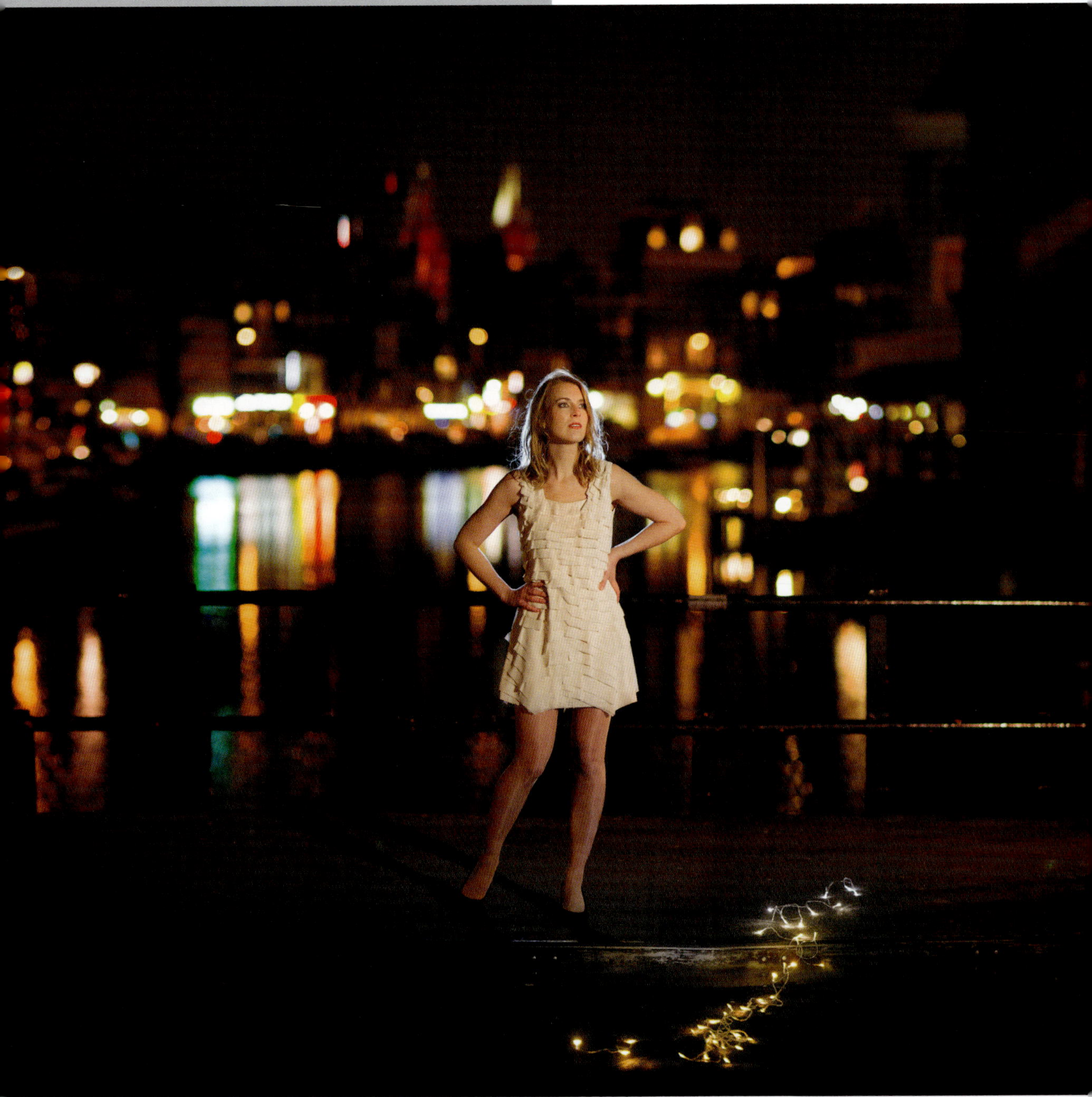

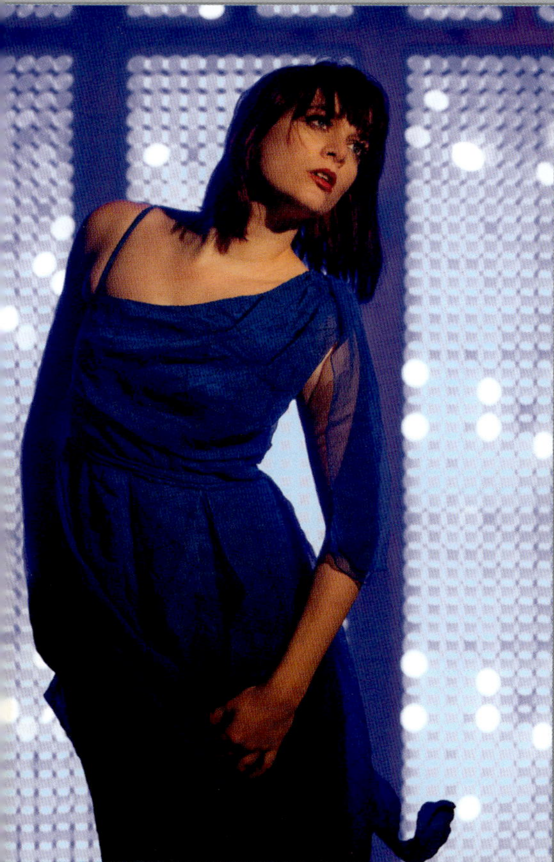

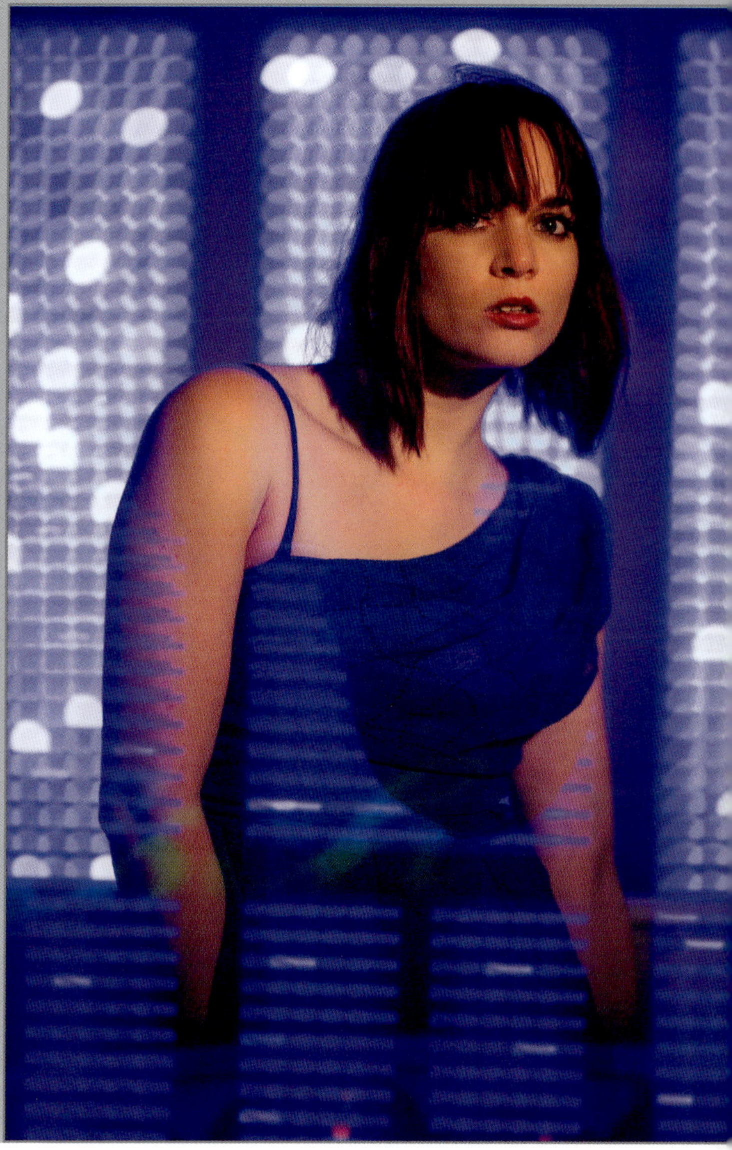

Images 7–15 and 7–16. A Lowel GL1 balanced the model against a wall of LED panels outside a nightclub. *Tech Specs:* Nikon D4s, 4000 ISO, Lens: 85mm f/1.4, Aperture: f/1.4, Shutter speed: 1/2500 second, Mode: M.

further point of interest. The fairy lights are actually daylight balanced; however, I asked my digital artist to change them to a warmer color in postproduction, as I felt that they looked too blue in contrast to the tungsten-balanced GL1.

Amsterdam Night Club

The images of Nadine (**images 7–15** and **7–16**) were shot outside a nightclub in Amsterdam, where the striking LED panels made for a great background. I illuminated her with the Lowel GL1, which produced a kind of Hollywood lighting effect. For the second image, I incorporated a prism to reflect the LED panels. As you can see, the result is quite interesting.

Mist in the Streetlight

This image of Ineke at the end of the bridge railing (**image 7–17**) was lit by a nearby streetlight, as you can see from the accompanying behind-the-scenes shot. The light catching her hair was from the Lowel GL1 and my assistant blew a little talcum powder into the air to create the moody "mist" effect.

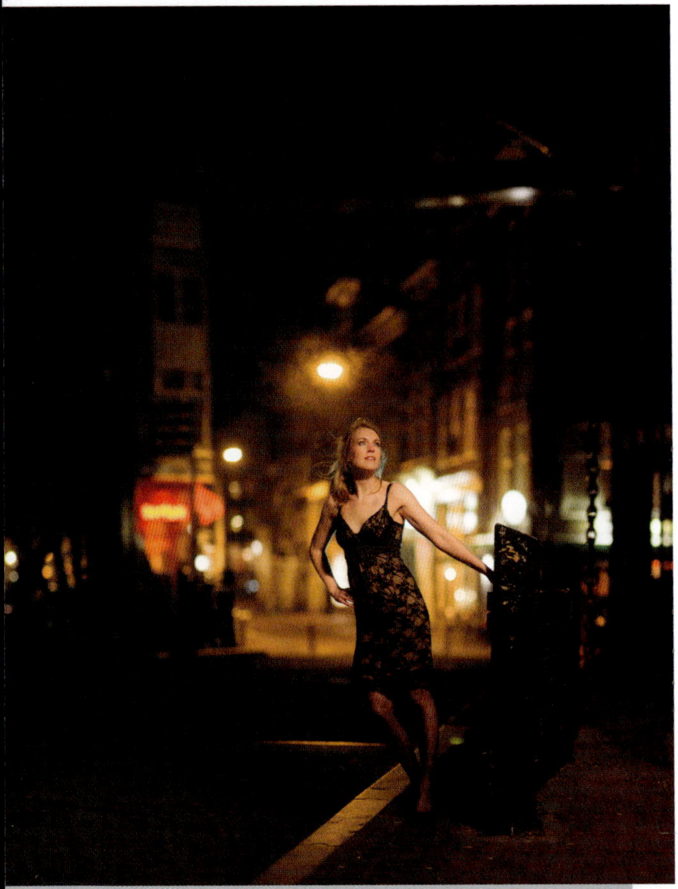

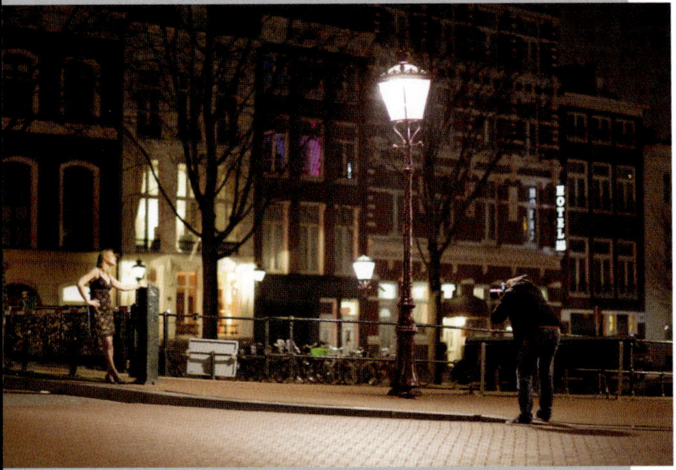

Images 7–17 and 7–18. Talcum powder blown into the air enhanced the mood of this street image. *Tech Specs:* Nikon D4s, 2000 ISO, Lens: 85mm f/1.4, Aperture: f/1.4, Shutter speed: 1/200 second, Mode: M.

The Brooklyn Bridge

This is probably my favorite image from a shoot I did at New York City's Brooklyn Bridge. I love the sense of romance that the city light added to the image—and the intimate moment that the "bride" is having. It reminds me of a movie poster for a romantic comedy.

Images 7–19 and 7–20 (below and facing page). Two of my favorite night images from a shoot at the Brooklyn Bridge. *Tech Specs:* Nikon D750, 2500 ISO, Lens: 85mm f/1.4, Aperture: f/1.4, Shutter speed: 1/200 second, Mode: M.

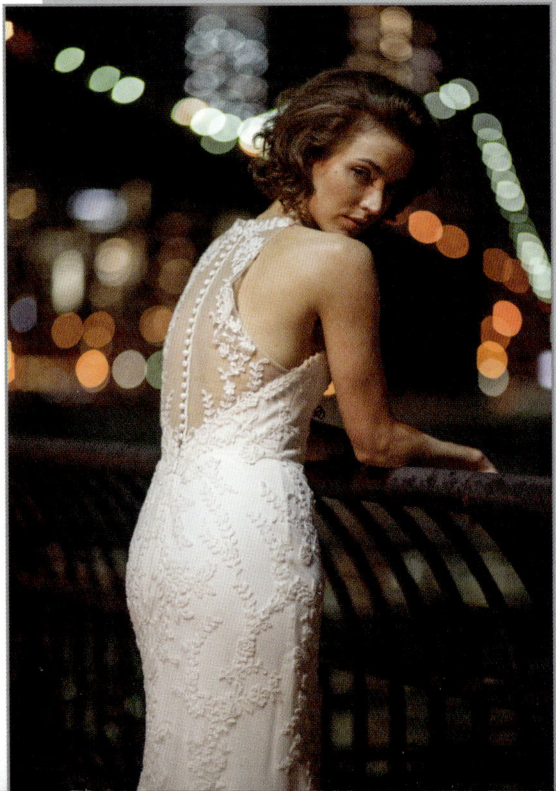

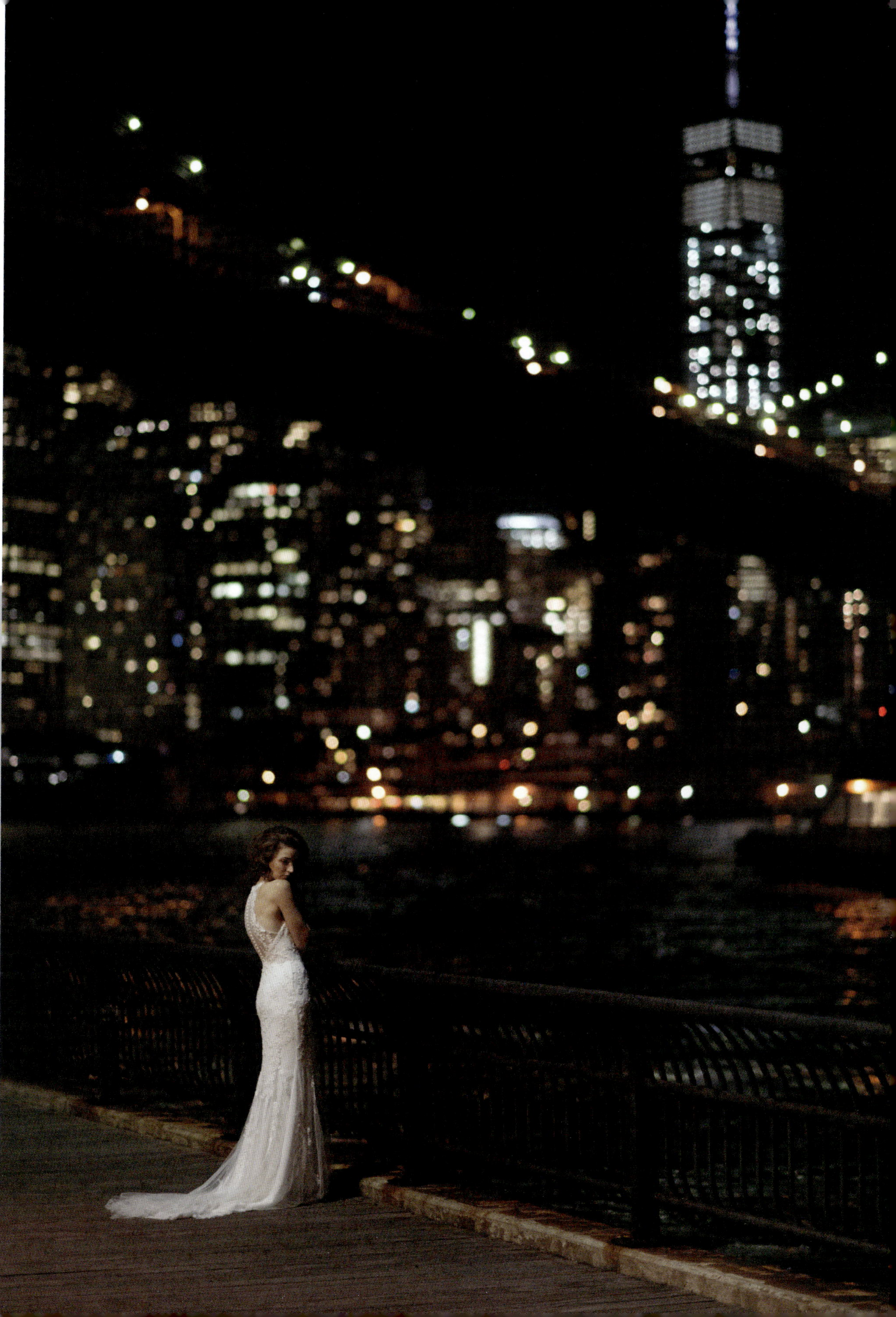

In a Dark Hallway

The dark hotel hallway, the bride's incredibly beautiful dress and veil, her classic French chignon and makeup—it all made me think of times gone by. That feeling of old-world Hollywood glamour and elegance was what I wanted to capture. I set up my lighting to reproduce the typical black & white portraits of those times. Wanting plenty of tonal contrast, I had my assistant hold a Fotodiox LED light quite close to the bride and almost directly above her. This accentuated the falloff and didn't illuminate the background too much. I asked the bride to turn her face to a three-quarter view and lift her chin so she was looking directly into the light. This produced the great highlights and shadows that give her face a three-dimensional structure and powerful elegance. The light captured all the crystal beading on the intricately detailed dress, so that it shone in true Hollywood style. I also love the way the intense lighting caused the lace detail on her dress to create shadows on her chest. I converted the image to black & white using Silver Effex Pro from Nik Software and intensified the contrast to produce what I deem to be an incredibly striking image.

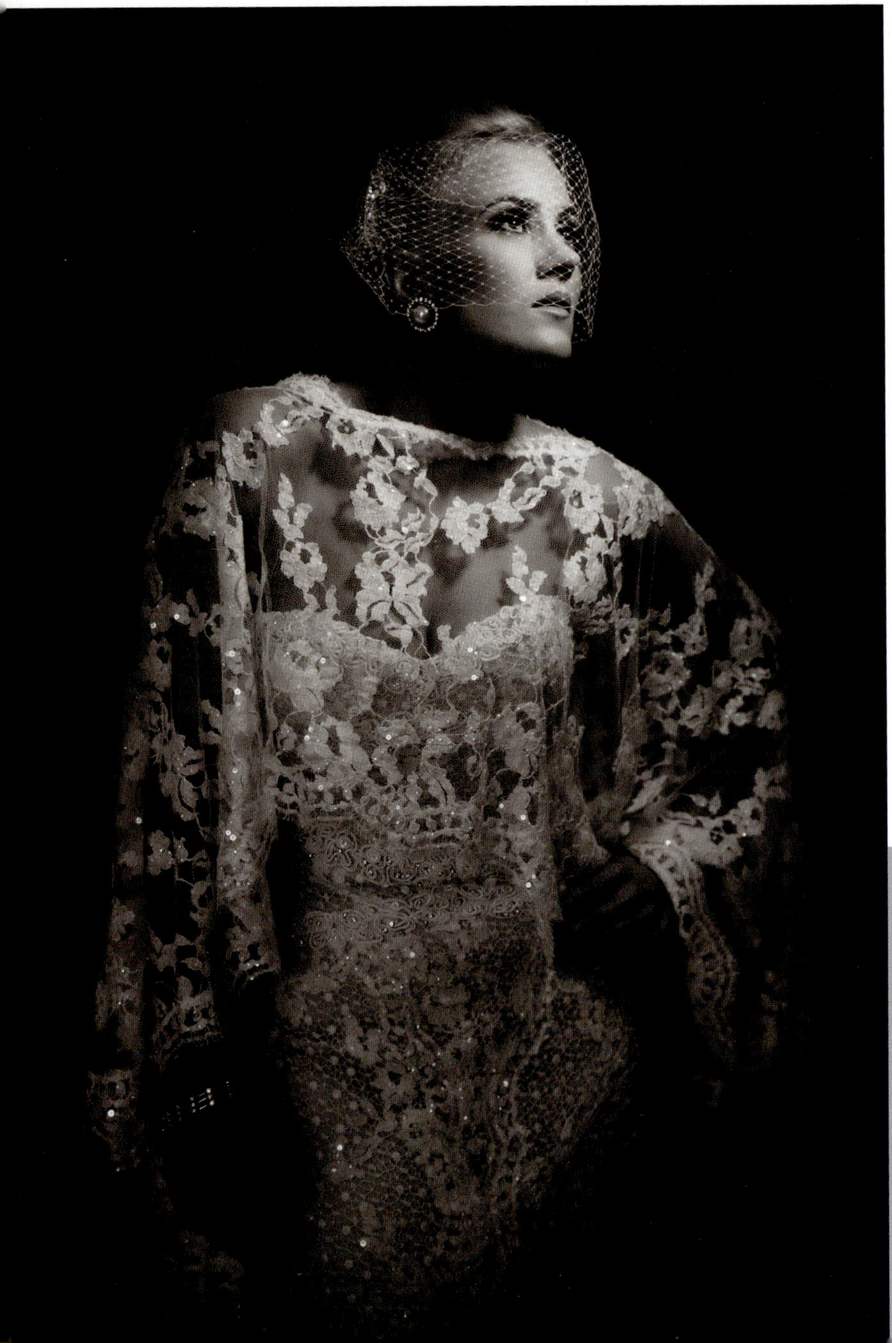

Image 7–21. I created this classic Hollywood look in a dark hotel hallway, using a Fotodiox LED as the main light. *Tech Specs:* Nikon D4, 800 ISO, Lens: 70–200mm f/2.8, Aperture: f/2.8, Shutter speed: 1/500 second, Mode: M.

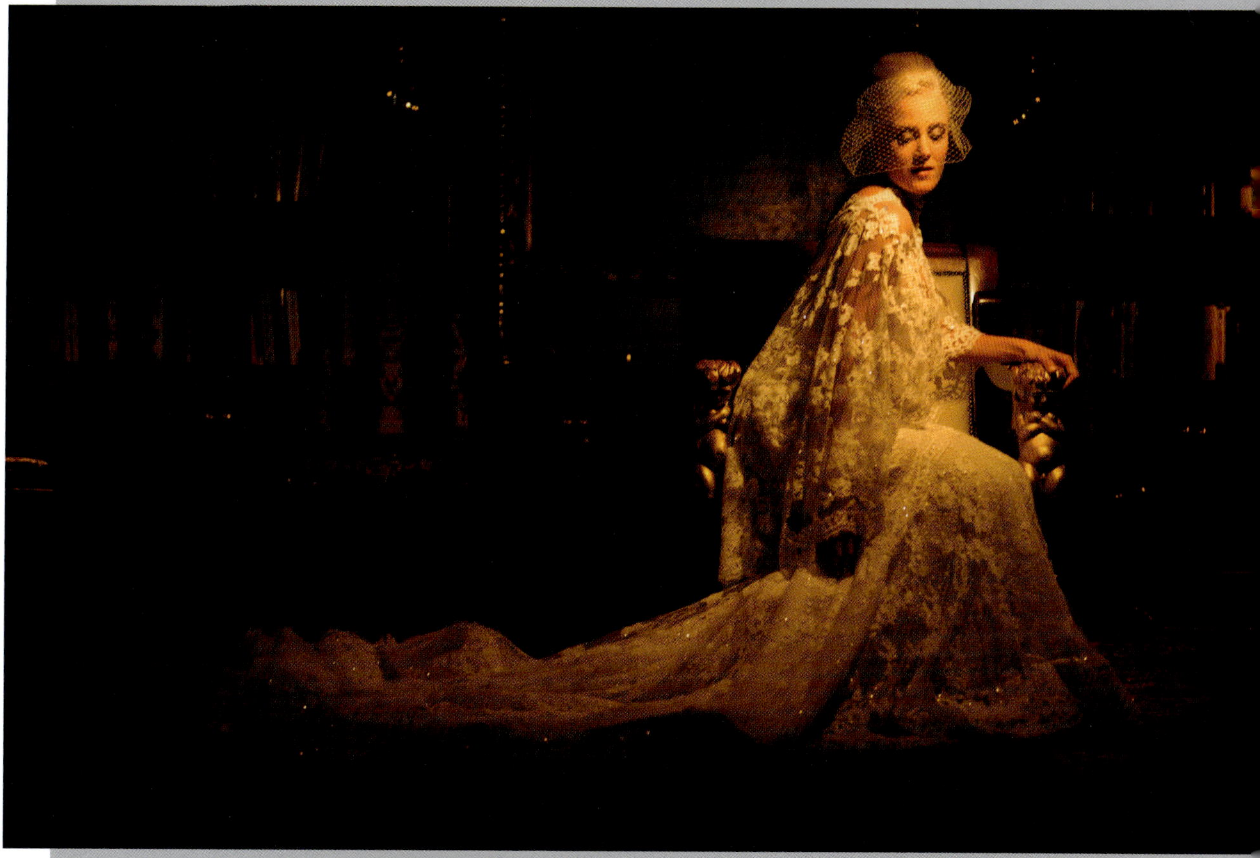

Image 7–22. We darkened this library, then added a Fotodiox LED to produce a chiaroscuro look. *Tech Specs:* Nikon D4, 2500 ISO, Lens: 24–70mm f/2.8, Aperture: f/2.8, Shutter speed: 1/25 second, Mode: M.

Chiaroscuro

If you are familiar with Rembrandt's paintings, or the work of other artists from the 17th and 18th centuries, you may know the artistic term "chiaroscuro." This Italian word, which literally means "light-dark," refers to the very clear tonal contrasts in the artwork. It was almost as if someone had shone a spotlight onto a particular subject while the rest of the room remained in the dark, giving the paintings a very dramatic appearance. The colors were generally very yellow and black, while the atmosphere created was very moody and intriguing. For this image, I knew that re-creating the chiaroscuro effect would be incredibly impactful—and unusual, as far as bridal portraiture is concerned. After closing all the doors and all the heavy curtains to the library, then switching off the lights, we worked a room that was gorgeously dark and gloomy. To camera right, my assistant held a Fotodiox LED that was set to create a warm yellow glow reminiscent of the chiaroscuro paintings.

Theatrical Flair

Images 7–23, 7–24, and **7–25** were shot at a local theater. The bride was a ballerina and the location was very sentimental to her. We were fortunate to get the stage lighting turned on, which provided a dramatic backdrop for the images. I had my assistant throw some talcum powder up into the air to create the smoke effect. He also held a small LED flashlight (the Lenser T7) in position behind the subjects. When I color corrected the image to compensate for the very warm stage lighting, the light from the LED flashlight shifted quite blue. I like it. The shot with the bridesmaids was particularly effective; it looks like a chorus line from a big production. Because I was shooting in relatively low light with a wide aperture, I had to keep the ladies equidistant from the camera to ensure that they were all in focus. Because there was a lot of darkness in the background, I shot with –2EV exposure compensation (but I could have shot in manual and dialed in the same exposure).

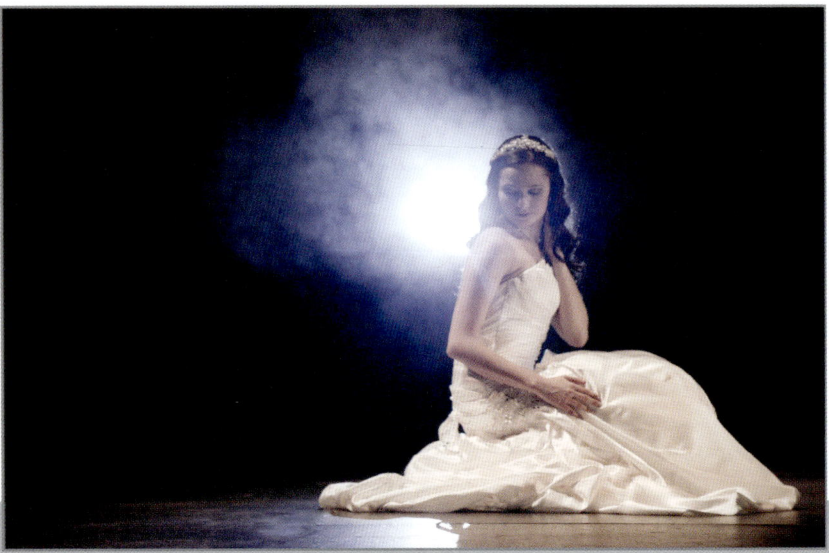

"We were fortunate to get the stage lighting turned on, which provided a dramatic backdrop for the images."

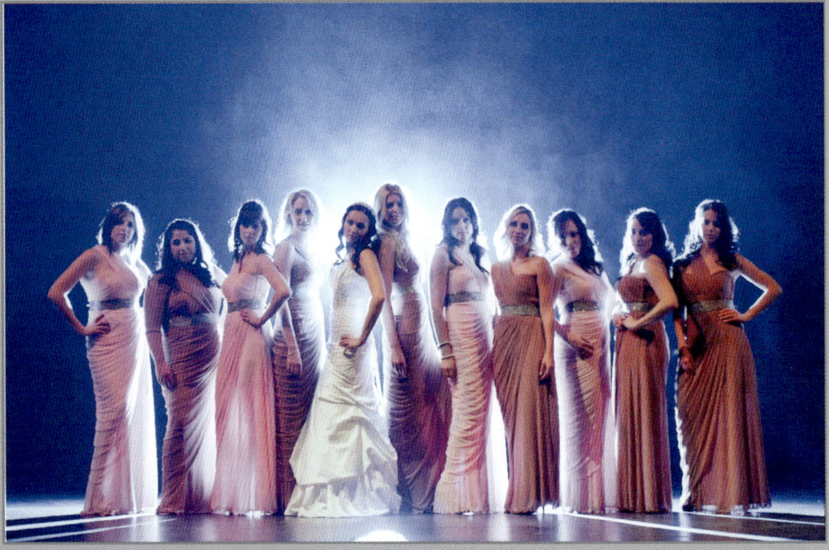

Images 7–23, 7–24, and 7–25 (left and facing page). With stage lighting and an LED flashlight, we created theatrical images for this ballerina bride. *Tech Specs:* Nikon D4, 800 ISO, Lens: 70–200mm f/2.8, Aperture: f/2.8, Shutter speed: 1/200 second, Exposure compensation: –2EV, Mode: A.

Foreground Bokeh

By introducing a transparent object—here, a prism—in front of the lens, I managed to create an image with further depth and interest. Without it, **image 7–26** would have been nice and acceptable; the added dimension of the foreground element elevated it to an image that is compelling and out of the ordinary. This was lit from the side with the Manfrotto LED.

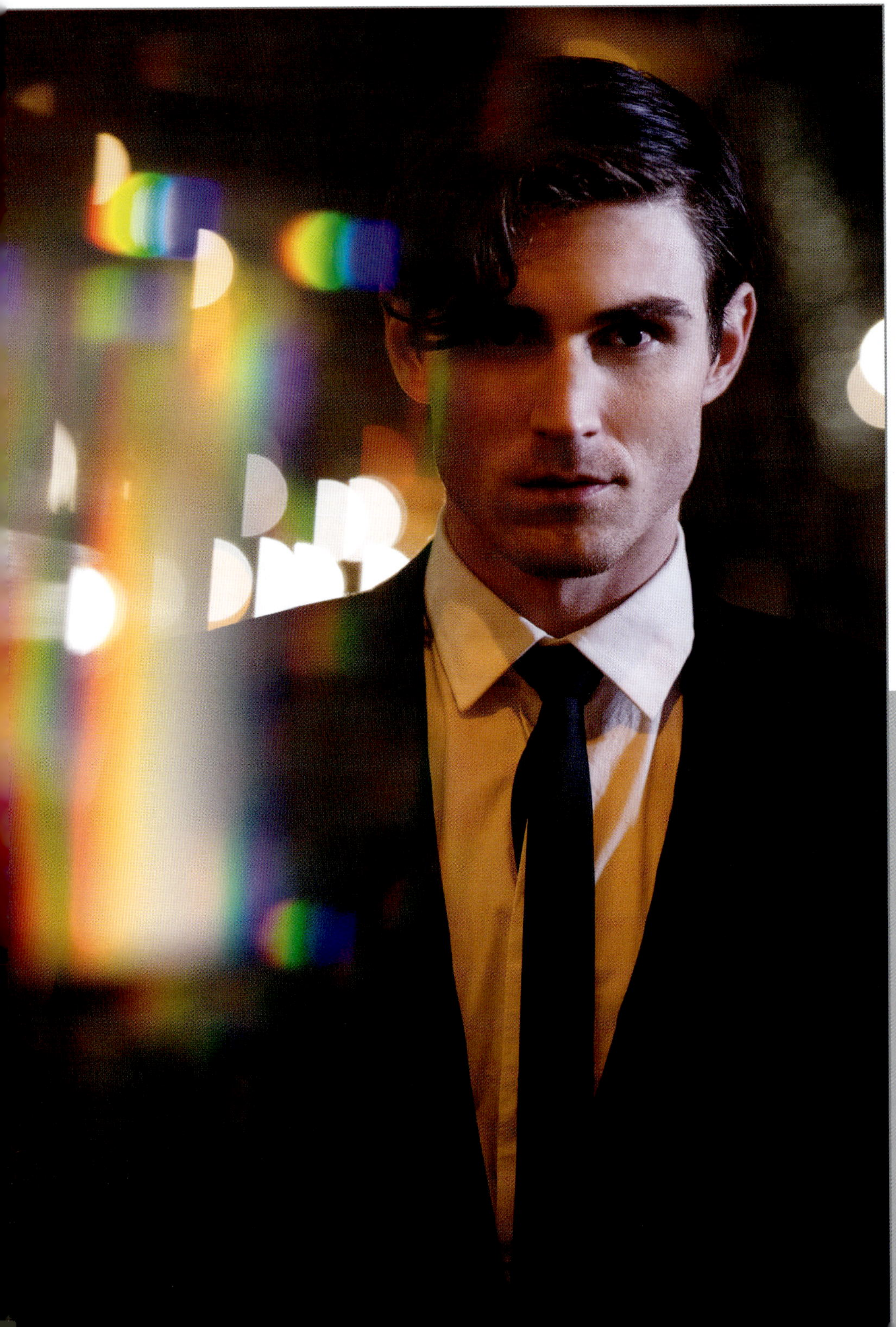

Image 7–26. Adding a prism in front of the lens elevated this low-light image. *Tech Specs:* Nikon D4, 2500 ISO, Lens: 85mm f/1.4, Aperture: f/1.4, Shutter speed: 1/400 second, Mode: A.

Index